CULTURE**SHOCK!**

A Survival Guide to Customs and Etiquette

EGYPT

Susan L Wilson

Marshall Cavendish
Editions

This edition published in 2006 by:
Marshall Cavendish Corporation
99 White Plains Road
Tarrytown, NY 10591-9001
www.marshallcavendish.us

Other Marshall Cavendish Offices:
Marshall Cavendish International (Asia) Private Limited. 1 New Industrial
Road, Singapore 536196 ▪ Marshall Cavendish Ltd. 119 Wardour Street, London
W1F 0UW, UK ▪ Marshall Cavendish International (Thailand) Co Ltd. 253 Asoke,
12th Flr, Sukhumvit 21 Road, Klongtoey Nua, Wattana, Bangkok 10110, Thailand
▪ Marshall Cavendish (Malaysia) Sdn Bhd, Times Subang, Lot 46, Subang Hi-Tech
Industrial Park, Batu Tiga, 40000 Shah Alam, Selangor Darul Ehsan, Malaysia

Marshall Cavendish is a trademark of Times Publishing Limited

ISBN 10: 0-7614-2497-0
ISBN 13: 978-0-7614-2497-0

Please contact the publisher for the Library of Congress catalog number

Printed in Singapore by Times Graphics Pte Ltd

ABOUT THE SERIES

Culture shock is a state of disorientation that can come over anyone who has been thrust into unknown surroundings, away from one's comfort zone. *CultureShock!* is a series of trusted and reputed guides which has, for decades, been helping expatriates and long-term visitors to cushion the impact of culture shock whenever they move to a new country.

Written by people who have lived in the country and experienced culture shock themselves, the authors share all the information necessary for anyone to cope with these feelings of disorientation more effectively. The guides are written in a style that is easy to read and covers a range of topics that will arm readers with enough advice, hints and tips to make their lives as normal as possible again.

Each book is structured in the same manner. It begins with the first impressions that visitors will have of that city or country. To understand a culture, one must first understand the people—where they came from, who they are, the values and traditions they live by, as well as their customs and etiquette. This is covered in the first half of the book.

Then on with the practical aspects—how to settle in with the greatest of ease. Authors walk readers through topics such as how to find accommodation, get the utilities and telecommunications up and running, enrol the children in school and keep in the pink of health. But that's not all. Once the essentials are out of the way, venture out and try the food, enjoy more of the culture and travel to other areas. Then be immersed in the language of the country before discovering more about the business side of things.

To round off, snippets of basic information are offered before readers are 'tested' on customs and etiquette of the country. Useful words and phrases, a comprehensive resource guide and list of books for further research are also included for easy reference.

CONTENTS

INTRODUCTION

This third edition of *CultureShock! Egypt* brings with it what I hope is an even better understanding of what it is like living in Egypt if you are a Westerner. I have been going to Egypt since 1988 and have had the privilege of living there in fairly typical, upper-middle class Egyptian neighborhoods (Garden City and Zamalek). I purposely chose not to live where most Americans live because it felt 'right' to me to be where I was. A new friend recently confirmed my impression that something 'happens' to some of us when we go to Egypt—we feel like we have 'come home'. If this happens to you, please recognise that you are not alone and enjoy.

Just the word 'Egypt' brings to mind visions of pyramids, grand temples, gigantic monuments, mummies and king-gods, all relics of one of the oldest civilisations in the world. To many, it will forever be the 'land of the Pharaohs', a place where agriculture and advanced mathematics developed. But the long reign of the Pharaohs and grand monuments passed away nearly 2,000 years ago. Life in Egypt has changed, and changed a lot, since the time when grand temples and statues were built to worship its king-gods.

Today, Egypt is a developing North African country of over 60 million people facing new challenges as it moves through the 21st century. Egypt is a land of proud, honourable families, each trying to do the same things families do everywhere in the world within the confines of their government, religion, culture and values. Like people everywhere, they concern themselves with love, work, family, doing the 'right' things and having their children grow up to be 'good' people.

As humans, each of us faces the world within the confines of our culture (that complex mixture of beliefs, behaviours and societal rules which tell us what is right and wrong, good and bad). Hopefully, this book will bring greater understanding of the Egyptian culture: of 'who' modern Egyptians are, how they view life from their cultural perspective, and how they go about facing challenges in a rapidly changing world. In the words of modern Egyptians: *Ahlan wa sahlan*! (AH-lan wa-SAH-lan)—Welcome! You are welcomed to Egypt!

Above all, I thank the people of Egypt who are patient with my questions, share their lives with me, are kind and generous, and who always make me feel welcome. Much of the data gathered for this book results from directing two field schools in Egypt sponsored by the University of North Texas, Institute of Anthropology and the Study Abroad Program. Special thanks to Dr David Keitges for helping make these field schools happen. Thanks to all my students who went to Egypt with me. Their remarkable incidences of culture shock showed me that culture shock is not just a long-term response, but one likely to clobber even those aware of the phenomenon and who are there for short periods. Their questions and observations reminded me of what Egypt looks like when you are 'new' to its environs, no matter how 'cool' you think you are. A special thanks to Violet Sparks and Michelle Robicheaux for their assistance and support throughout the field schools and subsequently. Also, a special thanks to Cynthia Talbot for suggesting that I write this book, and for her help.

I would also like to thank my Egyptian and Chinese students in Egypt at ESLSCA's (Ecole Supérieure Libre Des Sciences Commerciales et Appliqués), Advanced Management Institute in Mohandasin. It is entirely possible that I learned more from them about cross-cultural communication than they learned from me.

Over the nearly 20 years of my Egyptian experiences, two people have been there with moral support, understanding, humour and kindness: Ambassador Hussein El Kamel (International Co-operation Senior Advisor, Prime Minister's Cabinet Information and Decision Support Centre) and Mr Medhat A-Monem (Egypt's greatest tour guide. Call Medhat on his mobile phone at tel: 012-367-6574). They helped me in more ways than I can think to mention and I am forever in their debt.

Thanks to Her Excellency Dr Amal Osman and her staff whose hospitality made possible visits to special schools and NGOs in Egypt. I especially thank my friends and colleagues Mr Mohamed Dahawi; Mrs Riri el-Aasser; Dr Khalid Dahawy; Mrs Amany Khalil; Mr Amr Dahawy; Mr Mortada Mohamed; Dr Nabil Mansour, Dr Mahmoud M. Amr and Dr Ali ElMaligui.

Finally, in addition to my friend Medhat, three individuals especially helped me 'see' Egypt from the perspective of those who face their own cultural challenges dealing with the various culture shocks Westerners exhibit while in Egypt. Thank you Ayman, Arabi and Ibrahim. They can be reached as follows:

- Mr Ayman A Mohamed in Maadi
  Desert Fox Club
  Tel: 012-354-6491 (mobile phone); fax: (02) 525-0886
  Email: info@dfcegypt.com
  Website: http://www.dfcegypt.com
- Mr Mohamed Arabi in Aswan, the 'Bird Man' of Aswan,
  tel: 012-324-0132 (mobile phone)
  See my article about Arabi on the TourEgypt.net website at:
  http://www.touregypt.net/magazine/
  mag06012001/magf2.htm
- Mr Ibrahim Amin in Alexandria and Cairo
  Tel: 012-347-6343 (mobile phone)
  Email: morgan_eg@yahoo.com

In the US, I would like to thank Jimmy Dunn at InterOz, Inc, in Lubbock, Texas. West Texas may seem a strange place from which to design the most informative website about Egypt on the Internet (http://www.touregypt.net), but Jimmy has done it and maintained it over the years. He is always ready to help with information and a contact when I need one (he seems to know just about everyone or know how to find them in Egypt).

Thanks to all the folks at Marshall Cavendish whom I have neither met nor spoken with, but who worked on this book. Special thanks to Patricia Ng for her help with the third edition and to Shova Loh, Jonathan Griffiths, Cheong Yaun Marn and Oh Hwee Yen for their help with earlier editions of the book.

My loving family deserves special recognition and the most thanks. Throughout it all, they have been there for me and it helps.

For my sons,
Edward and Darrell Spragins
and
for my friend and 'brother' in Egypt,
Medhat A-Monem

MAP OF EGYPT

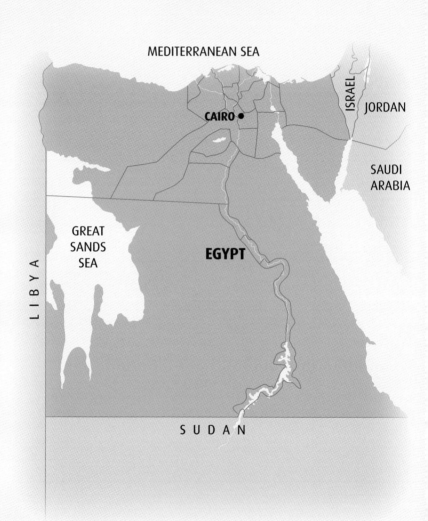

MEDITERRANEAN SEA

CAIRO •

ISRAEL

JORDAN

SAUDI
ARABIA

LIBYA

GREAT
SANDS
SEA

EGYPT

S U D A N

FIRST IMPRESSIONS

CHAPTER 1

'All men dream; but not equally. Those who dream
by night in the dusty recesses of their minds
Awake to find that it was vanity;
But the dreamers of day are dangerous men.
That they may act their dreams with open eyes
to make it possible. This I did.'
—T E Lawrence, *Seven Pillars of Wisdom*

LIKE MOST PEOPLE, I ENTERED EGYPT BY AIR through the Cairo airport. There are other ways to enter Egypt, of course—by air at another airport, by boat or over land. Since most people enter through the Cairo airport, I will devote this arrival discussion to that port of entry. Four things come to my mind when anyone asks me about my first impressions of Egypt. Wherever and however you enter Egypt, your first challenge will be to go through customs to get your feet on Egyptian soil. You will encounter most of the situations listed below no matter how you arrive.

My First Time

I would be remiss if I didn't say my *very first feeling* when arriving in Egypt the first time (in 1988) was one of sheer panic—panic at the sudden realisation that I did not know how to communicate what I needed or wanted. I did not know where to go, what to expect or what to do. I did what is normal for an American travelling—I looked for a sign with directions. But when I looked around, I didn't recognise (for the most part) any letters or words. Sounds were different. I was truly humbled at my ignorance! I felt the way I imagine a child feels before they learn to read but after they have figured out that the symbols they see 'mean' something. Of course, there were many welcoming Egyptians speaking to me in English (my native language) to help me as my feet touched Egyptian ground, but I still remember that short moment of unbelievable panic. Egyptians who were total strangers made me feel at home and welcome when things around me didn't look familiar!

(Continued on the next page)

(Continued from previous page)

My second first impression happened on the way into Cairo from the airport. Yes, we really did drive up the wrong side of a divided street and no, we did not have lights on even in the darkest stretches. My first trip into the city was via a small tour bus. It was night, so the lights remained on in the bus as we went into town. The bus was fantastic, though I felt that I was a rolling exhibit. As beautiful, comfortable and modern as the tour buses are, I truthfully never grew to like them because I wanted to be on the ground or pavement with real people. Of course, the other important thing about that initiation was my first experience with Egyptian driving. Coming from a country where one doesn't veer from one's traffic line without signalling and where one never 'creates' a new traffic lane just because there is room to do so, I was more than amazed by the bus's manoeuverability.

My third first impression was astonishment at how incredibly busy the city was. Cairo is alive and teeming with excitement any time of day or night. I was not prepared for the mass of people out-and-about, the congested traffic, nor the noise—the sheer *vivacité* that is Cairo. I loved it, but it was definitely new for me.

Finally, the smog was overwhelming and gave the city a burned diesel odour that permeated even the most inviting food or flower smells. What I really didn't like was blowing my nose and finding a blackened tissue from the air particles. The good news is that, since 1988 when I first travelled to Egypt, the air quality has improved considerably. I personally believe that a lot of the improvement resulted from switching from leaded to unleaded gasoline. However, there are still times when the smoke or smog is so bad you cannot see clearly across the river in Cairo.

If you are not accustomed to travelling in the Middle East, you may find it surprising if your plane does not pull into a gateway at the terminal. Some do and some do not. In many cases, the aircraft will park and passengers will disembark from a remote spot on the tarmac. Buses will arrive to shuttle passengers to the terminal. Once you are in the terminal, you are in a secured area and queue to go through customs. Immediately upon arrival, you will be escorted to the customs area where your passport and visa will be examined and stamped.

After clearing customs, you will go to another secured area for baggage claim. Before leaving the baggage claim area, you must go through one other checkpoint prior to admittance to Egypt. At this juncture, you will be asked about certain items you are bringing into the country. Occasionally, bags are searched. Personal effects and cameras are exempt from duty, but items such as electronic equipment and video cameras should be declared and listed on a Form D. If you lose them during your visit, it will be assumed they were 'sold' when you leave the country (unless you have police documentation of the theft). In this case, you will be required to pay 100 per cent duty. On items with a high resale value, you may be required to pay a deposit, which is refundable on departure from Egypt. If, for some reason, Customs insists on impounding any of your personal goods, get a receipt and contact your Consulate as soon as possible. That being said, I have taken my laptop computer into the country several times and have never been asked to declare it; perhaps next time. If there are specific items that need to be declared, you will be notified by officials at the airport. Somewhere I read that you should be sure to keep all money-change receipts and the custom Form D or other declaration forms (filled in upon arrival) as you may be required to present them upon departure. I have no idea why nor have I ever had anyone ask me for money-change receipts.

On your way through the airport, you will pass several banks or money exchanges. Unlike many other countries, the exchange rate you get at airport banks will be comparable to that elsewhere, so if you need to, exchange money into Egyptian pounds (E£) at the airport. If you prefer, you can wait to exchange money at your hotel or a bank near to your lodgings. Most taxi drivers will take major foreign currencies, as will baggage handlers, because they can now easily exchange them into Egyptian pounds. Hard currencies are at a premium throughout the country, so Euros or US dollars are greatly appreciated. However, you are likely to pay more for the service using foreign currency than you would if you tipped in Egyptian pounds—I think this is simply because you are still 'thinking' in your native language and customs rather than switching to Egyptian ones.

Do not be surprised, when you finally walk out onto the pavement, to find numerous men running towards you and grabbing your bags. No matter how many times I go there,

I have not been totally successful at stopping this. This is your first experience with what is fondly termed 'running the gauntlet'. Sometimes two or more people will seemingly fight over which one carries which bag, all the time yelling at one another in a language which you don't understand (unless you came to Egypt well prepared with a knowledge of Arabic). Each will try to take you to a special taxi driver that will undoubtedly give you the 'best price, no problem'. The important thing to remember is to negotiate the price before you get into the taxi and before you let someone store your bags in the taxi. This can be difficult because you are tired, confused and in the midst of a torrent of people all trying to get your attention and 'help' you. It can give you the feeling of being a morsel of food on a hot summer's day with flies circling. Just hold your ground and continue saying '*la*'—the Arabic word for 'no'—if you don't want assistance. Be prepared, however, to pay a tip for any service you accept (and sometimes even if you don't want help, they will just pick up your bags and run—and will still expect a tip). This is where having small Egyptian notes can come in handy. The going rate is about E£ 1–2 per bag.

> **Tipping Tip**
>
> Do not tip in foreign coins as these cannot be exchanged. If you are curious about the current official exchange rates, you can check your currency against the Egyptian pound at:
>
> - http://finance.yahoo.com/currency
> - http://www.xe.com/ucc/

Should you need additional assistance, you can summon a tourist policeman in an emergency (you should also tip the policeman if he gives assistance).

At some point following your arrival (whether by air, sea or land), you will begin to notice many men in uniforms, frequently with assault weapons. A heavy security presence is apparent to travellers throughout the country, though it is clearly more apparent at some times and places than others. Shortly after the September 11 tragedy in 2001 at the World Trade Centers in New York, I needed a little break, so left Cairo for a short cruise in Upper Egypt. To me, security was strong, but did not look abnormally high. However, a South African lady I chanced to meet along the way, quietly pulled me aside and asked if this was 'normal'. Since it did not look unusual to me, I assured her that it was normal, just something she might not be used to. You will see uniformed guards everywhere in Egypt—on the streets, at all monuments, frequently at hotel entrances—basically everywhere. Some are police, some are tourist police, some represent various branches of the armed services, and some are special security forces. After a while, you will be able to notice if something looks 'unusual'. There is a standard joke in Egypt, which says that most of the people you see with assault weapons do not have bullets or if they do, the bullets don't fit the gun. I have never trusted this witticism, especially since it would be totally impossible to tell which is which even if it is true. Your best bet is to assume that if there is a gun, the holder has ammunition that fits the weapon.

If you are coming from a country where the presence of armed guards on every street is uncommon, the sight of so many guns will probably be a little unsettling until you get used to it. Also, if you are accustomed to going wherever you like in some buildings, you will quickly find that entry into many areas is restricted and armed guards are there to ensure security. I also find that security presence differs from town-to-town.

Occasionally, you will find traffic is at a total standstill because an important dignitary is going somewhere. Troops line the streets in riot gear in these situations. Occasionally, armoured personnel carriers with troops wearing riot gear sit at strategic locations. Their presence depends on several circumstances, for example, where you are in Egypt or special circumstances of which you may not be aware. New residents and visitors may be particularly alarmed to see an armoured personnel carrier outside their hotel. The word on the street is that 'they are there for your protection'. Frankly, sometimes it seems for show, a way to show tourists that they are on top of everything. In Alexandria, for example, the tourist police seem to have less to do than in other cities, and always make a big show. Other times, extra protection is there because of a potential threat of which you are not aware, and they truly are there as a deterrent and for protection. Assume they are there for your protection.

A Word of Caution

Just a reminder, there are restrictions on photographing military personnel and sites, bridges and canals, including the Suez Canal. Egyptian authorities may broadly interpret these restrictions to include other potentially sensitive structures, such as embassies, other public buildings with international associations and some religious edifices. It is generally recommended that visitors should also refrain from taking photographs of any uniformed personnel.

Personally, I know of one situation where a foreigner was too close to a military site while taking pictures of trains or a bridge (it was never totally clear what the object of the photo was), was observed by police and arrested. The reason I am telling you is that it is sometimes very difficult to tell what is allowed and what is not allowed. As a general rule (this is definitely not an absolute), if you are trying to take a picture where it is not allowed, someone will tell you. If in doubt, you may ask—just be careful approaching anyone wearing a uniform unless it is clearly marked 'tourist police'.

On the way out of the airport, don't forget to stop by the duty-free stores, both inside and outside the Customs area of the airport, if you want any of the items sold there while you are in Egypt. Otherwise, you have 24 hours to go to one of the duty-free stores after you get into Egypt. For those who smoke imported cigarettes, they are sometimes cheaper at the duty-free outlets. If you want to have imported liquor while you are in Egypt, it is best bought by the bottle at duty-free. Otherwise, you can only get it by the drink at specific locations and it is very expensive. The local spirits stores typically sell products that have been bottled and labelled to look almost exactly like imported liquors. It is hard to say just what is actually in those bottles without a chemist, but in addition to appropriate food colouring, some are rumoured to contain formaldehyde and perfume. You probably want to avoid these products.

A TOUR OF EGYPT

'For anyone who sees Egypt, without having heard a word about it before, must perceive, if he has only common powers of observation, that the Egypt to which the Greeks go in their ships is an acquired country, the gift of the river.'
—Herodotus, Book II

EGYPT IS AN INCONGRUOUS MIXTURE OF OLD AND NEW. Considering that Egypt has one of the oldest civilisations known to the world and that it is home to the last standing Seven Wonders of the Ancient World, it is not surprising that just the word 'Egypt' fascinates and intrigues people. Looking around Egypt, one minute you think you have walked through a time warp straight into Biblical times; ten minutes later, you may find yourself negotiating a high stakes deal in an ultra-modern meeting room, teeming with skilled entrepreneurs dressed in the latest European fashion. Intertwined with remnants of time-worn lifestyles, Egypt is a nation seeking its place in a modern world of computers, telecommunications and banking. Lifestyles are so intermixed that it is difficult to define where one lifestyle ends and another begins. A booming tourist industry that introduces Egyptians to the world adds another dimension to the amalgam of lifestyles. While many Egyptians remain insulated from direct contact with outside forces, few are far from its influence. Most tourists remain somewhat isolated from real Egyptian life. They stay principally in modern facilities away from the poverty and exhausted infrastructure. Rarely do tourists experience the everyday struggles to move into the 'modern' age that affects the lives of Egypt's recently estimated (2005) 77 million people.

The modern Arab Republic of Egypt identifies itself as an Arab nation, though its people are 'Arabised' rather than true Arabs. The distinction between Arab and Egyptian is well recognised among Egyptians and Arabs alike. Egypt perceives its role in the development of the Middle East as one of leadership, peacemaker and negotiator. Egypt's rich educational heritage gives it a valuable export—skilled labour. Many Egyptian professionals, doctors, nurses, engineers, teachers and agricultural specialists work in other Arab countries. They make significant contributions to development throughout the Arab world and bolster Egypt's economy by sending wages back home.

In the following chapters, I will try to add order to seeming inconsistencies in Egyptian life. First, however, we must lay the groundwork by briefly describing the country, giving a few statistics, and pointing out some of Egypt's most pressing developmental concerns.

GEOGRAPHY AND NATURAL RESOURCES

Egypt is located on the far north-east corner of the African continent. It is about the size of Texas, Arkansas and Oklahoma, combined, or 1,001,450 sq km (386,662 sq miles). Egypt provides the gateway connecting the African continent with the huge Eurasian land mass. It controls the strategically and economically important Suez Canal and Sinai Peninsula. The Mediterranean Sea marks the northern boundary of Egypt. The Gaza Strip, Israel and the Red Sea border it on the east; the Sudan stretches across the southern border; and Libya lies west of Egypt's borders.

Egypt is a vast desert plateau interrupted by the Nile River valley and delta. Topographically, it is almost entirely desolate, with barren hills and mountains in the east and along the Nile. The Western Desert comprises slightly over two-thirds of the nation. The Sinai Peninsula and the Eastern Desert add another six and twenty-three per cent, respectively, to the desert landscape. The result is that less than four per cent of the total area is in the arable Nile Valley and Delta. When viewed with this perspective, it is easy to see why Herodotus so aptly noted in the 5th century BCE that Egypt is the 'gift of the Nile'. Like an emerald green ribbon, the Nile flows 880 km (550 miles) from Egypt's southern border with Sudan, through its desert heartland to the Mediterranean bringing life to an otherwise desert wilderness. The Nile forms at Khartoum, Sudan, when the Blue Nile and White Nile (whose sources are deep in Africa) converge. It separates the Western (Libyan) Desert from the Eastern (Arabian) Desert. As a result of its unique geographical configuration, most Egyptians live in the Delta and along the narrow irrigated strip on either side of the Nile.

Another prominent geographical feature is Lake Nasser, an artificial lake resulting from the construction of the Aswan High Dam. Historically, the Nile flooded annually, depositing needed silt all along the Nile's path. Whether Egypt had a high or low flood year depended on rainfall in other parts of Africa. Early in the 1900s, the first Aswan Dam (now below the High Dam) was completed to try to control annual flooding. It was subsequently raised, but still could not control the Nile's raging flood waters. Only after completion of the Aswan High Dam in the 1970s was the Nile finally tamed. The High Dam was built not only to control flooding, but to increase arable land and generate electricity to

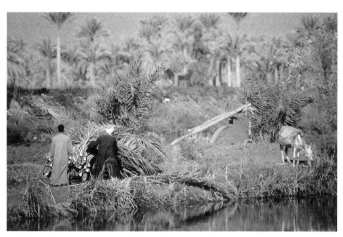

Traditional irrigation methods include the use of water wheels, like the one shown here, to lift water to crop fields. Donkeys and camels are still used as beasts of burden.

facilitate Egypt's move toward modernity. Considerable international controversy resulted from the former Soviet Union's financing of the dam after refusal by Western institutions. The Dam became operational in 1971 and by 1974, revenues had exceeded construction costs. Subsequently, increasing costs of reclamation have offset the value of providing a regulated flow of Nile water for irrigation.

Though it is ecologically controversial for several reasons, the High Dam rapidly increased modernisation throughout Egypt by providing an accessible source for electrical generation. Older people will tell you that food just doesn't taste as good as it used to when the Nile flooded. This is probably a result of the subsequent need to use chemical fertilisers that were never needed when rich soil was deposited annually.

Schistosomiasis

One interesting health result has been an increase in an ancient disease named schistosomiasis or Bilharzia (named after the German-born scientist, Theodor Bilharz, whose work in intestinal parasites rewarded him with a prestigious position at the Kasr el Aïny Faculty of Medicine in Cairo until his death in 1862). Apparently, the annual flooding washed away the snails that host the parasite eggs, thus, annually removing some of the means of infection.

Culturally, construction of the dam was also controversial. As a result of rising water in Lake Nasser, numerous small Nubian villages had to be relocated north of the dam. Historians and archaeologists worldwide were up in arms because many ancient ruins could not be saved from the rising waters. Seemingly superhuman international efforts saved some historical sites by rapid excavations or by systematically disassembling, moving and reconstructing them at a new site, such as the great temples at Abu Simbel. Increasing desertification and prolonged droughts in the Sahel and Sahara Deserts seriously threaten Egyptian water management and use of its water resources. In 1987, Lake Nasser's water level was at its lowest since the lake filled—at a level actually below the amount needed to run the Aswan power station.

Oil and natural gas are two of Egypt's most important natural resources although their quantities do not compare with the high reserves of their neighbours on the Arabian Peninsula. Proven reserves are estimated to be some 6.2 billion barrels of oil with some 500 cubic metres of natural gas reserves. Recent oil discoveries in the Gulf of Suez and the Western Desert suggest these figures will increase. Production of natural gas is sufficient to meet domestic needs and provides a surplus for export. Egypt's other natural resources include iron ore, phosphates, manganese, limestone, gypsum, talc, asbestos, lead and zinc.

ENVIRONMENTAL ISSUES

Egypt's environmental problems revolve around a rapidly increasing population, poverty, ignorance and historic lack of concern for environmental integrity. The current government is seeking measures to clean up Egypt's massive environmental problems, but many traditions are deeply ingrained and the existing infrastructure is severely in need of modernisation, so progress is extremely slow. Experimental projects look for new ways to maintain environmental integrity while allowing for productive growth.

Of course, the fact that much of the land is effectively uninhabitable presents other environmental challenges—like how to develop sustainable desert reclamation. On top of this, add the fact that the little agricultural land that does exist throughout the country is being lost to urbanisation. Oil pollution and new tourist sites along the Red Sea threaten Egypt's coral reefs, beaches and marine habitats. Natural fresh water resources away from the Nile (the only perennial fresh water source) are very limited although recent underground finds in the Western Desert may provide new sources for limited agricultural development. Agricultural pesticides, raw sewage and industrial effluents further threaten water supplies.

Natural environmental hazards include earthquakes and occasional flash floods and landslides, along with wind and dust storms. A particularly vicious hot, driving sandstorm, called a *khamsin*, occurs in spring, making the air thick with sand, limiting visibility and causing breathing difficulties among many.

REGIONS OF EGYPT

For planning purposes, the Egyptian government divided the country into seven major regions: Upper Egypt, Middle Egypt (Assiut); North of Upper Egypt; Greater Cairo; the Canal; Alexandria and Matrouh; and the Delta. Local tradition generally recognises slightly different regional classifications, so I will stick with local tradition, while recognising planning needs may require different categories.

Lower Egypt and the Delta

The terms Lower and Upper Egypt, which are used today, have their roots in ancient tradition before the first unification of the two regions of Egypt around 3200 BCE. Based on contemporary maps and global logic, one would expect Upper Egypt to be in the north. However, to ancient Egyptians reality revolved around the perceptions of the life-giving Nile whose source lies deep in the heart of the African continent (the Nile flows south to north). Since their world revolved around the flow of the Nile, quite logically, Upper Egypt was in the south and Lower Egypt was in the north. These designations are still in use today.

Lower Egypt begins at Cairo and ends at the boundaries of the Mediterranean Sea. Just north of Cairo, the Nile divides into its two tributaries, the Damietta and the Rosetta, forming the huge Delta alluvial flood plain. Extensive networks of canals and channel irrigation provide the Delta area with needed water resources for cultivation. The area provided such high crop yields that in Roman times, Egypt became known as the 'bread basket of the world'. Now, Egypt is no longer able to be self-sufficient in its food production. Throughout the country, maintenance of high agricultural yields depends heavily on the use of agrochemical products. The larger, more modern farms tend to be located in Lower Egypt. Most of the cotton, for which Egypt is famous, grows in this region.

The moment you leave the Delta proper, you are back in the desert again. Desert extends west from the Delta and eastward, turning into salt marshes along the eastern sea coasts. Desert reclamation farms in Upper Egypt have slightly increased the amount of arable land in the area. Local entrepreneurs have begun developing small fish farms along the shores of the Mediterranean near Port Said. One new corporation, using modern scientific methods, developed an experimental shrimp farm that was quite successful. This ecologically sensitive project, designed to be a long-term sustainable enterprise, is now being expanded to provide a vital new use for salty lowlands.

Upper Egypt

The area from Cairo south to the Sudanese border is called Upper Egypt. The green area from Cairo south is mostly a narrow band of irrigated land along the Nile's shores, rarely extending in breadth for more than a couple of miles. The Western Desert (Libyan Desert) regions of Upper Egypt have begun to experience some development. A lot of government attention is presently directed to the new cities with special emphasis given to the master development plans for the 'New Valley' in southern Egypt. The four New Valley oases are situated along a dead, prehistoric branch of the Nile. They depend on springs and wells tapping into water under the desert. The four oases are isolated from each other but may be reached via a loop road starting at one end in Cairo and ending in Luxor. The government has undertaken several agricultural initiatives to encourage settlement near oases and desert reclamation projects.

In 2001, a great archaeological find was announced in Bahariya Oasis, about 380 km (236.1 miles) west of the Pyramids at Giza. The tombs in the Valley of the Golden Mummies were discovered in 1996 when a donkey, ridden by an antiquities guard along the dusty road to the small town of Farafra, tripped after its leg slipped into a hole leading to the entrance. An entire undisturbed forgotten population of mummies in porcelain caskets or canvas wrappings were found. The mummies are covered with a thin layer of gold and wear gypsum masks. Sumptuous gilded death masks depict lifelike faces of real people, rather than stereotypical images. It is estimated that as many as 10,000 mummies may be found once the necropolis is totally excavated.

Farming in Upper Egypt generally tends to be small scale, often family subsistence farming. The landscape of Upper Egypt is dotted all along the Nile with small traditional villages and several small- to medium-sized cities. Large villas, markets, shops, streetlights, several universities, small hospitals and large apartment blocks distinguish the urban areas from the poorer *fellahin* (small-scale famer) and Nubian villages.

Middle Egypt

Although the whole area from Cairo south is called Upper Egypt, many also recognise a distinction in the centre of the country called Middle Egypt which includes the area around the governorates of Minya, Assiut, and Qena (Qina). However, most people from this area of Egypt also consider themselves to be Upper Egyptians.

Bani Hasan al Shurraq

If you are interested to find out more, read my article about a not-so-visited, but very interesting, Middle Kingdom site at Bani Hasan al Shurraq near el-Minya at:

> http://www.touregypt.net/featurestories/banihasan.htm.

Suez Canal

Located at the crossroads of Europe, Asia and Africa, the Suez Canal is one of the world's most important artificial waterways. It connects the Indian Ocean via the Red Sea and the Gulf of Suez with the Mediterranean Sea. The city of Port Said is located at the northern terminus on the Mediterranean Sea. Ismailia, the administrative headquarters, is about midway through the Canal. The southern terminus is at the city of Suez.

Prior to the peace treaty between Egypt and Israel, the Suez Canal held centre stage in several confrontations. The Canal provides the single largest source of foreign currency in Egypt's economy. Going through the Canal shortens the distance from the Far East to Europe by 8,047 km (5,000 miles), thus vitally affecting commercial shipping.

This tanker makes its way through the Suez Canal, the artifical waterway which brings in most of the foreign currency for Egypt. The Canal has helped to revolutionise shipping by shortening the distance from Europe to the Far East.

Built by French companies starting in 1859, it opened on 17 November 1869. Great Britain acquired the Canal in 1875 and Egypt subsequently nationalised it in the 1950s. A sea level artificial waterway with no locks, its total length is 169 km (105 miles) including approach channels. Renovation of the Canal widened its narrowest point to 60 m (196 ft) and increased its depth to 16 m (53 ft) to accommodate larger ships.

Sinai and Red Sea

The Sinai Peninsula is the place to go for the newest in Egyptian beach resorts. Other than that, it is mostly a barren desert wilderness with some oil rigs, military outposts and a few historic sites. It is strategically important because it is the only land bridge connecting Africa with the Eurasian continent and provides the eastern boundary to the Suez Canal. The Sinai is economically important because it contains much of Egypt's proven oil and gas reserves. A few Bedouin (desert nomads) live in the area, but other than that there is little habitation except in the developing tourist villages. Projects are in development to provide a fresh water source for more desert reclamation agriculture.

The Red Sea coast is rugged and scenic. It also has a very good highway.

The Red Sea area has beautiful blue-green waters with some of the best scuba diving in the world. Government efforts for national parklands are being implemented to protect some of the more environmentally sensitive areas.

MAJOR CITIES
Cairo (al-Qahirah)

Cairo, known as al-Qahirah in Arabic, throbs and pulsates with life 24 hours a day! Even those of us who like small-town living cannot fail to be captivated by her. Teeming with approximately 11 million people in the metropolitan area (and a best guess estimate of 2–4 million daily migrants), Cairo writhes as she strains to burst at the seams. The metropolitan area's population ranks 17th in the world. For comparison, Cairo proper has approximately the same population as New York City or London or Beijing. The population density is approximately 25,000 persons per square kilometre in Cairo (more than twice as dense as greater London and two and-one-half times as dense as New York City, for example). East and West butt each other face-to-face in modern Cairo. Few places in the modern world exhibit the inherent clash between the ancient and modern worlds seen in Cairo.

The beautiful city of Cairo by nght.

To Egyptians, Cairo is Egypt (Misr), the Mother of the World, and 'the victorious'.

The site of Egypt's capital (though not the name) can be traced back over 6,000 years. Around 4225 BC, on the western bank of the Nile a few miles north of present-day Cairo, East Delta people built the first capital of a united Egypt. Today, the oldest reminders of ancient Cairo are found in Old Cairo.

Getting oriented to the maze of Cairo is not as difficult as it seems at first glance. First, get yourself a good map and orient yourself to the major sections of the city. Start at the centre—Tahrir Square (Midan Tahrir)—and work your way out moving clockwise.

Online Maps

A good place for free, online maps is at the TourEgypt site:

http://touregypt.net/maps.htm.

I have found these maps to be clear and most print well. In fact, the TourEgypt site (http://www.touregypt.net), developed and maintained by Jimmy Dunn at InterOz, is the absolute best site to visit first for most kinds of information about Egypt from hotel reviews to feature articles about antiquities.

North

From Midan Tahrir, go north. Here you will find the neighbourhoods of Bulaq and Shubra. When you reach Ramses station, this is the boundary between Bulaq and Shubra. Bulaq was the old industrial centre of Cairo; however industrialisation subsequently moved northward to Shubra. A very traditional area of Cairo, today's Bulaq is one of the most densely populated districts of Cairo. It is also noteworthy because this area bred much of the recent Islamic unrest.

East

North-east from Midan Tahrir, you will find Midan Talaat Harb and Ezbekiya Gardens, an area full of Western-style shops and inexpensive, old hotels. Further east, you will find the area known as Islamic Cairo. This area encompasses the Citadel, some of Cairo's poorer districts, and a couple of important medieval neighbourhoods. Continuing east and south, you will find the Cities of the Dead. In the Cities of the Dead (huge necropolises), living inhabitants scurry through the vast array of mausoleums rearing children among the funeral vaults. Moving north-east from here, you will reach Heliopolis (where the airport is located), a wealthy district also known as New Cairo.

South

Directly south of Midan Tahrir is Garden City, home to embassies and expensive residences. From Garden City, bridges cross the Nile to Roda Island. On Roda Island you will find Manyal Palace, Cairo University's Faculty of Medicine, the Old and New Qasr al-Eini Hospitals, and the Nilometer. The sprawling suburbs of Old Cairo continue south from Garden City, encompassing the small area known as Coptic Cairo. The next major district moving southward is Maadi. A wealthy district, expatriates tend to congregate in this area.

West

Crossing Al-Tahrir Bridge, you come to Gezira Island in the middle of the Nile. The residential suburb of Gezira occupies the southern part of the island. Gezira is home to Cairo's elite, including some leading diplomats. On the northern half of Gezira Island is Zamalek, another expensive area of town which houses embassies and modern apartment buildings. The famous Gezira Sporting Club connects the two suburbs.

Across the river from Gezira are several districts on the west bank of the Nile. The southernmost district is Giza (home of the Great Pyramids), which stretches to the edge of the desert. Just north of Giza is Doqqi (Dokki). Doqqi houses the rest of Cairo University, and several districts including Imbaba (old home of Cairo's camel market). The camel market has now moved to Birqash about 32 km (20 miles) north-west of the city.

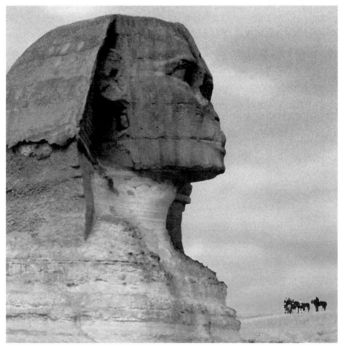

The majestic Sphinx stands guard on the Giza plateau. The horseback riders on the nearby ridge give you an idea of the immense proportion of the last remaining Seven Wonders of the World.

The Corniche winds along Alexandria's irregular coastline.

Alexandria (al-Iskandariya)

Beautiful Alexandria! After conquering Egypt south to Memphis in 332 BC, Alexander the Great (Iskandar al-Akbar) chose the site of current-day Alexandria to be the capital of his empire. What became known as Alexandria (al-Iskandariya in Arabic) was positioned on the west side of the Nile Delta at the site of a small fishing village. Alexandria was envisioned by Alexander to be not only the political and economic centre of his empire, but a naval base and great trading port. Alexandria was nearly destroyed when the Arabs captured it in AD 642. An earthquake devastated the famous lighthouse in 1324, another of the Seven Wonders of the Ancient World built on the Island of Pharos in 280 BC.

Alexandria was well designed with streets crossing at right angles. It is wide, stretching some 20 km (12 miles) from west to east. The hub of Alexandria is the Midan Saad Zaghloul, which runs to the waterfront. Just to the east is the Midan Ramla, where Ramla station is located. Alexandria's culture has many distinct Mediterranean influences such as in the European quarter as well as its characteristically Egyptian areas. The bulk of Egypt's foreign trade passes through its port. The population of Alexandria currently exceeds two million.

Luxor

Located in Upper Egypt, the contemporary city of Luxor was built on the ancient site of Thebes. Luxor now has a population of around 200,000 persons, most of whom seem to be rather sagacious hawkers and vendors working in the tourist industry. Here, modern Egyptians combine an exotic history with modern commercialism. Hordes of foreign visitors throng the streets, even in the scorching summer heat. What most people think of as Luxor is actually three distinct areas: Luxor city (including Luxor temple), the village of Karnak, and the necropolis of ancient Thebes. The sheer magnitude of Karnak's intricate temple complex boggles the mind. On the west Bank of the Nile, directly across from Luxor, the famous Valley of the Kings, Valley of the Queens, Temple of Hatshepsut, and many finely decorated tombs draw eager tourists anxious to explore the remnants of Egypt's intricate funerary practices. Howard Carter's 1922 discovery of King Tutankhamun's (King Tut's) tomb filled with treasures still remains one of the most internationally celebrated sites to visit.

For Tutankhamun Enthusiasts

If Tut is your interest, two websites are a must! National Geographic has a fully interactive site featuring the original February 1923 volume at:

http://www.nationalgeographic.com/egypt.

The Ashmolean Museum at Oxford, England, also has a website that contains the complete text of Howard Carter's Diary and links to other Egyptian sites at the museum. Visit:

http://www.ashmol.ox.ac.uk/gri/4sea1not.html.

Aswan

Gateway to Africa, frontier city and prosperous market at the crossroads of the ancient caravan trade route, Aswan is undoubtedly one of my favourite places in Egypt. It has a sleepy, almost tranquil atmosphere, in contrast to the rest of Egypt. It is here that the Nile is the most enchanting and magical as it weaves through the mass of boulders and small islands, glistening sparkles dancing off its surface.

View of Elephantine Island in Aswan.

The culture here is a fascinating mixture of Egyptian and Nubian heritages. Aswan is located on the eastern shores of the Nile about 9.6 km (6 miles) north of the First Cataract, one of the six major rock outcroppings situated between Aswan and Khartoum. A 'must-see' in Aswan is the beautiful Nubian Museum, (Nubia means 'gold') completed in 1997, which displays thousands of antiquities that would have been lost under the waters of Lake Nasser had not a major international effort salavaged them during the 1960s and 1970s. Speaking of the international effort to save Nubian artifacts, the UNESCO-supported effort to move the Temple of Ramses II and Temple of Queen Nefitari dedicated to Hathor above the flood waters of Lake Nasser is located 280 km (174 miles) south of Aswan. During the salvage operation which began in 1964 and continued until 1968, the two temples were dismantled and raised over 60 metres up the sandstone cliff where they had been built more than 3,000 years before.

ANCIENT AND RECENT PAST

A minimal understanding of Egypt's ancient and recent past is useful to the foreign resident for several reasons. First, the major issues affecting contemporary Egyptians, and thus anyone living in the country, have roots in her history. This is especially true when you consider that tourism is one of Egypt's top economic producers. Second, it is impossible to go down any street in Egypt without some kind of recognition of her ancient glory as one of the five centres in the world where civilisation developed. Third, ancient Egypt's monuments, temples, mosques, monasteries and pyramids provide the basis for a substantial portion of her current economy. For a short summary of Middle Eastern dynamics and history, see the work by Spencer listed at the end of this book, which served as the source of much of the recent historical information included in this chapter.

The accomplishments of the ancients defy description. Words like 'awe-inspiring' or 'incredible' or 'spectacular' cannot come close to describing the emotions running rampant through anyone confronted with his or her first

The breathtaking statue of Ramses II at Abu Simbel, a historical site which was systematically reassembled when the Aswan Dam caused Lake Nasser's rising waters to threaten its existence.

view of the great Hypostyle Hall of Karnak or the Great Pyramid of Khufu. No matter how hard you try to snap a photo that shows what you see, that feeling of being small and inconsequential eludes the camera's eye. Underlying the sheer majesty of Egypt's megalithic monuments is the inevitable acknowledgement of the powerful political and social mechanisms that must surely have been in place to organise such gargantuan projects. You cannot view monuments like the Pyramids, the Valley of the Kings, or the Temple of Karnak without humility and without recognising Egypt's contribution to the development of all human society.

That being said, I do not intend to write a description of monuments nor an in-depth diatribe on Egypt's history. Instead, I will highlight only the main eras recognised in Egyptian history. If you are interested in a comprehensive treatment of Egyptian history or prehistory, start with the works listed at the end of this book and work your way forward through the myriad of tomes on the subject.

Predynastic and Dynastic History

People were living throughout the Nile valley for several thousand years before Egypt as we know it became a unified state. This is generally termed the prehistoric, archaic, and Predynastic periods of Egyptian history. The Predynastic period lasted from about 3150–3050 BC. By around 3150 BC, highly stratified states existed in the two separate kingdoms of Upper and Lower Egypt. The boundaries were pretty much as recognised today. Upper Egypt constituted the area from the beginning of the Delta southward, whereas Lower Egypt covered the Delta region. Just as settled village life was inextricably tied to the narrow, elongated fertile strip along the Nile, the river also provided the avenue for traffic and communication.

Most of Egypt's outstanding monuments were constructed during her Pharaonic period. Egyptian dynastic history reckons that Egypt became a unified kingdom at about 3150 BC when King Menes (Narmer) succeeded in unifying Upper and Lower Egypt. There is no historical record of King Menes who placed his capital at Memphis about 40 km (25 miles) south of current-day Cairo. Some think the unification credited to Menes may be more a symbolic than a political act. However, Egypt's initial unification appears to have lasted through the end of the Old Kingdom (ca 2575–2150 BC).

Egypt's most enduring icon, the Great Pyramids, are a legacy of the Pharonic era.

In any event, the unity of Egypt seems to have been shattered during the First Intermediate Period (ca 2150 –2040 BC) which lasted about 100 years. During this time, the central power of the king broke down. Though nominally in service to the pharaoh, *nomarchs* (rulers of individual nomes or divisions of Egypt) operated virtually independently from central rule.

The anarchy of the First Intermediate Period was followed by a period of restored order under the Pharaoh Mentuhotep I or II (some controversy as to which one). This period was called the Middle Kingdom (ca 2040–1783 BC). Mentuhotep consolidated the administrative power of Egypt at Thebes (modern Luxor). Although the seat of political power shifted on several occasions throughout Egyptian history, from the Middle Kingdom onwards, religious influence emanated from Thebes. The pharaohs of the Middle Kingdom were able once again to institute major architectural projects, which had lapsed during the First Intermediate Period. By the last 50 years of the Middle Kingdom, once again central authority gradually waned.

The Second Intermediate Period lasted nearly 200 years (ca 1783–1550 BC). Somewhere around 1663 BC, Egypt was invaded by a group of somewhat mysterious people known as the Hyksos. The term 'Hyksos' comes from the Greek meaning 'rulers over foreign lands'. It is not totally clear exactly who the Hyksos were, but they were apparently of Asiatic origin, perhaps from Turkey. Some activities of the Hyksos are very confusing. Even though they continued to tolerate legitimate Egyptian kings, they apparently desecrated monuments and reduced major landowners to poverty. However, importantly, the Hyksos introduced several new technological innovations. Paramount among these was the

For Your Reading Pleasure

If you like historical fiction or dramatisations of this period, check out Wilbur Smith's book entitled *River God* and the sequel, *The Seventh Scroll*. Great reading and well researched, but not necessarily totally in line with history! Another really fun series is the five-volume title, *Ramses*, written by Christian Jacq. Again, not necessarily an accurate account of events, but great historical dramatisations and good research on Egyptian life make this an exceptionally readable series.

horse and chariot, which subsequently became a formidable weapon for Egyptian warriors.

The Hyksos were eventually forced out of Egypt around 1550 BC, which commences the period termed the New Kingdom. The New Kingdom lasted some 500 years during which time Egyptian dominance reigned throughout the region. In popular terms, the New Kingdom is synonymous with the Egypt described in the Old Testament. New Kingdom pharaohs abandoned pyramid-building in favour of massive tombs carved into the sandstone cliffs of the Nile's west bank. It is also during this period that the great temples of Thebes were built—Luxor, Karnak, Deir el-Bahari, Medinet Habu and the Ramesseum.

Until the invasion of the Hyksos, Egypt had been spared large-scale foreign invasion. After that time, Egypt became part of the overwhelming wave of aggressors throughout the Middle East. Under Tuthmosis I (1504–1492 BC), Egypt became an imperial power, pushing her borders far into Nubia in the south and to the Euphrates in the north-east. By the time of Ramses II (1300–1233 BC), Egypt's monarchs extended their power over much of the Middle East.

Power Points

Except for the Roman Empire (governed from outside the Middle East), major empires of the region centred successively from four focal points: Mesopotamia (current-day Iraq), Asia Minor (Turkey), the Nile Valley (Egypt) and Persia (Iran). Each of these areas served as a power focus two or three times over the ages. Interestingly, at one time or another each major power locus has controlled much or most of the rest of the region, thus providing many of the historical cultural links seen today.

By the beginning of the Third Intermediate Period (ca 1070–712 BC), Egypt no longer dominated the Mediterranean but instead retreated to her natural geographic boundaries. During this period, technological advances in the aggressive civilisations throughout Mesopotamia did not spread to Egypt. Consequently, Egypt was unable to wage war successfully against these powers. Once again, relative anarchy ensued, providing the milieu for Libyan mercenaries, who assimilated into Egyptian society during the New Kingdom, to assume powerful positions. Prior to the Third

The remains of Medinet Habu—one of the great
temples of the New Kingdom—seen at dawn.

Intermediate Period, much of Egyptian history is a result of archaeological and artistic reconstruction. From this period forward, however, documents remain that provide a much more traditional historical record.

Finally, Egypt began what is termed the Late Kingdom (ca 712–332 BC), a period of reunification established under rule of the Nubian pharaoh, King Shebaka. Twice during the Late Kingdom, Egypt came under Persian rule. The Second Persian Invasion succeeded in 343 BC, but lasted only a short time before Egypt came under the rule of the great Macedonian warrior, Alexander the Great.

The Second Persian Invasion marks an important point in Egyptian history. It signifies the beginning of 2,600 years of foreign domination. Independent rule was not reinstated in Egypt until Gamal Abdel Nasser's expulsion of the British puppet, King Farouk, in 1952.

Greco-Roman Period (332 BC–AD 395)

Alexander marched unopposed into Egypt in 332 BC. At the mouth of the Delta, Alexander founded the city of Alexandria designed to be the capital of his empire. For the next nine hundred years, Alexandria was the great centre of learning in the Middle East.

When Alexander died in 323 BC, he was succeeded by his able general, Ptolemy, under the nominal rule of Alexander's brother Philip. Once Philip died, Ptolemy became sole ruler, establishing a dynasty that lasted until the death of Cleopatra VII in 30 BC. Alexander's immense empire barely survived his death. His generals carved up the empire and fought among themselves to try to conquer more territory. Ptolemy embraced the Egyptian religion, a practice followed by his successors. Whether for political reasons or sincere belief, the practice helped secure the lands of Egypt under Ptolemaic rule.

The Ptolemies ruled from Alexandria, but became increasingly out of touch with the Egyptian people. In fact, until the last Cleopatra, the Ptolemies did not even speak the Egyptian language. It is during this period that Egypt undertook the last of its grand architectural and sacred artistic

Greek-influenced architectural reliefs can be seen at the temple of Philae.

development. Temples built in this era have Greek-influenced reliefs as seen, for example, in Edfu, Esna and Philae.

The Ptolemaic era saw Egypt fully integrated into the affairs of the Near and Middle East. Unlike earlier periods, technological, agricultural and trade innovations became assimilated into Egyptian life. Egypt still, however, resisted Greek philosophy and religion. Essentially, the Ptolemies kept Egypt independent from other outside rulers. But it was the death of the most famous, and perhaps cleverest, Ptolemaic Queen Cleopatra VII (69–30 BC), that marked the demise of Egypt's independence once and for all.

Cleopatra's Last Days

Octavian (later Augustus) defeated Cleopatra's military forces under the command of Marc Antony at Actium in 31 BC. Unable to seduce Augustus and thus maintain power over the throne of Egypt, Cleopatra VII committed suicide by clasping the infamous asp to her breast in 30 BC. If you are interested in reading the earliest accounts of Cleopatra VII, see Plutarch's *Parallel Lives*, originally written in the first century.

Under Roman rule, Egypt had little or no political autonomy. Rome used Egypt as its bread basket. Even though Rome ruled Egypt with a tight grip, it was largely tolerant of

Egyptian religion. Christianity finally dealt the death blow of Egypt's ancient religion, beginning when Constantine declared it to be the official religion of the empire in AD 333. As can be expected, the new religion took its fastest and firmest hold in the north, where Alexandria became a centre of Christianity. It took some two hundred years before the last of the Isis cult died on the island of Philae.

Egyptian Coptic Church

The Egyptian Coptic Church was one of the earliest organised Christian Churches in the world. Today's Copts are considered to be direct descendants of the ancient Egyptians. When Arab invaders in the 7th century brought Islam to Egypt, they were welcomed by the Copts living there. In return, Arab Islamic leaders did not require conversion to Islam. Instead, they protected the Copts, respecting their Christian heritage. Many Copts did eventually convert. They remain the principal minority in Egypt today. Until very recently, Egypt also had a small but established Jewish community. They were treated with similar respect under Islamic rule. However, most of Egypt's Jewish community immigrated to Israel after its establishment as an independent state in 1948.

Recent History

Following the Islamic armies, numerous nomadic Arabs settled in the Nile Valley. Egypt came under the rule of the Muslim caliphs ('successors' of the Prophet Muhammad) until the 10th century. At this time, a Shia group broke away, forming a separate government. This group established a new capital, al-Qahirah, in the desert south of Alexandria. During the 16th century, Egypt came under the control of the Ottoman Empire, then under the rule of the Mamluks. Originally slaves or prisoners, the Mamluks were eventually freed, subsequently forming a military aristocracy. The Ottomans essentially ceded control of Egypt to the Mamluks, requiring only periodic tribute and taxes from the citizens.

It was during the 18th century that Egypt became embroiled in European political dynamics. By this time, the French and British challenged each other for control of trade in the Mediterranean and sea routes to India. In 1798, Napoleon Bonaparte invaded Egypt. However, the British joined forces with the Mamluks and successfully drove the French from Egypt. This left the British and Mamluks in a power struggle over Egypt.

The Ottoman sultan appointed Muhammad Ali to the post of governor in Egypt in 1805. In the end, he was the successor to the disputes between the Mamluks and the British. Although Muhammad Ali was not Egyptian (he was Albanian by birth), his great organisational skills and vision for a rich and powerful Egypt provided the impetus for suppressing the Mamluks. Muhammad Ali's successors ruled in theory on behalf of the Ottoman sultan, but in reality functioned as independent rulers (called *khedives* or 'viceroys').

The Suez Canal was opened in 1869 during the leadership of Khedive Ismail. Unfortunately, for Egyptians, Ismail overextended Egypt financially and was forced to sell the Egyptian government's share of the Canal to the British. As a result, British control over Egyptian finances ensued. A popular revolt threatened an overthrow of the *khedive* system in 1882, but was halted when the British intervened. The British then established a de-facto protectorate, but kept the *khedive* office in place.

As most know, the Ottoman Empire, long in decline, finally collapsed totally with the end of World War I. The British used Egypt as a staging ground against the Ottomans throughout the War, insuring their interests in the Suez Canal were protected. Since Egypt was technically still part of the Ottoman Empire, Britain officially declared its intention to 'defend' the country. Following the end of World War I, a nationalist movement took form in Egypt. Egyptian nationalist leaders formed the Wafd ('delegation'), which presented demands to the British. They wanted complete independence for Egypt. When the British refused their demands, the Wafd turned to violence, organising boycotts, strikes and terrorist attacks against the British.

Under pressure, the British formally dissolved the protectorate in 1922, but retained certain controls over Egyptians through regulation of foreign policy, defence and communications. Thus, Egypt's 'independence' was a thin shell. Through this process, Egyptians did regain control over their internal affairs. A new constitutional monarchy was established under King Fuad. Neither King Fuad nor his son successor, King Farouk, trusted Wafd leaders.

During the years of the monarchy, the Egyptian military developed a strong corps of professional officers, most of whom were from lower- and middle-class backgrounds. Among this group of professional officers was Gamal Abdel Nasser, who was already an active anti-British demonstrator by the time he entered the newly formed Egyptian Military Academy. When World War II ensued, the British needed a military staging base in North Africa to ensure their control of the Suez Canal. As a result, the British officially reinstituted Egypt as a protectorate. This action energised Egyptian officers into forming a revolutionary movement.

Following World War II, the establishment of the state of Israel in May 1948 resulted in Egypt, along with other Arab countries, embarking on an attempt to destroy the new nation. During this action, the Egyptian army was defeated. Officers were appalled at the evident corruption and ineffectiveness of their own government. Nasser and his compatriots attributed the defeat to their government's failures, not their own weaknesses. They formed a secret organisation, the Free Officers, determined to overthrow the monarchy. Other groups seeking to overthrow the monarch existed but the Free Officers developed the best internal organisation and support of the army.

The Free Officers launched their revolution on 23 July 1952. In an essentially bloodless coup, King Farouk abdicated the throne. The coup came only six months after 'Black Sunday', the burning of Cairo by mobs protesting the continued presence of British troops in Egypt. By the time the monarchy was officially abolished in 1954, Nasser emerged as the clear leader and became president, prime minister and head of the Revolution Command Council (RCC) which was set up to run the country after the success of the coup.

Nasser established ambitious goals for Egypt: to restore dignity and status to Egypt; to eliminate foreign control; and to establish Egypt as the leader of the Arab world. During

Nasser's 18 years at the helm of Egypt, many of his goals were accomplished. Nasser finally succeeded in removing the last vestiges of British rule from Egypt. Valiant efforts failed to unify the Arab world, however. The nadir in Nasser's presidency was the 'catastrophe' of the Six-Days War with Israel in June 1967.

Egyptian-Russian Ties

Under Nasser, Egypt developed a close alliance with the Soviet Union between 1956–1967. The World Bank, under strong pressure from the United States, refused funding of Nasser's most important infrastructural project (construction of the Aswan High Dam) due to Egypt's expressed hostility towards Israel. This action triggered Nasser's turn to the Soviet Union. The Soviet Union agreed to finance the dam, which was completed in 1971.

Even though he had been in poor health for some time, Nasser's death came as a shock to many Egyptians. Following his death in 1970, Anwar el-Sadat, his vice president, was installed as president as per constitutional procedure. Sadat, long thought by many to be Nasser's 'yes' man, soon showed his strength.

Very shortly after assuming the presidency, Sadat introduced a 'revolution of rectification' which he said was needed to correct the errors of his predecessor. Seeking to ally Egypt more closely with the United States, in 1972 he ordered 15,000 Soviet advisors to leave Egypt. In October 1973, Egyptian forces crossed the Suez Canal and broke through Israeli lines in the occupied Sinai. This attack was co-ordinated with an attack from Syria on Israel's eastern border. The surprise attack initially pushed the Israelis back, but they later regrouped and subsequently regained most of the territory they had lost. Following that, a stalemate highlighted Arab-Israeli affairs until Sadat took a dramatic chance announcing at a meeting of the Egyptian People's Assembly that he was ready to talk to the Israelis in their own house—the Knesset. And he did so. Sadat's foreign policy successes culminated in the 1979 peace treaty with Israel and, subsequently, the Nobel Peace Prize.

On the home front, Sadat was not as successful. Internally, religious leaders and conservative Muslims objected to many of his practices and policies. The poor resented having to pay more for less. The educated classes were angry about claims that the political system was more open when it was not. Sadat's economic policies also worked against him. In 1974, he announced his new policy for opening the door, bringing to an end Nasser's state-run socialist system. Under this plan, called Infitah, the economy should have broadened throughout Egypt. Instead, a few people got richer, while the majority of Egyptians were no better off than before. By 1977, the economy was in such a bad state, that Sadat increased bread prices until riots forced him to cancel the increase.

On 6 October 1981, President Sadat and government leaders reviewed an armed-forces parade in Cairo. Suddenly, one of the trucks stopped, men alighted from the truck and headed for the viewing stand from which Sadat and other dignitaries viewed the parade. In the confusion, it seems that Sadat thought the soldiers were coming over to shake his hand. In any event, a hand grenade was lobbed at the viewing stand, but did not explode. A second followed, which again did not explode. Finally, the third grenade exploded. At the same time, the assassins leapt out of the truck, and with automatic guns fired into the viewing stands, killing Sadat.

Vice President Hosni Mubarak succeeded Sadat without incident. Mubarak was given emergency powers and approved death sentences for five of Sadat's killers. Mubarak continued the path started by Sadat, that of opening Egypt's economy and government. He continues progress towards eliminating socialism. Though progress sometimes seems slow to the outsider, his policies are carefully designed to allow step-wise progress without undermining cultural values among the populace. Mubarak, like any leader, has his detractors. Principal among these is the conservative religious element that would like to see Egypt's government become less secular. President Mubarak is now serving his third term as President of Egypt.

GOVERNMENT AND JURISDICTIONS

The Permanent Constitution of the Arab Republic of Egypt, adopted on 11 September 1971 and amended on 22 May 1980, provides the basis for Egypt's political system. Egypt's government is a democratic republic with its legal system based on English common law, Islamic law and Napoleonic codes. According to the Constitution, sovereignty is for the people and they are the source of authority. Egypt has 26 administrative divisions or governorates, each a corporate body. Executive power resides in the chief of state—the president—who may be elected to an unlimited number of six-year terms. The president is nominated by the People's Assembly and then must be validated by a national, popular referendum. The head of the government is the prime minister, who, along with the Cabinet, is appointed by the president.

Legislative authority resides with the People's Assembly (Majlis al-Cha'b) which has a total of 454 seats (444 elected and 10 appointed by the president). Under the Constitution, the People's Assembly should not be less than 350 persons, half of whom (at least) should be workers and farmers chosen by direct secret public ballot.

The Advisory Council (Majlis al-Shura) functions only in a consultative role. It was formed to widen the participation of intellectuals in shaping the nation's future. The Advisory Council has a total of 264 seats (176 elected and 88 appointed by the president). The Shura is an age-old tradition in Muslim societies.

The Supreme Court and Council of State conduct judicial review. There are three levels of regular criminal courts: primary courts, appeals court and the Court of Cassation, the final stage of criminal appeals. Since the judicial system is based on Napoleonic tradition, there are no juries. Misdemeanors punishable by imprisonment are heard at the first level by one judge and at the second level by three judges. Felonies, punishable by imprisonment or death, are heard in criminal court by three judges. The Court of Cassation hears contested rulings. If a defendant does not have a lawyer, one is appointed at the court's expense.

The judiciary in Egypt is generally credited with conducting fair trials. However, under the Emergency Law, cases involving terrorism and national security may be tried in military or state security courts in which the accused do not receive all the constitutional protections of the judicial system. During 1996, most terrorist cases were referred to Supreme State Security Emergency Courts; high-profile cases involving Muslim Brotherhood members and a large number of terrorists went to military courts. (*More about the Muslim Brotherhood later in this chapter, page 46.*)

Egypt's political system is based on a multiparty system within the framework of what is considered 'acceptable socially responsible parameters'. The National Democratic Party (NDP) is the dominant party. Despite a constitutional ban against religiously-based parties, the technically illegal Muslim Brotherhood constitutes a significant influence.

ECONOMY

Egypt's principal sources of revenue are from the Suez Canal, agriculture, textiles, food processing, tourism, chemicals, petroleum, construction, cement and metals. Tourism passed petroleum as the second largest hard currency earner in 1995. After a slight dip in tourist visits in 2001 (about

4.6 million), the number of tourists visiting Egypt has risen to more that 8 million visitors in 2004. The complexities of the Egyptian economy cannot be addressed in a few paragraphs. Some things in Egypt seem to be changing rapidly and others at a very, very slow rate. Due to the dynamic economic development policies, I hesitate to put hard figures into a discussion of the economy. Rather, I will give you the government's stated economic reform strategy along with highlights of a few characteristics that affect economic development.

Egypt's economy is in the process of liberalisation in an effort to transfer the national economy from the government sector to the private sector through guided central planning. A number of steps have been introduced to open the economy to encourage growth. Over the past five years, the government enacted significant economic reforms which have reduced the budget deficit, stabilised the exchange rate, reduced inflation and interest rates significantly, and built up substantial reserves. The government has undertaken several steps to grow the economy in recent years. For example, the passing of decree number 95 of 1992 organised the stock market and streamlined procedures for foreign investors, including the granting of residency permission for six months until projects are registered. A centralised authority to streamline company incorporation procedures was also established. Privatisation efforts continue to move Egypt away from a centralised economy. Encouraged by the government's privatisation programme, the Egyptian Stock Exchange (ESE) ended 1996 nearly 40 per cent up on the year, leading all Middle Eastern stock exchanges. Foreign investments increased significantly and by early 1997, Egypt's Standard and Poor's ratings improved substantially.

Egypt has a tradition of entrepreneurship and capital markets, but shifted to a socialised, government-run economy in the 1950s. Centralisation affected the population in many ways; nevertheless, a healthy entrepreneur class continued within the constructs of a planned central economy. In this sense, the shift back to a market-driven economy would seem to be an easy one. However, the mass of the population was (and is) dependent on elements of a planned economy. The government's economic strategy is to introduce a gradual change programme in measured stages. It is not considered a practical or real option to hastily shift to a liberalised economy. Therefore, Egypt adopted a policy of economic reform based on several characteristics that include some very important real practicalities. The comprehensiveness of the plan not only considers the need for economic changes, but also the social and political dimensions associated with all economic sectors. They are quite aware that sustainable economic growth must be accompanied by sustained social stability or they may lose everything.

To many middle- and lower-income Egyptians, the transition seems especially slow. These groups often realise only the immediate results of inflation and a slowly responding job market. Agriculture is the largest employer in the economy and is almost entirely in private hands. Egypt's oversized bureaucracy employs some one-third of the population's workforce through government jobs, public sector enterprises and the armed forces. Privately owned service and manufacturing enterprises account for roughly another 20 per cent; the remaining labour force is unemployed.

Many skilled labourers work abroad (at least 2.5 million) or are underemployed in Egypt. In talking with middle-class, university educated young Egyptians, many claim they are unable to find work in their chosen professions. Often people will tell you that although the government promises a job after graduation from a university, a person must sometimes wait seven or eight years to actually get a job. As a result, the tourism sector harbours large numbers of the highly educated who are unable to find work elsewhere. Consequently, don't be surprised to find a tour guide who has graduated law school, but cannot practise law due to the high costs of establishing a practice. Alternatively, you may find an accountant or schoolteacher working in tourism as secondary employment to raise their family income. Most commonly, among the middle- and lower-classes, you will find people working two or three types of jobs to try to make ends meet. In spite of significant actions taken by government which have increased per capita income, the overwhelming majority of Egyptians still live in poverty.

TOURISM

Tourism is a mainstay of the Egyptian economy. Some estimates suggest that one in seven working Egyptians are somehow involved in the tourist industry. Current estimates suggest that direct and indirect employment in the tourist sector exceed one million workers. Egypt possesses a tremendous cultural heritage drawing tourists from all over the world to see its Pharaonic, Roman, Greek, Coptic and Islamic monuments. The total number of tourists in 1995/1996 climbed to around 3.1 million with some 20.5 million tourist nights, up considerably from the previous year. Revenues from the tourism sector reached approximately E£ 11 billion or US$ 200 million in 1995/1996, growing some 27 per cent over the previous year. Egypt is also seeking to expand its tourism sector by developing additional types of tourist attractions, such as those for the arts, sports and adventure. To improve competitive capabilities in the international tourism market, Egypt is upgrading tourist facilities and elements throughout the country.

Five-star cruise ships dot the Nile waiting for their passengers. Tourism is a cornerstone of the Egyptian economy.

When you are in Egypt, it is impossible to avoid or ignore the role tourism plays in the economy. Tourism and its effects are seemingly everywhere. Although only 263,600 workers are estimated to work directly in tourism, the downstream effects are felt throughout the population, with the possible exception of the small-scale traditional farmers. From hawkers to tourist buses to taxi drivers to bank clerks, almost everyone seems to be affected by the hordes of foreigners visiting Egypt each year. Tourism slackened substantially in the early 1990s due to adverse reactions to terrorist activity, but this pattern reversed beginning in 1995.

Tourist Attack

On 17 November 1997, local criminals carried out the most serious and horrendous terrorist attack against tourists ever perpetrated in Egypt. This event occurred on the west bank of the Nile across from Luxor at the site of Queen Hatshepsut's tomb. Six gunmen, dressed in police uniforms, rampaged through the ancient site brandishing automatic rifles, hand grenades and knives. The semi-official newspaper, *Al Ahram*, reported that 42 Swiss nationals, ten Japanese, four Britons and four unidentified foreigners were killed along with several Egyptians. Among the Egyptians killed were the gunmen who perpetrated the crime. (*For more information on Terrorism, see the section further in this chapter.*)

CRIME AND VIOLENCE

Violence and violent crimes in Egypt are extremely rare. When they do occur, they tend to be family related or between individuals who know each other. Rape and attempted rape are quite rare by Western standards. Punishment for these crimes is extremely severe, including the death penalty in some cases. Women, even unescorted, are generally safe on the streets of Egypt although caution is prudent especially when visiting the less touristy parts of major cities.

Being Cautious

Especially when women are alone on the street, it is important to follow local customs regarding dress and appropriate behaviour. Proper dress and behaviour demonstrate respect and deter cat-calls and other unwnted comments. In point of fact, except in extremely rare circumstances, you will be safe on the streets—even at night. There just seems to be no need to try to provoke locals with what they would consider inappropriate behaviour.

Sometimes Egyptians seem to be in a heated argument right in each other's face. Frequently, well-wishing passers-by get involved in the dispute and before you know it, there will be a whole crowd of people shouting, yelling and waving their arms. This kind of confrontation can be disconcerting and often scares the uninitiated expatriate because it is easy to misinterpret. In fact, it is fairly common just about anywhere in Egypt and is simply a traditional way of communicating that almost never leads to violence. The best thing to do is to just ignore it and go on about your business. If, for some reason, you happen to be the centre of one of these discussions, just stand aside and let them settle it. This could happen if, for example, you asked for directions and two people disagree on what you should do. Another situation where I see this potential is if someone thinks you are being mistreated, cheated or otherwise treated disrespectfully and feel it is their responsibility to take your side.

Pickpocketing, purse snatching and petty theft are not uncommon, though they tend to occur most frequently around tourist areas. Obvious precautions certainly reduce or eliminate the risk of petty robbery. One thing that again happens infrequently, but which you must be aware of, is unapproved charges to credit cards. Again, this occurs only rarely and certainly not in the better shops in Egypt.

TERRORISM

Terrorism is a difficult topic to explain not only because it is seemingly random in nature, but also because when acts occur, the number of casualties is typically higher than individual acts of violence. Besides, the very word 'terrorist' is enough to scare anyone! One never knows when or where a terrorist will strike or who will be affected. The Egyptian Penal Code defines terrorism to include the acts of 'spreading panic' and 'obstructing the work of authorities'.

The Egyptian government's anti-terrorist campaign is taking very strong measures to reduce risks of random terrorist violence. Under provisions of the Emergency Law (in effect since 1981), the police may obtain an arrest warrant from the Ministry of the Interior upon showing that an individual poses a danger to security and public order. This act thus nullifies the constitutional requirement of showing that an individual has likely committed a specific crime. The following section is a very general timeline of major terrorist events and groups in Egypt. During 1996, security forces and police arrested at least 120 members of the Muslim Brotherhood as well as 200 members of a new group, called the Qutbiyoun, which is an offshoot of the Brotherhood. Charges ranged from distributing illegal leaflets, to membership in an illegal organisation and inciting the masses against the government.

The Muslim Brotherhood is a political and religious organisation founded in Egypt in 1928. Generally anti-Western, it advocates a society based on Islamic principles of social justice as opposed to secular nationalism. Since the 1950s, the Brotherhood and many of its radical offshoots received funding from Saudi Arabia. Initially, this was due to their anti-Communist stance; later it was due to a need to counterbalance Iranian-backed Shi'ite radicals and the Palestine Liberation Organisation (PLO) and its offshoots. The Islamic Group (Al-Gamaa'a al-Islamiyya) broke from the Brotherhood in the mid-1970s. Al-Gamaa'a al-Islamiyya is the group responsible for the attack that killed 18 Greek tourists in Cairo (April 1996), which was until November 1997 the largest casualty count from a single incident in Egypt's modern history. Terrorist groups killed 132 persons in 1996, compared with 200 the previous year. Persons killed included 48 security or police officers as well as 84 civilians. Most attacks were against either authorities or Coptic Christians in Minya, Assiut, Sohag or Qena (Qina). Groups also attacked churches and other properties owned by Christians. These attacks are partially the result of a feud between authorities and families located in these areas stemming from their goal to establish an Islamic state and the perceived economic repercussions of a secular government.

Ten people were killed and numerous wounded on 18 September 1997 when individuals tossed Molatov cocktails under a tourist bus outside the National Museum at Midan Tahrir in Cairo. Two brothers were arrested for this action, one of whom had previously lashed out at a major hotel that refused to give him a job and killed three people in the process. (The brothers have since been sentenced in October 1997 and executed in May 1998.) Therefore, this action appears to be separate from any organised anti-government groups that have previously sought to undermine the government of President Hosni Mubarak. Indeed, no known anti-government group has claimed responsibility for the event or association with these criminals.

A new round of attacks began in a little publicised event in Minya in October 1997. At this time, criminals dressed in police uniforms set up roadblocks and killed nine Egyptians, including four off-duty policemen. Since most recent terrorist events have occurred in this region of Egypt, perhaps little thought was given to the expansion of this mode of attack to other areas. For whatever reason, security (which was historically less intense in and around the major tourist sites from Luxor south to Aswan) proved to be insufficient when six men attacked tourists on Luxor's west bank on 17 November 1997, killing 64 people. The six perpetrators dressed in police uniforms, believed to be members of Al-Gamaa'a al-Islamiyya, were killed during the subsequent gun battle between the terrorists and police forces. On 18 November, a rival militant group, Talaa Al Fath, headed by Ayman Al Zawahari living in Switzerland, reportedly issued a statement to an international news agency warning tourists to stay out of Egypt. According to Richard Engel writing in the *Middle East Times*, the statement said, 'Today's military operation in Luxor won't be the last one. Foreigners per se are not targets, but we have warned them about giving money to the Egyptian regime.'

Egyptian government officials responded immediately with massive police support in and around all tourist sites in Egypt. Changes were made at the ministerial level when a new Minister of Interior was appointed following the immediate resignation of his predecessor. New plans were developed to re-evaluate and refine security measures at all of Egypt's tourist sites. For example, several military sites were built above the Valley of the Kings where guards overlook the whole valley on a 24/7 schedule. Initially, tourist groups found their movement restricted as forces sought to secure their safety through increased security forces. In March 2006, I toured Upper Egypt as a standard tourist with my sister. What I observed at that time was actually more freedom for the tourists to climb the hills on the West Bank in Luxor, more people taking donkey rides, more balloon rides and, generally speaking, more flexibility for tourists to wander among villages and streets than I had seen prior to that time. Security was present more than pre-1997, but seemed slightly subdued compared to times more closely associated with the 1997 event. When I would point out something I thought looked different, I usually got a shrug and a 'well, you know—1997' for an explanation.

International governments also reacted immediately to events in Luxor, which occurred at the beginning of the high tourist season in Egypt. Many governments issued travel advisories and one began special flights to evacuate citizens on the ground in Egypt. Egypt's anticipated greatest tourist year ever fell far short of expectations as a result of many tour group cancellations.

Like an awakened volcano, the Middle East once again spews violence. Israel and the Palestinian intifada remind us that all is not well in the region. The death of Yasser Arafat (2004), illness of Ariel Sharon, subsequent election of the 17th Knesset, and recent election of a Hamas government in the Palestinian area (2006) leave this situation wide open. Terrorists bombed American embassies in Africa on 7 August 1998 and the USS Cole in Yemen on 12 October 2000.

The heinous events of 11 September 2001 not only devastated the United States, but also rocked the Middle East and all of the world. Egypt seemed to be especially hard hit, but maybe that is my opinion because I was living there at the time. As I have mentioned, Egyptians love rumours and and conspiracy theories. The gossip grapevine ensures that all titbits, no matter how outrageous, get rapid circulation. Before it became clear exactly what happened in New York and Washington DC, the rumour-mill was only reporting that the 'World Trade Centre' was hit. Well, there is a 'World Trade Centre' in Cairo on the Corniche el Nil. At first, some people thought this was the centre that was hit. This was followed by total disbelief that anyone would do what was done in New York and DC. People were constantly hugging me and crying for and with me over the tragedy. It seemed incomprehensible to most Egyptians that anyone could perpetrate such a horrid event. When it was announced that some of the perpetrators were Egyptian, this was (by many; or maybe even most) considered to be just plain wrong and absurd because 'no Muslim could kill innocents like that'. At this point, I heard every conspiracy theory imaginable. Well, without going into more details about this event, let me say that tourism once again declined, hurting Egypt's economy.

The attack on the United States and the subsequent wars in Afghanistan and Iraq appear to have preceded, if not precipitated, more open expression of discontent within Egypt as cited below.

All in all, the number of terrorist incidents have declined significantly since the 1980s and early to mid-1990s making travel throughout Egypt safer for tourists and guests. It is widely thought that the government's tough tactics against terrorists during this period removed most terror threats within the country. In fact, since 1997, there were no acts of terrorism against tourism within Egypt until 2004. There were two terrorist events in Egypt in 1998, but there were internal attacks against police and private citizens. It appears that the predominant terrorist threat prior to 1998, al-Gama'a al-Islamiyya (GAI) , was eliminated either through members going to prison, emigration to other countries, affiliation with other groups, e.g., al-Qaeda, or conciliation with the government.

Unfortunately, new efforts apparently designed to destabilise the Egyptian government have resulted in renewed terrorist attacks starting in 2004. The following is a listing of events that have occurred since 2004. (Note that one additional event is listed by some as a terrorist act where an 'Egyptian' stabbed and killed an Israeli man in 2002, but this is certainly not a mass-casualty event generally thought of as terrorism.) Most consider these new events to be attempts to weaken the Mubarak government. Since attacking the government or military directly would be unlikely to be successful, an attack on Egypt's economy appears to be the route of choice. These 'new' attacks target Egypt's US$6 billion tourism industry, Egypt's leading source of hard currency.

On 7 October 2004, in a co-ordinated attack, three bombs went off almost simultaneously in the Sinai Peninsula resorts of Taba and Ras al-Shitan killing 34 and wounding upwards of 100 individuals. According to RAND Corporation information reported by MIPT TKB (http://www.tkb.org): 'investigators believe the attacks were motivated by the deterioration of the Palestinian situation, rather than the global jihad. Multiple groups claimed responsibility for the attacks, though none were ever substantiated'. One group that claimed responsibility was the Battalion of the Martyr Abdullah Azzam, which also has other aliases such as Al-Qaeda in the Levant and Egypt, and Al-Qaida in Syria and Egypt. The group was founded to 'oppose Middle Eastern governments that the group deems to be aligned with the West (such as the Mubarak government in Egypt), the Zionist movement, and non-Muslim forces in the Middle East' according to the above quoted source.

On 7 April 2005, a suicide bomber from a previously unknown group (the Islamic Glory Brigades in the Land of the Nile) killed himself, an American and two French nationals in an attack on Cairo's Khan el-Khalili bazaar. The police believe they have captured the suspects, but continue investigations in the villages of Ammar and Ezbet al-Gabalawi, where the attackers originated.

On 30 April 2005, two women and one man (brother to one of the women and fiancée to the other) attacked almost simultaneously. The two women opened fire on a tourist bus wounding no one before they turned the guns on themselves which resulted in their deaths. The man, with a bomb strapped to his body, killed himself and wounded seven as he jumped from the 6 October Bridge onto the Midan Abdel-Moneim Riyadh below, near the National Museum. Multiple groups have since claimed the attacks; however, it is unclear if any of these individuals had links to any organisation.

Unknown terrorists plotted and carried out three simultaneous attacks on the tourist infrastructure in the Sinai towns of Sharm el-Sheikh and Taba. A total of 88 people died and approximately 200 were wounded, among them six tourists. Police state the responsible parties were a Sinai-based group with no ties to any international group who responded to the jailing of their leader. Others suggest the responsible party was Battalion of the Martyr Abdullah Azzam. The jury remains out on this issue.

On 24 April 2006, a third co-ordinated attack on the Sinai Peninsula resort towns occurred at Dahab. At the time of this writing, the number of casualties is not confirmed; however,

A building in Midan Tahrir, Cairo. Today all is normal but in September 1997, an isolated attack on a tourist bus outside its National Museum left ten people killed and several others wounded.

it is thought that at least 23 people have died, and more than 68 have been injured.

Tourist travel into certain areas of the country (specifically, Middle Egypt) still requires extra caution. The government continues to prefer that Westerners, especially Americans, stay out of Middle Egypt. If you plan to travel to this area, it is prudent to seek advice from your local embassy, licensed tour operators, and/or tourist police authorities responsible for the area. Following events in Luxor, standard security measures for tourist groups at all tourist sites have been increased and will likely remain so in the foreseeable future. As always, check for government warnings and advisories to determine relative risks before travelling to the area. Any number of factors not directly related to events in Egypt can make travel to the area unadvisable.

As a side note, I would feel remiss if I did not point out that travel within Egypt, even given the most recent drastic events, presents less hazard based on statistical probability of experiencing a violent event, than living in most major US cities. I say this not to diminish the importance and horror associated with the recent attacks or the attack in Luxor. It is only presented as a reminder to look at real events and occurrences rather than responding emotionally to the unknown. In March 2006, I took a 'classical' tour beginning in Cairo, travelling by train to Aswan, cruise boat to Luxor, and returning to Cairo by air. In the intervening 15 days, I felt welcomed. At no time did I feel, in any way, threatened or unsafe. I did not find the security overwhelming or stifling, but clearly present. As in any potentially risky situation, keep your antennae tuned, constantly monitor the situation and maintain situational awareness to give yourself a greater probability of a safe journey. Or, as my sister reminds me, "Keep your ears up and your head down."

Another reminder—it is always a good idea to keep vigil on international events when living or travelling abroad. For current information and links, check the US Department of State site at:

http://www.state.gov/www/global/terrorism.

Terrorism in Egypt:
17 November 1997 to 24 April 2006

Here's a summary of the attacks.

Date	Perpetrator	Place
24 April 2006	Unknown	Dahab (Sinai Peninsula)
15 August 2006	Unknown	El Arish
23 July 2005	Sinai-based group	Sharm el Sheikh (Sinai Peninsula)
30 April 2005	Unknown group	Cairo
30 April 2005	Unknown group	Cairo
7 April 2005	Islamic Glory Brigades in the Land of the Nile	Cairo
7 October 2004	Jemaah Islamiya (JI) and Tawhid Islamic Brigades	Taba (Sinai Peninsula)
7 October 2004	Unknown	Nuweiba (Sinai Peninsula)
7 October 2004	Battalion of the Martyr Abdullah Azzam	Nuweiba (Sinai Peninsula)
19 April 2002	Unknown	Sinai
5 April 1998	Unknown	Ibshadat
22 March 1998	al-Gama'a al-Islamiyya (GAI)	Bani Mazar Village
17 November 1997	al-Gama'a al-Islamiyya (GAI)	Luxor

Target	Tactic	Total Fatalities/ Injuries
Tourist	Bomb	At least 23/ at least 160
Military	Bomb	Unknown/ two Canadians
Tourist	Co-ordinated three bombs	68/ unknown
Tourist	Bomb	one/ seven
Tourist	Armed attack	two/ none
Tourist	Bomb	four/ 18
Tourist	Co-ordinated three bombs (Nuweiba)	34/ 159
Tourist	Co-ordinated three bombs (Taba)	none/ none
Tourist	Co-ordinated three bombs (Taba)	two/ 12
Individual/ Property	Knives and sharp objects	one/ none
Individual/ Property	Firearms	two/ unknown
Police	Armed attack	four/ 13
Tourist	Armed attack	74/ 24

Adapted from: MIPT Terrorism Knowledge Base
(http://www.tkb.org/Home.jsp)

THE EGYPTIAN PEOPLE

CHAPTER 3

'You can tell whether a man is clever by his answers.
You can tell whether a man is wise by his questions.'
—Naguib Mahfouz

RELIGION

If you do not understand the basic beliefs of Islam and the important effect religion has on the life and actions of all Egyptians, I firmly believe you are destined to never understand anything that goes on around you in Egypt. I say this even though there are some six to seven million Coptic Christians living in Egypt. It is estimated that 94–96 per cent of the population of Egypt is Muslim, therefore much of the government and everyday life of all Egyptians (as well as foreign residents) are affected by this important aspect of life.

The word Islam means 'having peace with God' or 'submission to God'. A Muslim is a follower of Islam. Do not confuse the term Muslim with the term Arab—they are not synonymous. Muslims inhabit all parts of the globe and may or may not be Arab. An Arab may be a Muslim, a Christian, a Jew or an atheist. Allah is the Arabic word for God. When people invoke the name of Allah, it is often stated as follows: 'In the name of Allah, the Compassionate, the Beneficent'. This is also the phrase you will see printed in Arabic at the beginning of many letters or publications in the Islamic world.

The Qur'an (also spelled Koran), or holy book of Islam, represents the literal word of God as revealed to the Prophet Muhammad (peace be upon him) through the Archangel Gabriel. When the name of the Prophet Muhammad is said or written, it is customarily followed by the phrase 'peace be upon him' as shown in the previous sentence. The Prophet's 'sayings' or Hadith supplement the Qur'an as a guide to the correct conduct and behaviour of Muslims. The Hadith includes reported sayings, deeds and approvals of the Prophet Muhammad. This code is called the Sunna, literally translated to mean the 'Beaten Path'.

Muslims go to worship at a mosque; however, they may pray anywhere—in a house, an aircraft, outside. It is preferable to pray in a congregation, but a Muslim may pray anywhere in the world, alone or with others. Friday is the Holy Day for Muslims, so Egypt's 'weekend' is Friday and Saturday, rather than Saturday and Sunday, as is commonly practised in the West.

Before I explain the basic principles of Islam (and please remember I do not represent myself as an Islamic scholar), I think I should point out an aspect of Islam probably most difficult for non-Muslims to understand. Muslims do not partition life as Westerners do into religion on the one hand, and life, work and government on the other. This is because Islam is considered to be a total way of life. This fact is particularly difficult to understand for persons coming from countries with a strong heritage of separation between religion and state. Church and state simply cannot be separated in the minds of average pious Muslims—both are indispensable and mutually complementary.

The principal food restrictions among Muslims are not difficult. Islam does not allow Muslims to eat certain items, such as pork and its by-products. Muslims should also avoid alcohol. To some people, even handling alcohol is objectionable.

That being said, let's look at some of the important Islamic principles that guide the life of a believer.

- Most importantly, 'There is no God but God'. God is the One and the Only God. Jews, Christians and Muslims are called the 'People of the Book', the Book referred to being the Old Testament. However, Muslims reject the idea of the Trinity or any idea that implies there is more than one

God, believing Jesus was a Prophet, but not God incarnate as believed by Christians.

- Muslims believe God has sent several Messengers or Prophets through the ages. The Prophets of Judaism and Christianity, such as Noah, Abraham, Moses, David and Jesus, are also Prophets of Islam. However, importantly in Islam, Muhammad is believed to be the final Prophet or Messenger of God.
- Muslims believe God created unseen creatures such as angels for special missions.
- Muslims believe there is a Day of Judgement when all people throughout history are brought before God for accounting, punishment and reward.
- In Islam, prayer is to God and only God, and is made by the individual with no intermediaries.
- There is no 'Original Sin' in Islam. Humans are born free from sin, and it is only after they reach puberty and after they commit a sin that they are charged for their mistakes. Individuals can take responsibility for their own sins. They cannot take responsibility for the sins of others. The door to forgiveness by God is always open through repentance.

The Five Pillars of Islam

Five basic duties are required of the believer in Islam. These duties are typically called the 'Five Pillars' of Islam because they form the foundation of the House of Islam. The Five Pillars are:

- The confession of faith or affirmation of the creed (*shahada*)
  Muslims believe that 'There is no God but God, and Muhammad is the Messenger of God'.
- Prayers (*salat*)
  Muslims are required to pray five times daily, facing in the direction of Mecca, the holy city. The times for prayer are dawn, noon, mid-afternoon, dusk and after dark.
- Fasting (*saum*)
  Ramadan, the month of the Prophet's first revelations, is the month of fasting for Muslims. Many rules regulate

Ramadan, but basically all sane adults are obligated to fast between dawn and dusk during the month of Ramadan each year. Children are not required to fast until they reach a certain age; however, they are encouraged to fast when feasible. Certain people and people living under certain circumstances are excused from fasting, although some situations require that the individual make up for time missed fasting at a later time. As a general rule of thumb, the following people are excused: travellers; the insane, retarded or mentally impaired; invalids; and pregnant women and nursing mothers.

One of two religious celebrations (Eid) occurs at the end of the month of Ramadan—the Eid of Fast-Breaking (Eid el-Fitr). The second major celebration, the Eid of Sacrifice (Eid el-Adha), commemorates the Prophet Abraham's willingness to sacrifice everything for God, even his son Ishmael.

The month of Ramadan shifts each year with respect to the Gregorian (civil) calendar. This is due to the fact that the Islamic calendar is a lunar calendar based on 354 days. Leap years have 355 days with the extra day added to the last month. The Islamic calendar began in the 'year of the Hejira', or AH 1, which was the year the Prophet Mohammed moved from Mecca (Makkah) to Medina to escape religious persecution. AH 1 corresponds with the year AD 622 of the Gregorian calendar. In the 30 years of the Islamic calendar's cycle, 11 years are leap years. With the exception of leap years, the 12 months beginning with the New Year have alternately 30 and 29 days.

- Almsgiving, a tax or gift (*zakat*)
  It is the responsibility of all Muslims to give not less than 2.5 per cent of their earnings, savings and gold and silver jewellery (or its cash equivalent) to the community each year to help the poor. A different rate is levied for agricultural produce and cattle.
- Pilgrimage (*hajj*)
  Each Muslim is required to perform a pilgrimage to Mecca at least once in a lifetime if means are available.

DIVERSITY

Racism as known in the West does not occur in Egypt. This is not to say that social status distinction and even differential access to positions or power does not exist. What I am saying is that the distinction or discrimination that does exist is not based on skin colour or 'race' as commonly perceived in the West. Skin colour may be judged on aesthetic grounds to be more or less attractive, but is not considered important in establishing one's social status.

In describing themselves and the people around them, most Egyptians more or less acknowledge the following distinct groups: Egyptians, Bedouins, Arabs (people from the Arabian Peninsula), other Middle Easterners (usually by country), and foreigners (usually by country). Several sub-categories are recognised within the group generally called Egyptian. This can be viewed as 'ethnic' group distinction in some senses because people are assigned to these groups based on some common characteristics that distinguish them. However, in Egypt, people do not generally recognise the term 'ethnic group'. Instead, people are merely referred to as being in different 'groups'. The most frequent group distinction occurs simply between Muslims and Copts. Nubians and Bedouins constitute somewhat more distinct groups, although they also fall within the general grouping of Muslims.

Nubians

When plans for building the Aswan High Dam began in the 1960s, President Nasser was the first to use the term 'Nubian' to refer to all the dark-skinned, non-Arabic speaking peoples living between Aswan and the Sudanese border (now called 'Old Nubia'). With the exception of a small group of migrants and few tribal leaders, the people from Old Nubia very rarely interacted with or were exposed to other Egyptians (and vice versa) until resettlement moved them north of Aswan in 1963. Prior to that time, if the people now called Nubians felt any common identity with one another (they did not see themselves as a united group), it was probably only based on shared grievances against the Egyptian government.

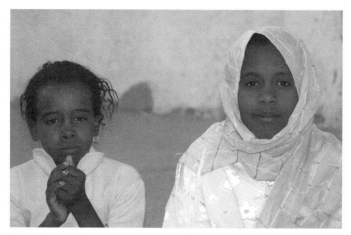

Today, Nubians, like these two young girls, are considered a part of Egyptian society and the distinctions between them and the other groups are not as pronounced.

Today, Nubians are a recognised ethnic group, and many of the distinctions and barriers that separated them from other Egyptians have lessened or disappeared.

Bedouins

The Bedouins (traditionally nomadic, but now both nomadic and settled) are perhaps the most distinct, though very small, group of Egyptians. Nomadic Egyptians live, to some extent, outside the confines of traditional Egyptian life and law. Bedouins maintain their ethnic distinction through marriage patterns, lifestyle and tradition.

SOCIAL CLASS, POWER AND WEALTH

Social class is the most important delimiting factor in Egyptian society, more so than any type of ethnic designation. Although social class and ethnic distinction overlap somewhat, social class structure determines access to power and position. Therefore, recognition of existing social class structure is what is important to Egyptians and to you in establishing relationships within Egypt. Probably 98–99 per cent of the population falls within the lower and middle classes, with the rest occupying what can be termed an elite or upper class (I never measured this, it is just a guess). Pragmatically, this means if you move to Egypt on a business or academic contract, you may be conducting business or socialising with only a very limited segment of the population in this realm of your life. At the same time, most of the people you see around you, and with whom you will interact daily, definitely reflect the poorer and less politically powerful majority of the population.

People in the United States prefer to see themselves as a 'mobile, classless' society in which determination and hard work designate one's ultimate social position. A poor person, through diligence and hard work, can become president. In the United Kingdom, however, social position more closely affiliates to birth. This can be seen by the fact that people often know their 'social class' and in the continuance of distinctions between 'royalty', 'nobility', and 'commoner'.

Egypt's social structure is somewhere between those of the United States and the United Kingdom. Importantly, no royalty or nobility classes exist in Egypt. Very distinct social class differences delineate everyday life and potential opportunity throughout Egypt. There remain remnants of the old ruling family, but most have either maintained their elite status through marriage or have taken a place among the 'less than upper class' as a result of social power being transferred to another group of people. Following the revolution in 1952, social and political power transferred to a new group who assumed the roles of the elite class in Egypt. While some members of the 'old' upper class certainly remained (as do their families now) among the upper class, a whole newly formed upper class took hold. Over the 50 plus years since the revolution, these statuses have become so ingrained, it is virtually impossible for the foreigner to actually tell who was among the old elite versus the members of the current elite. That is not to say that, even to the casual observer, one can delineate social class distinctions that everyday life and potential opportunity throughout the country. Revolution and elections notwithstanding, a relatively small group of old, very influential families still control the majority of wealth and power within Egypt.

Traditional stone carvers—class distinctions are clearly defined between Egyptians and dictate the terms of social interaction.

Most social scientists characterise Egyptian society into three basic social classes that correspond more or less with socio-economic status—upper, middle, and lower classes. Intragroup distinctions exist within each of these classes. This classification probably will work for you in most situations. In Egypt, status is sometimes more a case of family heritage than income. There are no hard and fast rules, but Egyptian society appears quite inflexible (by American standards), with little or no social mobility. Members of each class tend to socialise only within their group. Almost no cross-class marriages occur. As a result, though persons may amass wealth, gain an education or both, they will not move from one class to another. Compare this to the American way where wealth essentially determines social standing and access to power.

Egyptian upper-class individuals, as a total group, enjoy significantly better access to position and education than do members of the middle or lower classes. But even within this class, certain individuals have easier access. These people more often occupy higher ranking political or intellectual positions than do other members of the upper class.

Many upper middle-class individuals actually amass a great deal of wealth. However, as mentioned, acquisition of wealth does not provide a basis for moving one from the middle to the upper class—neither does education. Although members of the middle class increasingly receive a university education, their social position, vis-à-vis the upper class, remains constant. A university education certainly provides more opportunities for upward mobility within the middle class and may well increase a person's intra-group standing. University education also provides greater opportunities to migrate for work and achieve distinction in other countries.

The majority of Egyptians fall into the lower class. These people are distinguished by low educational levels and poverty. Members of this class have very little real opportunity for social mobility, though the hard-working and clever among them do improve their family's living conditions. Rapid population growth among this group has led to greater migration to the cities for work as family farm land is filled. Most frequently, they occupy low-paying positions since they are, by and large, unskilled. Little difference is apparent to the observer as members of this class are among the poorest in the country. Increasingly, members of the lower class achieve a secondary level education. Most still receive little education above the primary level and illiteracy levels (besides being able to write their name) continue to be quite high among this group.

Social gatherings tend to be among social status peers; rarely would one see a lower- or middle-class individual invited to a reception or dinner given by an upper-class individual at their home. Therefore, deferential behaviour tends to disappear or at least become less apparent in these settings. Respect due to age, of course, always applies. Certainly, it is appropriate to invite members of different social classes to your home for various events. However, whatever you do, do not mix people from different classes at a social gathering. Inviting your driver to join a function with your boss or a high-ranking official would embarrass both guests.

Even within a grouping of social class peers, different relative status may still be represented within the group. For example, a high ministerial or elected official might attend a formal dinner or reception. While among members of the same social class (the upper class), this relatively higher ranking person would still receive deference and respect from members at the gathering to acknowledge his or her distinct position.

A Different Perception

Sometimes it is difficult for foreigners to ascertain just who represents the higher rank except by quietly observing group actions. You can count on the fact that relative rank or status is well known among the Egyptians. In fact, depending on the circumstances, you may find you are the object of deference from people at a gathering because of your foreign status. This may simply reflect Egyptians' value for hospitality and honesty or it may be a sign of recognition of your perceived importance. For example, since only high-ranking or wealthy Egyptians typically travel abroad, your very presence in Egypt signifies to many Egyptians that you must also be rather high-ranking and wealthy. Deference to your perceived position then follows logically in their world view.

FAMILY

Life in Egypt revolves around the family, and family concerns often assume greater significance than business relationships. It would not be uncommon for someone to cancel a business meeting because some pressing family matter took greater precedence.

All Egyptians seem to love children. One of the first things I noticed in Egypt was that children were everywhere. There seem to be few public places where you won't find children. When women shop or go visiting, the custom is to bring all the children regardless of their ages. Traditionally, the mother assumes major responsibility for assuring that children are raised properly. Because of this, many people think fathers are not close to their children. My observation has been that fathers often fondly hold small children and are frequently seen with them in public. As children age, fathers apparently bond more closely with their sons with regard to career and responsibility roles, but maintain a deep affection for all their children. Daughters become more closely aligned with their

You will find children of all ages everywhere in Egypt, like these boys I encountered when I went out to the pyramids one day.

Egyptians value marriage and take great pride in their families.

mother's role as they age. Mothers remain an important figure in their sons' lives at all ages.

Traditionally, the Egyptian standard was to live in the extended family setting usually comprised of three generations within the same household. This is still the preferred living arrangement among most Egyptians, but as crowding forces more people to migrate to urban areas to work, family living arrangements have dispersed somewhat. Unless they must migrate for work or education, most unmarried children remain in the family home until they get married. Very rarely do single women move away from their family residence unless it is to another family member's home.

Traditional family size is rather large in Egypt by Western standards. Preferred family size seems to be decreasing somewhat. Many people I meet say that they would prefer to have only two or three children rather than eight, nine or more, which was customary in the previous generations. Recent efforts by government sponsors to provide family planning to Egyptians has been met with mixed success. Some people judged limiting family size to be against their religion. Since the highest Islamic authority in the country has announced that it is not against Islam, more people are moving to control family size through various contraceptive means.

Complementary Roles for Men and Women

Most Egyptians I have talked to view men's and women's roles as complementary. Each person in the household has rights and responsibilities based on age and gender. Egyptian women are traditionally responsible for the household, whereas men are responsible for working and providing money for the family. Increasing urbanisation with its shift from an agrarian lifestyle throughout Egypt challenges traditional ways of life. Women among the lower classes increasingly find it necessary to work in the labour market or in small entrepreneurial enterprises. This is frequently insulting to the family male and often results in increased family friction and violence. It is also degrading to many women, who rather than seeing an opportunity for personal expansion, perceive working to be a necessity which keeps them from fulfilling their expected responsibilities for the family and home.

Lower- and lower middle-class women usually get work in the service industry, for example, as hotel maids or restaurant servers. Upper middle-class people are also on the move. Among this group, males and females now often receive a university education and work outside the home, thereby expanding opportunities for both partners.

In Upper Egypt, women rarely work in the fields as is seen in the Delta region. The main reason is that farming in Upper Egypt is very small scale, whereas in the Delta there are larger farms where people from villages go to work for wages.

Although nothing is cast in stone, usually the eldest female occupies the role of senior person responsible for the household whereas the senior male provides for the family (or their portions of the extended family). If the father dies, usually the remaining parent continues to head the household, even though many responsibilities pass to the oldest son if the father passes first and the son is of an appropriate age. If the mother dies first, one of the daughters may assume many of the responsibilities of the household for their father's well-being. If the children are all grown and married, the remaining parent may move in with the family of one of the children or may remain alone if none of the married children live in the family household. Upon the death of both parents, responsibility for younger siblings and/or grandparents generally transfers to the eldest son.

HONOUR

Never discount the value of honour in Egyptian society. Honour denotes respect, admiration or esteem for another. It can be seen as a right or as due. Intricate interactions among honour, family and family honour constitute some of the most important facets affecting Egyptian life.

In Egypt, an individual's honour cannot be separated from that of his or her family. As such, the actions of one family member bear directly on the reputation of all other family members. This concept is rather different from much of Western belief. In the West, an individual's reputation may well be viewed as a personal responsibility and can frequently be separated from the reputation of his or her family. For example, in the West, a brother is not usually held directly responsible for his sister's behaviour and/or reputation. In Egypt, the situation differs. Any behaviour on the part of an individual reflects strongly on the family. Behaviour of any family member is held to be the direct responsibility of the family. For example, the brother, father and all other family members bear direct responsibility for the actions of a woman, perceived actions of a woman, or any action directed toward a female family member. It is for this reason, among others, that family members concern themselves intimately with the actions of all family members.

Honour has so many implications in Egyptian life that it would be impossible to discuss them all. So I will discuss a few of the many intricately interwoven aspects of honour existing in Egyptian society.

First, honour means a code of integrity, dignity and pride. Honour, in a general sense, applies to both the feeling and the expression of the sentiment. Throughout Egypt, feelings of honour find expression in everyday language and demeanor. For example, Egyptians are overwhelmingly concerned with demonstrating their hospitality and generosity. Dignity and pride express themselves in all aspects of dress, manners, language, business, attitudes and behaviour. In daily life, Egyptians demonstrate pride and honour for their religious, political, social, and ancient heritage—in other words, their culture.

Understanding how appearance relates to honour requires using a broad perspective of how appearance integrates with behaviour to Egyptians. Outward appearance, i.e. how you are dressed, your grooming etc., is very important to all Egyptians, most especially to upper-class Egyptians. They strive to appear well-dressed and groomed at all times and cannot fathom why anyone would want to appear otherwise. As a result, dress appears to be a bit more formal than is common in the West. For example, casual dress in Egypt more closely relates to what is termed 'dressy casual' in the United States. What does this concern for appearance mean for you? Well, it means that you will also be judged by your public appearance. While you may prefer ragged jeans and sloppy shirts, appearing in public dressed like this gives a bad impression. You will be judged to have little pride, thus honour, in your personal appearance when you dress neatly.

Second, honour very importantly involves personal integrity. A person's word, honesty and good character are hallmarks of an individual's integrity, thus the family's honour. Trustworthiness, as evidenced through honesty and good character, are critical to developing both personal and business relationships throughout Egypt.

A Matter of Honour

I was reminded of the importance of honour during a discussion with a friend. When I mentioned that I wanted to bring some colleagues to Egypt, my friend reminded me, "You know I can help them, but I do not know these people. I know you very well and trust you. You must be certain they are right for this—it's a matter of honour, you know." Acknowledging my trustworthiness was indeed a great compliment and a great responsibility. Needless to say, I took a huge gulp of air and began pondering to myself whether I knew these people well enough to place my honour, indeed my integrity, on the line.

It is through personal honour that deference behaviour comes into play. Outsiders often wonder why Egyptians seem to defer to others at times when foreigners customarily would not. Deference reflects respect. It is a courteous regard for another person that often takes the form of yielding to his or her decisions or wishes. In other words, deference is an honourable way Egyptians use to show appropriate respect for someone in a perceived higher position, authority or who might be deserving of great respect for other reasons.

Two circumstances come to mind when I think of respect and deference in Egypt. While it is impossible to think of all the situations where respect/deferential behaviour might appear, hopefully the following examples will give you an elementary understanding of how this works. The easiest example is with age: Egyptians respect their elders. They rise when an older person enters or leaves a room. They defer to the elder person's opinion, especially in public. One would never contradict an elder in front of others. In fact, a principal requirement of 'good' children is to respect their elders.

Second, in the workplace, social setting or in trade, Egyptians tend to defer to someone perceived to be in a higher social, political or bureaucratic position. Subtle acts of deference abound in all sorts of human interactions. Expressing opinions in the presence of a 'superior' is not done. Coming from a culture where expression of one's opinion is highly valued, at first I found this quite disconcerting and could not understand such restraint. After all, if you had an opinion, why not express it? The reason is because honourable people in Egypt would never consider showing this type of disrespect to their peers or superiors. The person present with the most perceived social power should be the spokesperson, the one to express an opinion. I have noticed this often at business meetings. Frequently, persons who perceive their position to be below another will not express opinions in the company of the person above them. They might express their ideas to you individually, but if an opinion is presented publicly, the person of the highest rank will usually present it unless that person refers the question to an assistant. By the way, it does not matter whether the person in the superior position is a male or female.

Subtle mannerisms of the person in the lower position reflect his or her acknowledgement of status with regard to the other individual. For example, when asked a question, there might be a slight hesitation before answering or even a non-answer to indicate that the person feels he or she should not be answering the question. You may also observe eye shifting or position shifting as a sign of discomfort. By the way, you will also get some of the same responses when you broach an inappropriate topic, so sometimes it is difficult to determine which situation prevails.

Next, women in the company of a male may find that upon asking a question, the answer is then given to the man as if they were not standing there. Alternatively, if an Egyptian man wants to get an answer from a woman, he may well address the question not to her, but to the man she is with. Western women tend to find this action demeaning—an action of deferring to male superiority. Depending on the circumstances, this kind of behaviour may represent a sign of respect.

Finally, an extremely important form of honour relates to a woman's chastity or reputation for chastity. 'Appearance' applies not only to the way a person looks, but also to 'how things seem'. How things 'seem to be' can be much more important than actual facts. If a situation does not seem or appear to be appropriate, then it may be judged to be inappropriate. Any behaviour or suggestion of behaviour that compromises or 'seems' to compromise a woman's reputation for chastity is extremely serious. Gossip also comes into play here. The way I have had it explained to me is as follows. If, for example, a woman stopped to talk with a man, it is likely that someone might see her. That someone would then tell someone else. By the third or fourth translation, the woman was at the man's home alone with him. By the time all the gossip was through the town or village, this man made her pregnant. The woman's reputation could then be ruined over nothing more than a casual conversation. Although this extreme example is less likely among the upper-class, more Westernised in Cairo, most communities even in Cairo continue to be quite closed and subject to this kind of concern.

Another example, which may seem quite innocent in the eyes of foreigners, involves men and women being alone in a room. A man should not be in a closed room alone with a woman who is not his wife because this could give the appearance of compromising the woman's respectability. If you (a male) drop by a friend's house without an appointment, you might find the woman of the house (if her husband is out) either will not answer the door or will yell through the door that no one is home. This is because it would not give the proper appearance, would not seem appropriate, for a woman to invite you into her house without her husband or other relatives present.

Protecting Our Reputations

I learned this very quickly when inviting a male Egyptian friend to join some of my colleagues in a discussion in my hotel room one afternoon. He would not come into the room, but placed a chair just outside the door in order not to give the wrong appearance and risk compromising our reputations.

Incidents of 'honour killings', the murder of women for reasons of family honour, have been given a lot of international press in the past few years. The prevalence of 'honour killings' is quite low in Egypt. In the event they occur, punishments tend to be less stringent than in the case of murders for other reasons.

EDUCATION

Education is highly valued among upper- and middle-class Egyptians as well as among the Nubians. Primary education, though technically required for all children, is not enforced uniformly throughout the country. Education is often still seen as a luxury to poor Egyptians since children are often needed to help with family economic endeavours. Among farming families, boys assist their fathers in farming activities while girls assist their mothers with household responsibilities. Other children work in trades, such as carpet weaving, to provide both a future trade occupation and supplementary family income. It seems that no matter where you are in Egypt, regardless of time of day or year, children herd animals, perform household or farm duties, or work in and around the various tourist shops.

Primary education is compulsory in Egypt and is a high government priority, yet many of the poorest children still do not attend school regularly because they are needed to help with family income.

Sometimes only selected children get educated. Among farming families, parents often send only the oldest male children to school on a fairly regular basis. They believe these children must be somewhat educated in order to be able to get manual and other unskilled jobs in the urban areas.

Poor farming families educate only some of the children because of their values and expectations. Young girls are not perceived to need an education because it is most commonly assumed they will marry and bear household responsibilities typical of women in their villages. Therefore, they need to learn the skills that will help them with their anticipated familial and household responsibilities. For boys, it is different. Farm land can only be divided so many times and still support the needs of families. This means that all of a family's male children cannot be provided land for farming after they marry. Logically, then, some of the male children must acquire some other means of supporting their future families. For example, if farm land is only sufficient for one child to inherit, often the youngest male is selected to continue the family farming tradition and assume responsibility for the parents in their old age. Thus, this child is the least likely to be perceived to need an education. Of course, if there is sufficient land, families may perceive less need to educate children since they will be expected to continue the family farming tradition.

Education for girls among the lower classes in urban areas is also sometimes viewed as an extravagance and unnecessary. The major exception to this is some vocational training for some girls, for example, training in basket or carpet weaving. In any event, most children from less wealthy families are expected to spend some of their daytime hours contributing to family endeavours.

Among wealthier Egyptians, the picture acquires the extreme opposite position. 'The more education the better' seems to be the policy in this group for both male and female children. Education provides the route to well-being and progress and symbolises status. One or, preferably, more university degrees establishe the basis for getting that all important government or industry position. Education, including university education, is free to all Egyptians who

Dispensing knowledge in a different manner—children are taken on a field trip to learn more about their ancestors.

qualify (this does not include private or foreign education). However, all children are not selected for advancement to university candidacy. Although education is free, qualifying students may be forced to forego a university education because their families cannot afford to support them during this extended educational period. While the education is free from the government, the cost of living without an income is not supported by the government.

Structurally, the Egyptian educational system is somewhat similar to the British one. Primary school extends from approximately ages six through 12 years. Upon completion, students may enter a preparatory school, which lasts an additional three years. At the end of preparatory school, students sit an exam to determine whether they may continue to secondary school. Depending upon the student's satisfactory completion of the preparatory school examination, they will be directed into either a general secondary or specialised secondary school. General secondary schools prepare students for a university education in the sciences or humanities. Specialised secondary schools prepare students for trade or technical professions. As in the United Kingdom, secondary schools are called 'college'.

To acquire a Secondary School Certificate, students must pass a major qualifying examination which lasts about three weeks. A national secondary qualifying examination is given annually to all students seeking certification in this area. Depending on the student's ranking nationally (and a passing grade), certain students may then proceed to university level training. A student's ranking determines not only if he or she will be allowed to go to university, but also in which programmes he or she may enrol. Highest priority is placed on advancement to medical physician training. Only the highest percentage ranking students throughout the country are eligible for medical training. Another percentage group of students is eligible for the next category of training, and so on. A student who is eligible to go to medical school is not required to take this track and may, in fact, choose another. However, a person with a lower academic ranking would not be allowed to 'move up' and study medicine.

Incidentally, while in the United States the term 'faculty' refers to the professors of a university, in Egypt a faculty member is a student.

In addition to publicly-supported schools throughout Egypt, numerous private schools exist. Some are based on the Egyptian model, while others base their curricula on the American model. If you plan to go to Egypt for a university education and are coming from the West, options are somewhat limited. If you are planning to enrol children in primary or secondary schools, you should probably make arrangements from abroad. In this event, you will most likely find that the company sending you to Egypt will have listings for private schools from which to choose. The cost of private universities or other schooling will probably exceed US$ 10,000 for an academic year per student.

You will also find numerous facilities and/or individuals that provide tutoring services to assist students in exam preparation. If you seek intensive courses in classical or colloquial Arabic, several facilities exist which provide short-term courses at reasonable rates (I have listed a few in the Resource Guide). Check with your embassy, consulate office or tourist authority in Egypt for further information. Of course, the Internet is an increasingly good source of timely information.

SOCIAL INTERACTIONS

CHAPTER 4

'Most people seek after what they do not possess and
are enslaved by the very things they want to acquire.'
—Anwar el-Sadat

WARM, FRIENDLY, SMILING, HAPPY EGYPTIANS abound throughout the country. In keeping with the tradition of hospitality, a call of 'Welcome! Welcome my friend!' penetrates every exchange from well-known friend to total stranger. So why do I include sections on smiles, eye contact and touching? Mainly it is because a smile, a touch or eye contact at the wrong time and with the wrong person can get you into a situation you probably want to avoid. First, let's take a quick glimpse at common social interactions among Egyptians including their smiling, touching and eye contact behaviour.

In the course of normal conversation, Egyptians make intense eye contact, smile a lot and touch each other. Look carefully—most times you will notice these interactions involve same sex interplay, especially in public. Please note—this has nothing to do with homosexuality. I repeat, nothing to do with being homosexual. Normally accepted social rules for appropriate behaviour between same sex and male/female interactions differ substantially depending very slightly on the circumstances. The rules roughly fall out as follows. Don't forget these are only broad generalisations, but it should get you by until you get a feel for the territory.

It is always appropriate to smile, make intense eye contact and even touch frequently and warmly when in same sex groups. This applies for men and women. In Egypt, the standard greeting upon seeing someone you know, whether in business or social situations, usually includes kissing first on one cheek and then the other between persons of the same sex, often while shaking hands.

Handshaking patterns tend to differ between Westerners and Egyptians. Rather than a perfunctory, strong, short handshake typical in much of the West, Egyptians tend to have a less-gripping (even limp, by American standards) handshake. Sometimes, they may continue to hold your hand long after it would seem appropriate by Western standards, but this is normal in Egypt. Both men and women shake hands but in most circumstances, a man should probably wait for the woman to offer her hand in mixed company.

Since men do not typically kiss one another in many parts of Europe and the United States, this can be a little unsettling until one gets used to the practice. More shocking to the Western male, Egyptian men hold hands as they walk and talk. Contrary to some people's beliefs, holding hands among males and cheek-kissing does not mean Egyptian men are homosexuals. The only comparison I can think of in Western society translates to the type of camaraderie shared by men on sports teams where traditional Western touching barriers among men tend to disappear. It is perfectly fine for American men on a football team to hug each other following a touchdown. Once you begin to get accepted in Egyptian society, an Egyptian male friend may well begin to treat you as he would an Egyptian male friend and casually take your hand as you stroll along the street. In most cases, when this happens, it should be viewed as a sign that you are beginning to be seen as an equal, and not as an inappropriate overture. Never fear, a person interested in a homosexual liaison is likely to let you know in a myriad of other ways including an outright statement of intent.

Oddly, although Western women do not usually find the cheek-kissing greeting with other women uncomfortable, they frequently find arm-in-arm or hand-holding with women as they walk a bit unsettling. Normally, Egyptian women link arms when walking to bring them closer to their companion so they can talk more easily. Again, when an Egyptian woman takes your arm in the normal course of walking, it symbolises acceptance and friendship.

Mixed gender situations are where things can become problematic. So much of what is acceptable depends on how well you know the person and upon how familiar the person is with foreign social practices. Obviously, the more educated Egyptians accept differences in social interaction more easily without misinterpretation than do those who are not familiar with other cultures. Most social situations in which you are likely to be involved will tend to be a bit more formal than is customary in the United States. Therefore, I definitely recommend using some caution in interactions, particularly at first, until you become familiar with what is acceptable behaviour. Probably the best rule to follow is to let your Egyptian colleagues or friends establish the pace of interactions. In general, the following guidelines apply.

If you are in a social situation, whether for business or at the home of a friend, and spouses are present, male-female interaction stays on a rather formal level. Smiles between men and women may appear somewhat distant though sincere. Conversations revolve around non-personal topics. Male-female touching should be limited to a handshake. Eye contact in these situations should be rather limited, but you should not appear to be avoiding looking at someone with whom you are talking as this can be interpreted as aloofness and lack of sincerity. Once you become very good friends, these types of situations become more relaxed. Rather than being the initiator of a cheek-kissing greeting upon arrival or departure, just follow the Egyptian person's lead, especially in mixed company.

Men should always be somewhat reserved when interacting with Egyptian women, even with women they know fairly well. 'Showing too much interest' can compromise the woman's reputation and honour, and thus the man's as well. The concept of 'showing too much interest' is relative, but remember, even the slightest personal attention could compromise an Egyptian woman in the wrong situation. In most social situations, it is fairly easy for foreign men to avoid close interactions with Egyptian women because the women will generally keep fairly distant, either physically or by demeanour. Often men and women will retire into separate groups, after dinner for example, eliminating the issue. Does anyone recognise this pattern of behaviour from American parties? In Egypt, practice assists foreign women who might be placed in an awkward situation.

Say, for example, you are an unaccompanied man in a setting with an Egyptian man and his wife. In this situation, conversation should probably be kept at a fairly casual level. If the woman seems to not participate extensively in conversation, it is not necessary to try to involve her more in the conversation. By some standards, this might seem as if she is being ignored, but by Egyptian standards, it may be perceived as normal. Follow her lead and you probably won't go wrong.

If a woman accompanies a foreign male (again in a setting with an Egyptian man and his wife), the women will probably engage in a separate conversation from the men. More commonly, after perfunctory greetings and initial conversation are over, the men or the women will retire to separate rooms for conversation.

At the dinner table or at a reception when there is a mixed group, just remember to keep the conversation very casual and never try to engage an Egyptian woman in discussions of personal issues. If you do get off on a topic that is deemed too personal or one which is inappropriate for the setting, your Egyptian host will indicate this by giving you a totally non-committal answer or by casually changing the subject. Don't forget, topics considered as appropriate for casual conversation in the West can easily be out of bounds in Egypt.

Foreign men should never try to start conversations with Egyptian women to whom they have not been properly introduced, except as required for a business transaction. This could be interpreted as a sign of disrespect, and thus by extension risk compromising the woman's reputation. A foreign man's interest in an Egyptian woman could be interpreted (especially by less educated Egyptian men) to mean he wants the woman for his wife or worse, suggest less acceptable intentions. Unless this is what you want, it is best to avoid speaking to women who are strangers. However, should marriage be your intent, find the woman's appropriate male relative with whom you should negotiate to establish a marriage contract and proceed from there.

A foreign woman who starts a conversation with a male stranger also runs the risk of compromising her respect as well as her reputation if the conversation is for anything other than a bargaining, academic or business type interaction. Socially acceptable behaviour quite simply prevents Egyptian women from engaging unknown men in conversation. To do so, even as a foreigner, leaves you open to lewd suggestions or offers of marriage. Keep in mind that the goal of all Egyptians is to have a good marriage, therefore any unmarried female is fair game. (*More on the marriage issue later in this chapter.*) Most typically, immediate marriage proposals are intended only to flatter the unsuspecting foreign woman and mean no real intent. The reasoning goes as follows: if the woman's morals were high, she would not be engaging in this type of unacceptable behaviour, therefore any type of comment is OK.

While this may seem unfair, it is based on logic according to local perceptions of acceptable behaviour. On the whole, average Egyptian men on the street do not have a high regard for the morals of Western women. They are, of course, basing this judgement on their own standards as compared with their limited understanding of Western women and life. For the most part, average Egyptian men have few ways of learning about Western women. Direct learning is usually gained from interactions with or observations of tourists. There they may see women drink alcohol, wear revealing clothes, or behave in other ways unacceptable for respectable Egyptian women. Indirectly, many TV programmes and movies, broadcast via cable or satellite, provide another basis for judging the morals of Western women.

However, do not discount the fact that some Egyptian marriages are still arranged based on nothing more than a casual smile across a room. This doesn't occur as frequently as in the past, but the arranged marriage does still happen. Additionally, some Egyptian men, especially lower middle-class men, would like nothing better than to have a foreign wife, assuming it would provide them a passport to a more affluent life. Others simply think it would improve their social standing among their peers to have a foreign wife.

Unexpected Engagement
In her excitement for learning about everything Egyptian, one of my students pursued a conversation with a shopkeeper, asking 'all about Egyptian life'. Big mistake! To her surprise and embarrassment, she found herself accidentally 'engaged' within about one hour of arriving in Cairo and spent the next three weeks trying to avoid her would-be suitor who was extremely persistent.

So what do you do if you really want an Egyptian husband? Well, first, find other foreign women (American, European, Asian, etc) who are married to an Egyptian and ask them what everyday life is like. If you still think this is what you want, the next thing is to meet men through an appropriate introduction, for example through business, at social clubs, at university or through friends. Third, understand the nature of courtship, the marriage contract and how it is arranged in Egypt. Finally, have someone act as your intermediary, preferably a male relative or minimally an Egyptian friend who can act as your 'brother', to arrange the contract.

DATING AND MARRIAGE

Courtship rituals in Egypt differ significantly from those in the West. Young men and women do not have the range of opportunities to get to know one another as they do, for example, in the United States or Great Britain. As a rule, only a small portion of the upper-class population undertakes anything that roughly corresponds to what is termed dating in the West. Even so, these relationships tend to be associated with public activities. Rarely would couples spend time alone. Unmarried couples simply do not live with one another in Egypt.

Some young people do attend discotheques, movies, restaurants, social clubs and sporting events as couples. Access tends to be limited by both wealth and social acceptance. People who socialise at these places generally tend to be more educated, wealthier and wear Western-style clothing. Still, only an extremely small percentage of Egyptians consider it proper for young men and women to be out socially on a one-to-one basis. Western-style dating relationships are frowned upon by the majority of people in Egypt. This kind of behaviour is frequently seen as decadent and a sign of Western moral decay.

Negotiating Marriage

Under Islamic law, a non-Muslim man must convert to Islam to marry a Muslim woman. However, a non-Muslim woman does not have to convert to Islam to marry a Muslim man. It is permissible for a Muslim man to marry a 'woman of the Book', i.e. either a Jewish or Christian woman. That being said, it is preferable for a non-Muslim woman to convert for both social, cultural and inheritance reasons. Muslim marriages involve several steps. Significant differences in each phase of marriage occur depending on geographical region and local custom. Therefore, the following represents only a general procedural pattern.

First, the potential partner is selected; this is discussed in detail below. Second, the dowry must be negotiated. This step involves settling on an appropriate dowry that the groom must give to the bride. The bride is not directly involved in these negotiations. The dowry is given to the bride's family, which is then given to the girl. The dowry usually consists of some type of durable wealth. Depending upon the economic status of the families, dowries range from some fixed amount of gold to household wares. Among Bedouins, men usually give camels for their brides. The dowry is the woman's to keep and never becomes the property of her husband. Some social scientists call the dowry a 'bride price'. In many ways, this is a misnomer since the dowry eventually goes to the prospective bride. The groom is not 'buying' a wife. Neither is the family 'selling' their daughter. Giving the bride a dowry is better regarded as a statement of good faith and intention. It does not signify a transfer of ownership, rather a transfer of responsibility. In fact, the dowry establishes the girl's independence in some regards because it means she has her own wealth.

The third step, which is actually the first of the two-part marriage ritual, is the signing of the marriage contract. No vows are exchanged at any step in the Muslim marriage ritual. The marriage contract is both religious and secular. It can be viewed as both in that many parts of the contract are established by Egyptian family law, which is in turn based on Islamic tradition. The marriage contract is religious in that ritual agreement of marriage rights and responsibilities constitutes an old Muslim tradition. It is secular in that marriages must now be registered with authorities to preserve the rights of children born of the marriage. The marriage contract includes elements outlining which partner brings what durable goods to the marriage (for example, carpets, bedroom furniture, living room furniture, and so on). The marriage contract tends to remind me of prenuptial agreements in the West.

After signing the marriage contract, the couple is considered 'engaged'. Engagement is symbolised by wearing a wedding ring on the right hand. During the period between signing the marriage contract and the marriage celebration, the couple may be allowed to get to know one another by going places together publicly. Sexual intercourse is prohibited until the final marriage celebration occurs.

The final step, consummation of the marriage, occurs when all parts of the marriage contract have been fulfilled and the couple is ready to 'make house' together. It is celebrated by a wedding party after which the couple may live together as husband and wife. At the wedding celebration, the ring is moved from the right hand to the left, symbolising completion of the marriage. In some situations, the marriage celebration occurs directly after the signing of the marriage contract. In other cases, it may be several months to a year or more before the final step is undertaken.

Selecting a Partner

So, just how do Egyptians go about establishing a marriage relationship if they are not permitted to get to know one another in a dating relationship? Obviously, if the young people grow up among the group that allows young people considerable freedom in making relationships, the issue becomes more one of choice based on direct knowledge of the prospective partner.

In most cases, selection is by choice, but choice based on little or no direct knowledge of the person's habits or personality. Rather, selection is based on reputation and indirect knowledge. The following is a fairly typical middle-class scenario.

In his mid-30s, a well-educated and reasonably well-off man I will call Ahmed got increasing pressure from his family to take a wife. He, too, wanted a wife and family, so began looking for an appropriate mate. Although very sophisticated in manner and dress, Ahmed came from a very traditional family, so had almost no direct interaction with proper, eligible young women from his area of the country. He had several criteria that he wanted in a wife: proper upbringing, educated, preferably pretty and, most importantly, a virgin. While at a cousin's wedding, he saw a pretty girl, some ten or 12 years younger than he, across the room. They made eye contact and smiled at one another. After the wedding, Ahmed asked friends and relatives about the woman. What was she like? Was she nice? Was she educated? Did she have a good reputation? Upon getting all the right answers to his inquiries, he then arranged to have the marriage contract negotiated. Once the dowry was given and the contract signed, they were engaged. Then the couple took several months getting to know one another to determine if the choice was a good one. 'Getting to know one another' meant they were able to go places together in public, such as to a movie or shopping, and to find out if their personalities would work together. Subsequently, the marriage was finalised.

Arranged Marriages

The oldest tradition, that practised by the more conventional Egyptians, is arranged marriages. Arranged marriages are characterised by little or no choice for the woman and sometimes the man. In all types of marriage arrangements, it is customary for a family member to serve as broker for the marriage contract. Most commonly, the broker is the father. If the father is dead, another male family member, usually an uncle or eldest brother, may serve as broker.

In arranged marriages, the fathers of the prospective couple sometimes negotiate the contract without consulting anyone else. In these cases, the groom may or may not have some influence. The groom's mother also generally maintains significant influence in this realm. The old-fashioned way (which still goes on in many sectors of the society) is essentially for the mother of the boy/man to choose her son's wife. Since the man could not really get to know his prospective wife prior to the marriage, he has no basis from which to choose other than recommendations from family or friends. And since women socialise together and know each other's daughters, who is in a better position to make a good recommendation than the man's mother?

Women would get together over coffee or tea to discuss just which girls were available and who would make a good wife. After careful discussion, one would be chosen as the best prospect for the son's wife. Often, the girl would have been brought to meet the future mother-in-law if she were not already known. Most of the time, of course, the girl would be a cousin to the groom and, therefore, the future mother-in-law would already know much about how the girl was reared, including her temperament, reputation and beauty. Then the marriage contract would be arranged between the fathers.

In some ways, this process could work to the advantage of both partners. A factor that enters the equation is the fact that the man's wife would traditionally come to live in his natal home. She would spend much of her time under fairly direct control of her mother-in-law. It was, therefore, important to have a wife who was congenial not only with her husband, but also with her mother-in-law. And since the couple is not allowed to get to know one another through social interaction, who else knows the young man's behaviour and ideas better than his mother? On the other hand, this assumes that the boy's mother wants a good, loving wife for her son. If, to the contrary, the boy's mother was particularly jealous of losing her son's devotion to a wife, she might best choose a wife that was incompatible with her son's personality. By doing this, the mother could assure that her son's devotion was not diluted by the wiles of his new wife. According to people I have talked to, both situations occur.

For women, the issue is a little different. The possibility of being wooed certainly must enter many girls' minds at some point. However, for most girls, not getting a husband may be a more devastating prospect than marrying someone she doesn't know. Marriage is the only real way to ensure security, shelter and family in the future. Even marriage to a very old man one doesn't know is considered by many Egyptian women to be a better option than no marriage at all.

You almost have to be asking yourself how could the kind of male/female segregation replete with arranged marriages lead to some of the world's oldest, most tantalisingly romantic poetry. I think one of the reasons is because ideas of romantic love were left to the realm of the imagination. If you will notice, much of the love poetry revolves around unrequited love from afar. Usually, the romantic fantasy involves ardour for an imaginary, silk draped maiden or one seen momentarily in the distance. In this poetry, men use flowery language and gestures to win the love of the woman. With these ideas in a man's head, marriage to an unknown woman represents the occasion to wed the fantasy with the real. A woman known only through brief eye conversation, if at all, represents the ultimate in hidden treasures.

You may now be asking yourself if the girl has a choice about whether she marries the person chosen by her father? Well, sometimes yes and sometimes no. Sometimes a contract between families is arranged when the couple is very young. Some village girls wear an engagement earring even at the age of eight or nine years, indicating their parents have already arranged their marriage. With these types of marriages, the girl has no input or choice. At other times, the girl's mother had input in the negotiation, especially through the selection process mentioned above. The girl can indirectly influence the decision by showing unattractive behaviour in front of a prospective mother-in-law, thereby decreasing the chances she will be approved. Among other Egyptians, a girl has the right of refusal and/or selection. Technically, a girl is supposed to have the right of refusal, but this is not always the case in reality. Choice of marriage partners in arranged marriages is, more often than not, a matter of the father's discretion.

Although men may have up to four wives in Islam, most people seem to feel it is wrong for a man to have more than one wife. Most men will also tell you, in a sort of laughing reference, that it is neither financially nor emotionally feasible to have more than one wife. I have yet to find a woman who likes polygamy. All acknowledge it is legal and acceptable under Islam, but most abhor the idea of being the second wife, much less their husbands taking another wife.

Divorce

An Egyptian man can get a divorce rather easily. Under traditional practices, all he has to do is to state publicly three times in succession, 'I divorce thee, I divorce thee, I divorce thee', or words to that effect. If he makes the statement only once or twice, reconciliation remains a possibility. Family members often serve as intermediaries to try to arrange a reconciliation. It is still quite easy for a man to divorce his wife, though the traditional statements must now be accompanied by a legal document filed with the authorities.

For a woman, getting a divorce is much more problematic. A woman technically can get a divorce for 'just reason', such as impotence or mistreatment. Mistreatment can range from not getting enough food in the husband's household to beatings and so on. Current estimates hold that as many as one in three women have been beaten at least once during their marriage. Only about half of those ever beaten have ever sought help.

The social stigma of divorce is not terribly serious among most Egyptians and the woman's family can usually find her another husband. But some blame does follow the woman if the husband gets the divorce. Sometimes people think she 'could have done something to keep the husband she lost'. Also, since she is no longer a virgin, her value is less.

Economic factors constitute a more serious reason for families encouraging a woman not to divorce. Family pressures, especially from brothers or fathers, can be substantial. When a woman gets divorced, she then goes back to being the responsibility of her natal family, which means either her father, brother or uncle re-acquires financial responsibility for her. The family also assumes responsibility to help her get another husband.

Finally, having to leave her children with the husband acts as a deterrent to a woman. In many cases, the children stay with the father after a certain age, usually eight years old for boys and ten years old for girls. The mother might or might not be given the opportunity to see the children again. Most people will tell you that a woman will still see her children occasionally if the husband is a 'good person'.

A 1979 law, which strengthened a Muslim woman's rights to divorce and child custody, was repealed in 1985 after it was found unconstitutional for conflicting with Islamic law. The marriage contract law established in 1931 is now in effect, though a new law introduced in 1995 is pending. If the new law is enacted, it would allow premarital negotiations on a wide range of issues including a woman's right to work, study, and travel abroad. Currently, a woman must have the permission of her husband or father to obtain passports and visas to travel abroad.

Rising Divorce Rates

In spite of the many reasons not to divorce, the Egyptian divorce rate has risen significantly over the past few decades. No specific figures are available, but most people agree that it is more common now than it was in the past.

FEMALE GENITAL MUTILATION (FGM)

Female genital mutilation (also called female circumcision) still persists in Egypt today. International health organisations widely condemn the practice, citing its long-lasting physical and psychological damage. In July 1996, following the death of an 11-year-old girl from haemorrhaging, the Minister of Health and Population issued a decree calling for the end of the practice of FGM. Also, the decree called for a prohibition of performing the practice by non-medical and medical practitioners. The exact prevalence of FGM is unclear, but both government and private sources suggest that the practice is common throughout Egypt. It is done to young girls (usually between the ages of seven and ten years old). Best estimates suggest that the procedure is equally prevalent in Coptic and Muslim populations.

Currently, the government broadcasts bulletins condemning the practice. Numerous non-governmental organisations also attempt to curtail the practice by actively trying to educate the population about the hazards attached to FGM. The curriculum at medical schools and for trained birth attendants is being revised to address FGM and its dangers. Finally, the senior Muslim leader in Egypt, the Sheik of Al-Azhar, has stated that FGM is not required under Islamic tenets.

FGM is an intensely ingrained cultural practice that carries with it numerous symbolic traditional reasons for continuing the practice. Many women believe the practice is necessary to ensure that their young daughters will be able to get a good husband and that the practice is a 'normal' thing girls must go through as part of growing up. Therefore, in spite of government, religious and private efforts to eradicate FGM, it is unlikely to completely disappear in the near future.

NAMES

Some of the most common names used throughout Egypt give clues on how to fit people into the social structure. You can usually assume that a person with a name common in Islamic history, e.g. Mohamed, is Muslim. People with Western names are more likely Christian. Names that appear in both the Qur'an and Bible do not mark a person's religion.

In fact, Mohamed is probably the most common name you will hear throughout Egypt. It is so frequently used that the name is used in conjunction with the next following name or sometimes a person will simply go by their second name to avoid confusion with others named 'Mohamed'.

The use of titles is an important aspect of Egyptian society. The way people are addressed in Egypt is by Mr, Mrs, Madame, Dr or Professor followed by their first name. For example, a person named Mohamed would be addressed as Mr Mohamed or Dr Mohamed as the situation warrants. As a woman, I am sometimes called Mrs Susan, Dr Susan, Madame Susan or Professor Susan depending on the situation and how people know me. Ministerial and high ranking diplomatic officials are referred to as 'Excellency'. Definitely try to find out any title a person has because to omit their title can be insulting. If you have to err, try to err on the side of giving someone a higher ranking title, rather than a lower one.

A word of caution when meeting married couples. Women do not change their last names when they marry. As a result, it is sometimes difficult to find out a woman's appropriate last name. She may well be introduced to you simply as 'Mrs Fatima, Dr Mohamed's wife'. If you are caught in a rough spot and do not know the woman's name, it is probably better to refer to her as 'Mrs Mohamed' (if that is her husband's first name) rather than to refer to her as 'Mrs Husband's-last-name'. This last form of address is usually reserved for informal situations, so should be used only as a last resort in any other setting.

Egyptians are especially proud of being parents. They have a very pleasant, informal way of referring to a person as the 'parent' of someone, usually the oldest son or oldest child. For example, a man might be referred to as 'Abu Mohamed' or 'father of Mohamed'. A woman could be referred to as 'Umm Mohamed' or 'mother of Mohamed'.

People may have many names and recite them differently for different occasions. Don't be surprised if you meet a person under one circumstance and his name is Ahmed Ishmail, only to find that the next time you meet, he is referred to as Ahmed el-Kamel. Usually, sons are named after their grandfather or paternal uncles rather than their father.

DEATH AND INHERITANCE

In Egypt, a person should be buried as soon as possible after death, whether Muslim or Christian. Usually, family members wash the body, wrap it, and then it is interred, often within hours of death. If death occurs at night, it is not necessary to wait until the next day to bury the person as a night burial is appropriate.

A Muslim woman receives half the amount of a male heir's inheritance. By tradition, male Muslim heirs face strong social pressure to provide for all family members who need assistance. A sole male heir receives all of his parents' estate.

A sole female heir receives half of her parents' estate with the balance going to designated male relatives.

DRESS

What Egyptians wear and what you will feel comfortable wearing depends to a large extent on where you are and who you are with. In other words, this is another one of those 'look around and see what is happening' kind of topics.

The most visible piece of clothing seen in Egypt is the traditional cotton *galabea* (*jalabaya*). A *galabea* is an ankle-length, loose garment worn by men or women. Many of the *galabeas* sold in tourist areas have short sleeves, but long

This worker from Beni Suef (south of Cairo) is dressed in the traditional ankle-length long-sleeved cotton *gelebea*.

sleeves are preferred throughout Egypt by most people. Men usually wear white, beige, grey or light blue *galabeas*. More prominent men usually wear business suits or casual European- or American-styled pants or blue jeans with knit or woven fabric shirts (usually collared). Men generally do not wear shorts or tank tops in public unless they happen to be in a tourist area.

Except in the highest fashion areas and around universities, Egyptian women do not usually wear long pants or slacks. Well-to-do women dress in the latest European fashions. For social occasions, prominent Egyptian women wear high heels and expensive (often silk) Western-styled dresses and accessorise their dresses with good jewellery—usually gold, but almost never costume jewelry.

When women think of Middle Eastern clothing, the first thing that comes to mind is the long black cape-like outer garment worn in movies. This is actually seen very little in Egypt except among older women, Bedouins and among those from exceptionally conservative elements of the population. This type of dress is more often seen in Upper Egypt, though there are neighbourhoods in Cairo and elsewhere that conform to this traditional form of dress. Short of dressing in a black shroud, what do you wear if you want to blend in most effectively? And, how do you reduce or totally eliminate catcalls, hisses and propositions as you walk down the street? Essentially, there is no great secret here. Just dress fairly conservatively and direct your wardrobe choices to where you are.

What is least attention getting? Here you can combine comfort with style. It is not necessary to dress in a traditional, brightly coloured woman's *galabea* to fit in with middle or lower-class Egyptian women. Prominent women dress in Western fashion pretty much everywhere, so this is acceptable as long as you stay within some bounds. Women find wearing long-sleeved, looser fitting garments with all or most of their legs covered to be most comfortable and least likely to attract attention when getting around in Egypt. This can be as simple as placing the blouse on the outside of the waistband rather than on the inside. Short sleeves are certainly acceptable, but probably should cover most of the upper arm. What you will find is that wearing garments with long, loose sleeves (preferably made of cotton or some other natural fibre) is actually cooler in the intensive heat anyway. Loose fitting, natural fibre fabrics form a little air pocket between you and the cloth. Anything made of man-made fibres, such as nylon or polyester, is very hot. When you perspire, man-made fibres tend to stick to you, allowing no air space to evaporate moisture. Cotton underwear is also more comfortable in the heat.

Tight fitting pants are definitely miserably hot no matter what the fabric. For women, almost any kind of long pants (even loose fitting ones) are more appropriately worn with a long, loose over-shirt. Certainly, there is no legal prohibition against tight fitting jeans and low cut or open blouses, but women who wear these demonstrate a lack of respect for local values according to Egyptian perception. Male or female, if you are attending one of the Western universities in Egypt, dress is more typical to that found in North American or British universities (including the tight jeans). The principal exception is that clothing appears to be somewhat less casual. Jeans are the norm for both men and women in these settings.

Swimwear presents an interesting dichotomy. On normal, everyday beaches frequented by average Egyptians, children and men wear Western-styled swimsuits. Women, on the other hand, wear the same thing they do on the streets. And, yes, they do get in the water, long skirts and all, although rarely above their knees. Private beaches are different. Here, depending on who you are with and how private the beach is, the full range of beachwear is possible. Most mature Egyptian women still do not wear Western swimsuits in mixed company on private beaches, but a little more latitude can be found here. Having said that, I will remind you that in tourist areas, particularly on cruise ships or Red Sea villages, you can see anything from bikinis to short-shorts. Western swimsuits of any kind are also all right at swimming pools in hotels and clubs. Most of the time you will find that women's and men's times for access to the pool are separate anyway,

A typical beach scene in Alexandria.

so your outfit becomes more a matter of personal preference than propriety.

For men, business meetings and social gatherings require reasonably conservative attire. Here, you will find a business suit appropriate for many situations. Alternatively, nice slacks with a dress or sports shirt (with or without a tie) are also acceptable. Egyptian businesswomen dress rather formally, but do not typically wear business suits like the ones worn by women in the United States. They are more likely to wear either a nicely tailored outfit or a dressy dress. Again, natural fibres are preferred since they provide the best protection against the oppressive heat that exists throughout much of the year. Almost always, you will find arms covered. Short, dressy dresses and business clothes have skirts shorter than ankle length, but usually well below the knee.

When in doubt, ask your host or a friend what attire is appropriate for whatever function. There are a couple of important things to remember when asking. First, whenever you ask, 'Is such-and-such appropriate?', the likely response will be 'Yes'. You will get this response because your Egyptian friend does not want to insult or contradict you. Therefore, you might get a better answer by asking, 'What are you wearing to such-and-such?' or 'What will people be wearing to such-and-such?' Second, unless they give you a specific answer, remember that overdressing by your standards is probably preferable to underdressing.

Veiling

The practice of veiling intrigues Westerners beyond belief. Some think it represents the most horrible, archaic subordination women endure in a modern world. Others see veiling as mysterious. Few foreigners view veiling as practical or benefitting women in any way. Western ideas vary about what constitutes veiling in Egypt and throughout the Middle East. So, why do women veil and who veils?

Many scholars believe that veiling was a tradition much older than the Qur'an. Apparently, only very wealthy or influential women veiled at the time of the Prophet Muhammad's early life. When Prophet Muhammad fled from Mecca to Medina (AD 622), some of his followers suggested that his women should be placed in an honoured category, so they would be noticeable to all who saw them. Subsequently, veiling became a visible symbol to indicate their difference

Stopping to chat; these women are wearing the most commonly seen type of veil.

from others. Wearing the cloak or overgarment also signalled that these women should not be annoyed or given trouble. Later, the act of veiling was legitimised in the Qur'an. Interpretation of how veiling should be implemented in a modern society is a matter disputed throughout the Islamic world. It ranges from the mandated requirements in Saudi Arabia and Iran to personal preference in many other parts of the world.

For anyone interested in looking at the reference to the act of veiling in the Qur'an, see Surah XXXIII, verse 59. You should note that several translations of the Qur'an exist. Some translations are more acceptable to Islamic scholars than others. However, this passage does not vary too much from one version to another.

Not all women in Egypt wear the veil. Veiling can be anything from a large head scarf, pinned under the chin, to a long cloak, head and face covered, allowing only the eyes to show through a slit in the face covering, with gloves and socks. While this type of veiling does occur in Egypt, it is quite rare in the population as a whole. Among the few women who cover themselves completely, the colour of the veil may vary from black to lavender. Most Egyptian women who veil wear a large head scarf secured under the chin that falls over the shoulders in front and back. This veil may be white or coloured. Can you imagine how they could work in the fields covered in a full veil?

A Veiled Experiment

Reasons abound for wearing the veil in Egypt—"I wear the veil to show I am a practising Muslim."; "I wear the veil to be inconspicuous."; "I am wearing a veil today because I didn't want to fix my hair."; "Women wear the veil more now than they did in the past because the economy is not good and women cannot afford to go to the beauty shop as often as they used to." Among the reasons I find most intriguing are the ones relating to being inconspicuous or 'becoming invisible'. Some of my female students decided to try an experiment to see if they were treated differently when they wore a scarf than when they did not. They found that by wearing a scarf veil, they truly could walk among crowds in the most frequented tourist areas and basically become invisible. Wearing the same clothes as before but without a veil, they returned to a popular tourist area with shops, and hawkers and the usual gauntlet of people tried to get their attention. With their heads covered, most of the hassling seemed to disappear.

HOUSEHOLDS AND HOUSES

Although lifestyles vary considerably by social class and economic conditions, Egyptian tradition fosters extended family ties. It is not uncommon to find three generations of a family living in the same dwelling, whether rural or urban. The best way to look at it is that the more the family can live close together, the better. This means that a family may purchase several flats in the same building, have a villa with separate areas for individual families, live in a village comprised of male relatives with their families, or even live in one flat with separate rooms for individual families. This tradition provides both financial and emotional support for its members.

In urban areas, small, but distinct, areas (called quarters) developed around family groups. New conditions, created by rapid development and increasing urbanisation, challenge the ability of many families to maintain traditional living standards. Indeed, crowded conditions in the city also make it harder for urban families to stay together in their family's area of the city. As a result, marriages are delayed until couples can find the financial resources for alternative living arrangements. More and more frequently, marriages cannot be made until the man has sufficient money to get living quarters separate from his family.

When a man marries, his new wife is expected to leave her natal family and move in with his. The distance may not be far, but marriage for a woman means leaving her familial ties and moving into an established family with which she has no or few ties or history.

Traditionally, the new bride came under the control and direction of her mother-in-law who was responsible for the house and household functions. Since the senior woman in the house basically ran the household, daughters-in-law would be directed by their mother-in-law in many aspects of daily living. One may be told to go to market; another to do the cooking for the family; while a third did laundry. Certainly, many women were mistreated under this system. Others were treated equitably to maintain household harmony.

For rural people, the challenges are somewhat different. Limited land available for farming means that, in many cases, some males must migrate to the cities for work. In these cases, male workers may be 'target' workers or may migrate permanently, establishing new households in the city. Target migratory workers migrate daily, weekly or for longer periods. In these cases, married workers usually leave their wives and children in the home village, stressing family relationships.

One Egyptian tradition, which crosses all class boundaries, is the habit of adult children living with their parents until they are married. It is quite different from the Western tradition where adult unmarried children establish their own household. One principal exception occurs with migratory male workers. Since more and more rural adult males migrate to the cities to work for wages, increasingly, groups of single males rent flats in the city separate from their families. The same is not true for women—it is still an exception for them to live alone. Young women, even working women, usually live in the home of their parents or close relatives.

Upper-class or elite families have much more flexibility in living arrangements than do others. A family frequently owns villas (houses) and flats (apartments) in several locations

Citadel with high-rise buildings in Cairo. Multi-family flats (apartments) may be larger than single-family residences in the West.

throughout Egypt. Apartments or flats tend to be quite different from those in the West. Among the upper-class, flats are often larger than most single family dwellings, for example, in the US. Family living space is generally quite comfortable.

Sometimes a large, family-owned villa is divided into flats in which different family groups live. This arrangement facilitates continuation of the tradition of the extended family living in the same quarters. However, in this case, individual families have separate flats within the villa. For example, the parents (or widow) may have one floor, a daughter and her family another, and a son and his family still another. Due to recent construction, particularly in and around Cairo, more and more very large buildings house many luxurious flats purchased by the occupants. In these cases, extended family living may encompass a widowed parent living with children and their families or vice versa.

RURAL AND BEDOUIN LIFESTYLES

The *fellahin* (peasant farmers) who typically live in small villages generally practise subsistence level farming and

Hailing from the rural area of Beni Suef, this man makes his living as the owner and caption of a *felucca*, a narrow wooden sailing boat that is used to transport goods and people along the Nile River.

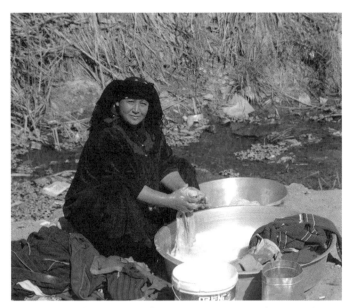

Electricity is available in most villages in Egypt. However, this woman's village does not have running water or sewerage, so she washes clothes by hand with water from the canal.

some fishing, or work for wages on large farms. Others rent farms from landowners and share profits from farm production. They are often quite poor but more commonly are able to maintain traditional family living patterns. Frequently, a village may be 40–50 people all belonging to the same family lineage. For example, one couple may have established the farm a few generations ago, had nine or ten children who, with their spouses, built additional houses, had their families, and so on through the generations.

Fellahin houses look like those that must have been around thousands of years ago. Although electricity is now available in all villages (though maybe not in all houses), many houses lack modern toilet facilities, sewage, and piped-in water supplies.

Throughout most of Upper Egypt, village houses are made from earthen bricks (much like adobe bricks in the desert south-west of the United States), sometimes with a mud plaster on the outside. They typically have flat roofs with

A *fellahin* house in a rural village—a building style unchanged for thousands of years.

mud staircases leading to the top. Some maintain areas attached to their houses for animals. Houses typically show little adornment on the outside. Inside walls are often painted with bright colours.

Nubian villages are distinguished from traditional *fellahin* villages by their architecture. Nubian homes tend to be more decoratively painted on the outside than most *fellahin* homes.

Bedouins, who are termed pastoral nomads, typically live in tents constructed of densely woven animal hair. The tent is struck according to prevailing winds to maximise air circulation in the summer and to protect occupants from blowing sand. In the winter and even on summer evenings, the desert can get quite cold, so tents may be erected close to some type of natural protection, such as in the bend of a *wadi* (dry river or stream bed).

Bedouin groups typically include 40–50 persons, usually related. Each family establishes its own small sub-area within the camp. Parents and children have separate sleeping tents. During the daylight hours, children can be seen frolicking around their family's area.

HOSPITALITY

'Welcome! Welcome!' Everywhere you turn, you will hear this comforting refrain in Egypt. Hospitality is a keyword in Egyptian life. The beginnings of some of the hospitality traditions are unknown, but possibly some began in the desert. People in the desert often offered shelter and food to strangers, assuming that next time, they may be the ones in need. No matter where it began, it is now an ingrained tradition everywhere.

Hospitality takes many forms. Some will tell you that by tradition, no matter what the cost to the host, one should provide a guest three days of hospitality. Even if hospitality is not taken to this extreme, you will see some form of typical Egyptian hospitality everywhere you turn. It may take the form of offering you tea in a shop. It may even take the form of sending children to walk with you if you are alone. A common form of hospitality is inviting you to join the family for meals. They may well spend what, to them, is an exorbitant amount on a meal for you, even if doing so means they would not have money left for other needed things.

Another form hospitality often takes involves being out in a restaurant or café. You may well have suggested going to the restaurant or café, expecting to pay for all persons. However, when the bill arrives, you may find that your Egyptian host insists on paying for all persons. It would be very embarrassing to your Egyptian friend for you to argue over the bill in public (regardless of whether they can afford the tab). When this happens, wait until you are out of the restaurant and quietly give your friend the money. It is at this point that you can insist without your Egyptian friend losing face. Even so, your Egyptian friend may well tell you that it is 'no problem' and that you shouldn't pay. Remember the rule of three's—allow them to refuse your offer twice, but continue to offer until the third time. If they refuse the third time, then it really is all right for you not to pay for the meal.

Getting Around a Sticky Situation

I find hospitality rules discomforting at times because I am a woman, usually travelling alone, conducting business throughout Egypt. As a result, I run into two factors. First, I am a guest in Egypt, therefore should be shown hospitality. Second, since I am a woman, there is the unwritten rule that men should financially 'take care of' women. Therefore, when I try to insist that I pay, I often meet resistance even with people I have known a long time. I have figured out that the way to get around this double problem is to insist, and I mean absolutely insist—several times if necessary—that they must let me pay because I am on an expense account (whether I am or not). This takes the obligation out of their insistence because I have introduced a third entity, so accepting my hospitality then becomes all right. As an 'independent woman', this allows me to feel I am making my contribution and not taking advantage of my Egyptian friends.

FRIENDSHIP

Most Western friendships require little in the form of responsibilities back to the other person—a friend is just someone whose company you enjoy. Being 'friends' in Egypt is very different than in the West. Like love, friendship develops rapidly in Egypt. There seem to be few grey areas—people are either friends or strangers. If you are a stranger, you can expect hospitality, but that is all. Once you become a friend, you acquire a complicated web of rights and responsibilities. Friendships require energy and constant nurturing.

Westerners seem to deplore asking friends for 'favours'. On the other hand, Egyptian friends expect to be able to ask favours of you and expect you to ask favours of them. This is part of the responsibility of friendship. What does this mean in terms of your life in Egypt? Well, if you are not used to having people ask you to do favours for them, a likely response will be to 'feel used'. You may simply feel imposed upon, but in any event, Egyptian friendships are likely to be considerably more intense than you experience at home. Just try to remember that if you weren't considered to be a friend, they probably would not ask. Furthermore, many times a request for a favour may simply take the form of suggesting 'I want' or 'I would like' to do something, to go somewhere or to have something. Believe it or not, you may be expected to help the person do, go or have whatever it is (assuming it is a reasonable request). At the same time, the slightest hint from you will often provoke a reciprocal action from your Egyptian friends.

Going the Extra Mile

Before I was well acquainted with how Egyptian friendships progressed, I was astounded to find that the responsibilities of friendship involved much more giving of one's time and energy than I was used to. One day, I simply mentioned to a friend that I 'wanted to go' shopping later that day. I was just making conversation. Certainly, I did not expect my friend to take the comment seriously or as a request for a favour. Next thing I knew, my friend and her children changed all their daily plans to go with me so I wouldn't have to be alone. She assumed that because I said I wanted to go shopping (rather than I was planning to go shopping), that I was expecting her—as my friend—to accompany me or even to provide a driver and car. Of course I wanted her to accompany me, but I would never have asked her to change important plans just to go shopping with me. How delightful for me that she went to that much trouble! I had my friend and her children with me to help find all the good bargains!

VISITING

Visiting friends and relatives is the mainstay of Egyptian social life. Rather than 'going' somewhere or 'doing' something together, as is a common Western custom, Egyptians relish getting together for the sake of being together. Nothing seems to give Egyptians greater pleasure than the company of others. Foreign cultures, on the other hand, often tend toward action. With this action-oriented basis for socialisation, people often take little time for activities that do not seem to produce some tangible result. Therefore, many foreigners have difficulty with the idea of just 'being' with other people. If you are accustomed to getting together with friends to 'do' something, 'passing by' someone's house for the afternoon or evening to do absolutely nothing but sit around and talk can be unsettling. Furthermore, visits frequently are expected to take several hours. Rarely do visits seem to last just 15–20 minutes (what might be considered to be a polite visit by some Western standards).

One of the Family

Probably one of the most disconcerting events I experienced when I passed by a friend's house developed when I was invited for the afternoon meal. I duly went for lunch, enjoyed the meal, and settled down for what I thought was going to be a short visit following the meal. After we had chatted for a few minutes, my hosts (who followed the Egyptian custom of napping in the afternoon) offered me a room to take a nap. My initial response was to panic and try to leave immediately, because I thought I had overstayed my welcome. I definitely had to fight the urge to run. In retrospect, I realise that they simply wanted me to stay for a longer visit, assumed that I followed their tradition of napping, and were treating me as a family member and valued friend. I was 'welcome' in their home. But to me, since I was not a house-guest, it was totally unfathomable that I should go to someone's house and take a nap.

BAKSHEESH AND TIPPING

Baksheesh and tipping are two entirely separate things to Egyptians although Arabic dictionaries and tourist guide books usually denote them as synonymous. It is especially difficult around tourist areas to distinguish *baksheesh* from tipping. This is compounded by the fact that every local knows the guide books use the words synonymously.

Baksheesh is technically gifts for the poor, a handout or alms. Beggars of all ages throughout Egypt approach you saying, "*Baksheesh*! *Baksheesh*!" At first it is very difficult to turn down someone who looks quite helpless and needy—especially if it is a ragged, dirty little child. Very rapidly you will be able to distinguish between the ones that are sent out to hit on any foreigner who appears from others. Let your conscience be your guide regarding giving money, but remember one thing: if you give to one person, you will likely find many others immediately surrounding you asking for money. If someone is truly handicapped, you should always give a little something to help them—this is likely their only means of support.

Tipping, on the other hand, is considered proper and appropriate for any small service rendered. They have given you something (a service) and you should reciprocate (a tip). Most of the time people are quite courteous if you fail to give them a tip when they deem it appropriate, and simply remind you with a palm up gesture. If they speak your language, they may well remind you with the word 'tip' in whatever language. If not, they may use the word *baksheesh* if you seem particularly ignorant to what they expect.

Since tipping is considered rude under some circumstances and simply not necessary in some cultures, foreigners often do not realise that in many situations in Egypt they are expected to give a tip, whereas they might not be expected to tip in their native culture. Furthermore, Americans may find it an affront, especially if the person seems to be doing nothing or is in some kind of uniform. A couple of examples should suffice to show how this works.

First, if you are at an ancient site where there are uniformed guards protecting the place or at an entrance/exit gate, a person from the United States would usually not consider that these people should be tipped. They are employed, getting a salary—just doing their job with seemingly no service provided. After all, they didn't bring you a meal or carry your bag, right? Besides, some are government employees or members of the military. In the United States, it is not only immoral, but illegal, to tip government employees. Why should you tip them? Well, in Egypt they are performing a service for you—they are protecting you or easing your stay or assisting you in having a good visit. It is true they may get a salary, but like people in the service industry, their income also depends on getting tips. Their employer is irrelevant. If you look closely, you will see people or tour leaders almost imperceptibly passing a small tip as they shake hands upon going through the gate or when they leave. The average visitor may never notice money exchanging hands.

The same goes for monument watchers or keepers at mosques. These men appear in total silence out of the shadows when you least expect them. They are there to keep disrespectful people from leaving graffiti or trash, or otherwise defacing public monuments. They also tell you in no uncertain terms when you are not supposed to be in an area. Again, you shouldn't make a big deal out of it, just quietly give them a small tip for this service. You will readily differentiate between these men and the ones that appear out of nowhere with goods to sell.

A final example relates to children. Once I was busily taking pictures around Khan el-Khalili Bazaar and, since you should always ask people if it is OK, I asked some children if I could take their pictures. All children love to have their picture taken (though women usually don't) and so, of course, they posed. Afterwards, they surrounded me asking for *baksheesh*. A nearby shopkeeper saw them around me and came out yelling at them to leave me alone. I insisted to the shopkeeper that they had given me something (their picture) and I wanted to give them something back. At first, he still did not want me to give them anything because they were 'begging', but finally he understood (I think) that it was really only reciprocation on my part.

GIFTS

Gifts are a tough one. Knowing who to give gifts and what to give sometimes seems challenging. Several occasions warrant small gifts. When leaving for Egypt, take small gifts for special people you will meet in Egypt. Gifts should be nice, but need not be terribly expensive. If you come from a particular region known for a special product, something along these lines would be quite acceptable. For example, I am from Texas, so I usually take along a variety of Texana gifts ranging from coffee-table books to trivets decorated with Texas wildflowers for special occasions. Fine writing pens are always a safe gift for men.

It is also a generally accepted practice to take something to your hostess when being entertained at someone's home. Taking flowers is a custom in many parts of the United States and other Western countries, but probably best avoided in Egypt unless it is something you absolutely know the hostess would like. Unfortunately, until you have been there quite a long time, you probably won't know the protocol regarding colour, flower variety or arrangement, and you could easily go to one of the local flower stands and get a funeral arrangement as a wedding or table arrangement. Sweets, candy or nuts are a good bet. Most sweet shops will package your gift in a box with a nice ribbon for you to take to your hostess. By the way, do not take something perishable or you run the risk of having it ruin. A proper Egyptian hostess will thank you for the gift and set it aside for opening later (as is the custom with most gifts). If you are hosting and people bring you gifts, you should follow the same practice.

Another category of gifts relates to children. It is acceptable to bring gifts for young children if you know the people well. I like to stock up before leaving home with colouring books, coloured marking pens or crayons, and little toys that may not be available in Egypt to give to children of my friends. Be careful not to take anything that has a religious connotation.

A final category of what may be considered gifts are the items you take along to give to people you may meet along the streets or when visiting tourist sites. For some reason, inexpensive writing pens and lighters seem to be premium gifts. Poor children everywhere will often hold out their hands asking you to give them pens. They seem to especially like the ones that click, though any pen can cause furious rivalry within a mob of children. With adults in tourist areas, these small items can often be used as bargaining aids as well as for tips. It is probably best not to take candy or chewing gum for these occasions. Many poorer people do not get their teeth fixed and may have dental cavities, so candy or gum hurt their teeth.

COMPLIMENTS

Complimenting someone on something they have or are wearing can be a little confusing in Egypt. While it is standard practice to tell someone in the United States, for example, that they have a beautiful necklace or ring or anything, you should be a little careful in Egypt. Why? Generosity to a guest is important to maintain a good reputation. As a result, if you are not careful, what is meant to be simply a compliment of good taste places your Egyptian hosts in the awkward position of needing to demonstrate their generosity by offering you the admired object, especially if it is a small, portable object.

The way it works is more or less like this. You can say something like, 'Oh, you have a lovely home.' People are not likely to try to give you their home. But if you say something like, 'This box is so beautiful. I have been looking everywhere for one just like it', watch out. The person you say this to may feel obligated to offer it to you. They want to make you happy and welcome. Now assume that you were not 'hinting' that they give you their treasure, you suddenly feel guilty because you realise that their innate generosity means they will offer the box to you. If you find yourself in an awkward

A Short Recap

- Be generous with tips
- Be cautious with smiles and eye contact with persons of the opposite sex
- Be respectful of the role of women
- Holding hands with a same-sex individual does not mean people are homosexual
- Being a friend can be very intense and involves a significant commitment
- Dress rather conservatively

position like this (and it can happen when you least expect it), thank them and refuse. It can get even trickier because they will then try to insist that you take it because they are generous. Again, refuse. Usually that will end the offering. A sort of rule of thumb is if something is offered to you the third time, you may assume the person really wants you to have it and is not offering out of social obligation. In this case, you may accept if it seems appropriate to you. You must, naturally, use your own judgement of good taste and propriety depending on the article offered. Just remember that admiration of something will often place your Egyptian friends in the position of having to offer it to you to maintain their social reputation.

A Lesson Learned

One of my most embarrassing moments occurred as a result of window shopping with an American friend along with a friend who was Egyptian. It was close to when I was getting ready to leave Egypt and I did not think about the fact that my Egyptian friend might want to get me a little gift as a going-away present. So as I blithely wandered through some gold shops in Khan el-Khalili (trying, I thought, to help my Egyptian friend find a token gift to send to someone else), we passed a shop window which had what I considered to be one of the most beautiful sapphire rings I had ever seen in my life. So, naturally, I pointed it out to my American friend with a comment like, 'Wish I hadn't bought so much, because I would give it all up to have that ring.' In my mind, it was so expensive as to be outside the realm of anything for serious contemplation, just one of those nonchalant comments we Americans often make when window shopping. I did not know my American friend was in a small conspiracy with my Egyptian friend. Apparently, all afternoon they had been just waiting for me to comment on some piece of jewellery that I really liked. Had I guessed they might have been looking for something for me, I would certainly have kept my mouth shut about the ring in front of them or would have pointed out something relatively inexpensive as being the absolute thing I most wanted in life. You can guess what happened next: my Egyptian friend presented the ring to me over dinner as a gift. The ring is, without a doubt, one of my most treasured possessions (it ranks right up there with the watch my grandmother gave me when I graduated from high school). I wear it with pride and am eternally grateful for his generosity. It is still the most beautiful ring I have ever seen, but you can just imagine my embarrassment when I realised what I had done. I am now much more cautious when I shop with Egyptian friends and am careful of what I admire in shop windows.

THE LOGISTICS OF SETTLING IN

'Why buy from abroad while you have all the products of Mango, Esprit and Guess right here? You can find it just few metres away from your house.'
—Elhamy El-Kerdany,
City Stars general manager for operations and tenant relations at City Stars Centre in Nasr City

FORMALITIES

Americans, Canadians and British may purchase a renewable 30-day visa at the Cairo airport. This must be paid in the hard currency of your country (approximate cost is US$ 15 in 2006). You should get a visa prior to arrival if you are arriving overland or if you have experienced trouble with your visa in the past. If you arrive from Israel at the Taba border crossing without an Egyptian visa, a 14-day visa valid for travel within Sinai only may be granted. Work permits must be obtained through the employer. If you plan to be in Egypt more than 30 days, an AIDS test is required. Proof of yellow fever immunisation is required if arriving from an infected area.

Latest Information

For the most current visa information, visit the Embassy of Egypt website at:

http://www.egyptembassy.us.

You may also check the US Department of State, Consular Information Sheet, which keeps up-to-date information. Go to:

http://travel.state.gov/travel/

and select Consular Information Sheets.

There are few jobs for foreigners outside Cairo, though some jobs require travelling throughout the country. There are two types of jobs: those paid in Egyptian currency (usually much lower paying positions) and those paid in foreign currency. Lucrative jobs that pay in US dollars usually need to be lined up before coming to Egypt. Remember you must have a work permit. Ministerial Decree No 43/88, applicable to Law No 137/81, Article No 1, states in part that 'foreigners shall not be allowed to work in the Arab Republic of Egypt without obtaining a work permit from the Ministry of Manpower and Immigration'. Foreigners can acquire a work permit from the Ministry of Manpower and Training to work in Egypt, and accordingly are authorised residency in the country. Work permits must be obtained through the employer. Foreigners are generally not allowed to change residency status from non-working to working status while in the country.

HIV-AIDS Test Required of Residents

The Ministry of Manpower and Immigration's circular No 1/1993 states that all foreign expatriates are required to submit an HIV-free (AIDS) test certificate when applying for a work permit. The HIV test must be done in governmental or university hospitals or laboratories. It is permissible to bring your own disposable needle. Work permit officials recommend GOE-owned Central Labs for the HIV test. The lab technicians are very well trained and familiar with work permit/HIV-relevant requirements. The address of the Central Labs is:

Central Laboratories
Ministry of Health and Population
El Sheikh Rihan Street
Garden City

If you are in Egypt and looking for a job, you are likely only to be able to get a job paying in Egyptian currency. As mentioned before, you can get a renewable visa at the airport if you are but for longer term living, you will need a residence visa. Job hunting in Egypt is networking—almost all jobs are filled by word of mouth.

NGO Job Opportunities

The largest foreign-based NGOs offer opportunities to arrange a job before arrival. Among the biggest are:

- Ford Foundation
  Website: http://www.fordfound.org/employment
- USAID
  Website: http://www.usaid.gov/careers
- AmidEast
  Website: http://www.amideast.org/employment/staff

Some expatriates do find jobs with these organisations after their arrival, as contractors for work ranging from grant writing to project management. Employment discrimination is common in Egypt, especially based on age or gender. It is not uncommon to see an ad for a male, aged 25–30.

DOCUMENTS TO BRING

PASSPORT!! Keep it with you in case; it is handy if you are stopped by the police. Even if I don't plan to drive, I always carry my driver's licence with me.

You will need a visa to enter Egypt, but don't worry, if you didn't get one before you left home, you can get a tourist visa at the airport when you get there. But, you must pay in hard currency! I also always suggest keeping a copy of all credit card or bank card numbers along with emergency telephone numbers to contact in the event of loss. I usually leave a copy of the numbers with a trusted friend or relative at home in case I lose the copy I have with me. It may turn out to be easier for a friend or relative to contact the company to report your card loss. Another thing I like to have is proof of medical insurance. It is not likely that any medical treatment you get in Egypt will file with your insurance, but I like to have it anyway. Not all insurances will pay for mishaps that occur abroad, so be sure to check if your insurance scheme/company does before you leave, and, if necessary, secure insurance that covers medical services outside your home country.

Note that US Medicare and Medicaid programs do not cover services outside the United States. Americans can get a copy of the Department of State's brochure, Medical Information for Americans Traveling Abroad, by calling tel: (202) 647-3000 or visiting:

http://travel.state.gov/medical.html.

PRE-ENTRY VACCINATIONS

In general, the best advice is to see your physician before getting any kind of immunisation. Now, that being said, go to the Centers for Disease Control and Prevention website at http://www.cdc.gov to get the latest information on requirements. (Select 'Traveller's Health', then select 'North Africa'.) In general, malaria is rare in Egypt (El Faiyum area only), and can be prevented with chloroquine. At this time, the Centers recommend the following vaccines:

- Hepatitis A
- Hepatitis B
- rabies
- typhoid
- boosters for tetanus-diphtheria
- measles
- a one-time dose of polio vaccine for adults

If you are staying for periods longer than one month, you will be required to produce proof of an HIV test.

HOUSING

Finding good housing in Egypt depends on what you want and where you want to live. If your company is sending you over, they may have a flat arranged for you. If not, the best thing is to plan to stay in a hotel for a few days or weeks until you have an opportunity to scope out the landscape. Whether in the Cairo or Alexandria metropolitan areas, the first thing you must decide is in which area you want to live. If you are moving to a smaller city, the options may be more limited than in the two major cities.

Where you want to live will depend principally on your purpose for being there, how long you plan to stay, and the standard of living you prefer. Usually, flats and villas can be rented for a minimum of one month. So, if you plan to be in Egypt for a shorter period of time, you should count on staying in a hotel or paying for a month's rent even if you leave before the month is up. If you really want the experience of living in an Egyptian neighbourhood, renting a flat or villa is preferable to a hotel. In any event, unless you have some contacts in Egypt prior to going who can arrange your living quarters for you, you will need to stay in a hotel for at least a few days until you can find an appropriate flat.

Housing in Egypt can be quite reasonably priced by North American or European standards. The main thing to ask before renting a flat is what is included in the price. I don't mean asking a general question like, 'Does this include everything?' If you ask a question like this, misunderstandings are likely to occur. What constitutes 'everything' by your standard may be entirely different by Egyptian standards. So, be sure to ask for every specific kind of detail you can possibly imagine. If not, you may find yourself handed another bill for services you thought were included in the rental price. What you need to know is: do I have to pay separate for electricity? Gas? Water? Rubbish pick-up? Phone? (*More about phones later.*) Excluding the phone, electricity, gas, water and rubbish removal can add up to several hundred Egyptian pounds each month. If the apartment comes with a phone, how many local calls or minutes are included? Is the phone set up to call international or to cell phones? Which modern appliances are in the apartment? Is the flat air-conditioned (important for summer stays). Who do you contact if (when?) something breaks, such as the air conditioner? Is any maid service included? Where can you get a good maid or nanny for the children?

You will most likely have one or more doormen (*boheb*) for the building. They are critically important to you and you should tip them nicely each month. If you take good care of them, they will take good care of you! Local flat owners can give you a general idea about how much to give them each month. I also tipped them whenever they did something nice for me, for example, if they took the laundry or picked it up for me or if they helped me get groceries from the taxi to my flat.

Another very important feature to consider is how far the flat/villa is from where you work. If you are in Cairo or Alexandria, getting a place to live that is close to where you will be working may be an important consideration. If you have to take taxis around the city all day, you can run up significant expenses on transportation before you know it. On the other hand, if you have a driver or car to move you around the city or live close to a Metro stop, distance from work may be relatively unimportant. Then the choice may be a time issue, how long are you willing to commute daily?

Family considerations also may come into play. Distance from work or usual daily activities may well be less important than having your family close to schools or recreational activities. For example, many Westerners with children prefer to live in the Maadi suburb as Maadi is relatively quiet compared to other sections of Cairo. It is a rather upper-class neighbourhood of large old homes and gardens. This is a very family-oriented neighbourhood where kids can ride bicycles and skateboard. Maadi has great shopping (check out the Maadi Grand Mall), local churches, a community centre and many other trappings of Western life. The Cairo American College (K-12) is located in Maadi.

Another area you might want to consider is downtown Cairo, close to Tahrir Square. If you like the noise, traffic and other trappings of city living, you will love this hub of city life. Activity abounds day and night. Many shopping and entertainment options exist. This area is probably not as good for families with children.

Garden City is quite close to downtown Cairo. It remains an elite residential, diplomatic and business address. Most of the neighbourhood

Entertainment for Children

Here are just some of the activities your children can look forward to in Egypt:

- Ice Skating
- Roller skating
- Bowling
- Bicycle riding
- Cinemas (check the listings on http://touregypt.net)
- Video arcades
- Swimming
- Fun Parks—Sinbad's and Merryland's are great!
- Zoo
- Horseback riding
- Soccer (football) leagues
- Magic Land at Media Production City

population is Egyptian; however, a few foreigners do live here. Goods and services are abundant throughout the neighbourhood. Garden City has no private school for English-speaking children.

Zamalek has some of the best shopping and restaurants in Cairo. It is located on the northern end of Gezira Island and is home to the famous Gezira Sporting Club, public green areas and a new public library (the Greater Cairo Library). The British International School is located in Zamalek.

All in all, living in Egypt can be relatively inexpensive, but the cost can rise rapidly depending on the choices you make. Prices can range from absurdly low to very high, depending on what you want. One thing for certain, if you hire a rental agent to find you a flat, once you tell them how much you plan to spend (or how much your company has allowed you), you may be assured that every flat you see will be within E£ 100 of whatever amount you told the agent, whether it is worth that amount or not. How do I know this is true? You guessed it—I learned the hard way! The questions I got from the agent that set me up to pay a high price for my flat were: do you have a housing allowance from your employer? How much? I answered each question truthfully and, funny, but

Finding Housing

- You may need your passport for identification.
- Find a building in a neighbourhood you like and ask the doorman (*boheb*) if anything is available or get a rental agent to find you a flat.
- A rental agent works on commission and will get a commission of one or two month's rent, so the higher the rent, the more money they make!
- Ask if the price includes electricity, water, gas, phone and trash pick-up (and get it stated in the lease).
- Find out from neighbours how much should you tip the *boheb* each month.

every single flat I visited (big or little) was about the same price—exactly my housing allowance or more. I am not totally sure how to get around this with an agent, but I suggest if you have to come up with a figure, tell them much less than you actually have in mind to pay. Instead, stress what you are looking for in a flat—two or three bedrooms, on Zamalek, modern kitchen, air conditioning, etc.

Also, if you tell them you will pay in US dollars, Pounds Sterling or Euros, the rate will go up. Try to negotiate a rate in Egyptian pounds. After you find the absolute 'right' place for you, then you can keep in reserve that you might be willing to pay in a hard currency (of course, this is only if you can actually pay in a hard currency).

Where do you find an agent? Ask the Concierge at any major hotel and they can find someone for you. By the way, if you find an agent this way, don't forget to tip the Concierge or doorman who made the contact for you. Next, be sure to clarify with the agent (before you start looking for a place to rent) if you are supposed to pay their fee or if they will get it from the apartment owner (if you find a flat). Also, find out if they charge a fee for showing you flats or if you pay only when you find one.

There is another way to do this that doesn't require an agent: walk around until you find a building you think you would like to live in. Talk to the *boheb* and ask if there are any vacant flats in the building. I can guarantee you that the *bohebs* know more about what is going on in the neighbourhood than anyone else, and that includes the agents. If there is not a flat available in their building, they may know where there is one for a reasonable rate. Don't forget to tip him for his trouble!

Renting in Luxor

I recently learned of a place to rent flats in Luxor (short or long-term). Contact Flats at Luxor:

Tel: 010-356-4540 (Jane) or 012-415-5057 (Mahmoud)

Email: info@flatsinluxor.co.uk

Website: http://flatsinluxor.co.uk/ContactUs.html

LAUNDRY

Forget laundromats—they don't exist in Egypt. On the other hand, getting your laundry done in Egypt is usually quite easy and relatively inexpensive. All major hotels have laundry service available. As a local resident, you can get laundry services (known as *makwagis*) in all neighbourhoods around Cairo. Other than doing laundry yourself, sending clothes to a *makwagi* is the traditional method. Things to remember when sending your laundry out are to communicate exactly what you want done and make a list of what you send. These days, clothes are sometimes dry-cleaned instead of laundered, even underwear. So, be sure to check! If you do not want clothes washed in hot water, tell them. If you do not want bleach added, tell them. If you want clothes dry-cleaned, tell them. Most clothes will come back ironed, so if you do not want clothes ironed, again, tell them. If you do not state precisely what you want, you may be surprised with the results. Unless you have someone that you know who hand washes clothes, do delicate items by hand at home. If you have a family or expect substantial laundry needs, consider purchasing a washing machine after you get to Egypt. A washing machine will cost a lot, but you can probably sell it when you get ready to leave. One of my flats had a washing machine in it and I admit it was great for sheets. On the other hand, it was cheap and easy to send things out, so I definitely wouldn't buy one for myself.

MEDICAL CARE

Especially in the major cities, access to fairly good general health care services is readily available. However, you should do some pre-planning to ensure you won't have to take whatever you can find in an emergency or when someone gets sick. Like almost everything else in Egypt, medical care facilities run the gamut from little or nothing to a few hospitals equipped with the most modern technology.

Just as in a move to any other new city, it may be best for you to make contact with a physician upon arrival to find someone you like and can trust. For example, many well-trained and knowledgeable specialised physicians are professors at the University of Cairo Kasr el-Aini Medical School or Ain Shams. These physicians typically also have a private practice office (called a surgery or clinic) where they see patients at various hours of the day. This is not eight-to-five medicine. Physicians may see patients at their clinics at all hours of the day and night, depending on their personal schedule. Make sure to find out when your doctor sees patients, how to contact him/her at all hours, and what you need to do to make an appointment. Also, find out at which hospitals the physician sees patients. This may make a difference in choosing a physician for a long-term relationship. Surprise of all surprises, many Egyptian doctors will come to your home or hotel to see you.

Generally speaking, Egyptian physicians practise a more humanistic type of medicine than most Western physicians. This means that they listen to your symptoms, may palpitate as needed, but rarely utilise extensive laboratory measures for most common ailments. However, there are excellent laboratory facilities available when needed. They do not have a queuing system such as occurs in Great Britain and in some managed care programmes in the United States. What this means, in practical terms, is that if what you need is available and you have the money to pay for it, you can reasonably expect to be able to get the service you need.

It is always advisable to discover the locations of hospitals in a new place. In the event you might need one, it seems best to know approximately where it is located in the city and which one you would want to go to. Numerous 'private' hospitals exist in and around Cairo and Alexandria. Designation as a private hospital may be somewhat different than you are used to in your own country. A number of these small private hospitals are owned by one or more physicians. Just because a hospital is called a private facility, it does not mean that it will be a big, technologically sophisticated facility. Most small private hospitals are essentially open-air medical facilities. That is, they do not have sophisticated, recirculating air heating and/or cooling units with closed, sterilised wards or rooms. Instead, most small hospitals are built more on the traditional Egyptian pattern, with open doors and open windows throughout. Most commonly, small Egyptian private hospitals are equipped to handle general medical problems, with only somewhat limited access to surgical procedures or physical therapy. Only a few major hospitals are built on the Western model and equipped with modern technology. Get an up-to-date listing of hospitals and doctors from your Embassy.

It will probably be in your best interest to make sure any specialised health services you will need on a maintenance basis are available before going to Egypt. For example, if you are going to need allergy injections on a regular basis, you may want to bring the vaccine with you to cover the time you expect to be in Egypt. In this case, you might also want to be sure to purchase a disposable syringe at a local pharmacy, just in case the doctor you go to only has reusable syringes. Similar precautions should be taken for situations such as diabetes.

Unless you are coming from a cholera prevalent area, no immunisations are required to get into Egypt. However, some potentially life-threatening diseases occur often enough in Egypt to warrant consideration of immunisation prior to arrival. Immunisations to consider include: Viral Hepatitis A (HAVRIX); Hepatitis B; Typhoid; Poliomyelitis; and Tetanus/diphtheria. A final issue to discuss with your physician is a pre-exposure rabies vaccine. Anyone having the pre-exposure rabies vaccination series will still have to undergo post-rabies treatment, but the treatment is milder than for someone who has not had the pre-exposure vaccine.

Immunisation Guidelines

The Center for Disease Control and Prevention (CDC) in Atlanta, Georgia, has immunisation recommendations for travel to Egypt. The latest assessment from the CDC can be accessed at:

http://www.cdc.gov/travel/.

Similar programmes and recommendations exist through major public health entities or from your government in most countries throughout Europe. Check with your physician before leaving for Egypt to ensure that you have all recommended immunisations.

Pharmacies

Small pharmacies are located throughout Egypt. Many medications that require a doctor's prescription in North America or Europe can be bought over the counter in Egypt. To purchase narcotics, you will need a prescription from an Egyptian physician. Frequently, there will be a physician at the pharmacy; in fact, the pharmacist may well also be a physician. In general, you can find most prescription medications at a good pharmacy in Egypt. You can usually also find foreign made, imported or less-expensive Egyptian made brands. Although I admit I have taken some Egyptian made medications with no bad effects, I suspect the quality control of the foreign brands is significantly higher. The difference in price is worth it for the quality control during manufacture. If you know you must have a specific brand or a very specialised medication during your residence in Egypt, best to bring a supply with you just in case that brand is not imported to Egypt. If you bring in meds, be sure to keep any prescription medication in its original container with the label attached to avoid any possible confusion at customs. It is usually recommended that you also bring a copy of the physician's prescription with you. I have never had anyone check, but just as sure as I say that, the next time through, my medications will be scrutinised!

Most commonly used medications, though definitely not all, are available in some form in Egypt. However, pharmacies may run out of the very thing you need or may have drugs commonly used for an ailment, but not the one you want. Also a particular medicine may be available in a syrup instead of a pill, or vice versa, but available. For example, I once desperately needed a specific kind of asthma inhaler. The pharmacist had inhalers, but none with the specific composition I needed. Another time, I needed an expectorant cough medicine and was able only to find a cough suppressant medication. In this case, I did not know a chemical name I needed, so the pharmacist kept bringing me the wrong medicine.

It is best to know what medicine you want to buy when you go to the pharmacist. But even if you do not know what medicine you need, the pharmacist will gladly recommend medication based on what you tell him/her you need it for. If you do know what medicine you want to buy, such as a type of antibiotic, be prepared to give the pharmacist the generic or chemical name of the medication. Do not count on being able to find the brand named drug sold in your country of residence. Those who use oral contraceptives or hormone replacement therapy should bring their own brand since local pills may cause side effects due to different compositions or dosages.

Optical Supplies

If you wear glasses or contact lenses, you will be significantly more comfortable if you bring spares with you to Egypt, just in case you break or lose them. At the very least, bring a copy of your lens prescription with you. Egyptian optical shops are sometimes difficult to find and often have erratic hours, but you can get both single and bifocal lenses replaced. Small repairs are relatively inexpensive and most optical shops can accommodate you.

When you try getting something like glasses replaced, remember that it probably means you will be operating on Egyptian time. So, if you should break your glasses and actually need them to function, you could be out of luck for some time. The alternative, of course, is to

Safety Tips

- Find a good doctor before you need one.
- Learn the numbers to call in an emergency.
- Learn where the hospitals are and which one you would want to go to in an emergency.
- Check with the Embassy for a current listing of doctors and hospitals.
- Bring spare glasses and/or contacts.
- Bring prescription medications with you if you must have a specific drug.

have someone from your home mail you a spare pair. This can be quite expensive, but you could probably get them faster than having a new pair made in Egypt. Never trust the regular mail with something like this, but use one of the express mail carriers. The same applies to prescription sunglasses. Good sunglasses are definitely a necessity to combat the glaring sun and blowing sand. You can find good sunglasses in Egypt, but they might be expensive.

If you wear contact lenses, take special precautions. You may experience discomfort wearing contact lenses in Egypt's arid environment. Add air pollution and blowing sand, and contact lenses rapidly become painful and in need of replacement. Even if you have worn contact lenses for years, you should bring a backup pair of glasses for those days when your eyes are irritated by the environment. Many people have found that they cannot wear contact lenses at all in this environment. You are able to purchase some imported disposable contact lenses in Egypt now, but not all and you cannot count on being able to get the strength you need in a timely fashion.

Also, be sure to bring any specialised cleaning equipment for contact lenses with you. Contact lens supplies such as sterilised wetting solutions can be found fairly easily, but as in the case of prescriptior drugs, specific brand names may not be available, so any specialised formulas you require should be brought with you.

BABY SUPPLIES

Baby formulas, such as Similac, SMA and Nestle are available in powdered form in Egyptian pharmacies or markets. You can also find items like cough syrups for infants and Vap-o-rub.

Things you should bring with you if you have small children include training pants, receiving blankets, crib sheets, a play pen, door gate, extra baby shoes (at least one size ahead), car seat or stroller, baby thermometer, diapers and rubber or plastic pants. Disposable diapers are available, but they are very expensive. I have seen suggestions to bring a blender to prepare baby food, but I personally think you are better off to purchase a blender once you get to Egypt.

TOILETRIES

You can find most types of toiletries and cosmetics in Cairo and Alexandria (but not necessarily in the smaller cities). They may or may not be the brand you are used to. If you prefer specific brands of, for example, antiperspirant, cosmetics or shampoo, bring them with you or take a chance of having to use another brand. You should also bring insect repellent and sunscreen lotion with you if you require anything above SPF15.

Even when I go for short visits, I always take a small first-aid kit with me. You can buy these ready packaged or you can make one yourself. Don't forget bandages, individually wrapped alcohol swabs and, especially, an antibacterial cream. If you have very sensitive skin, take a tube or two of some type of cortisone ointment for those pesky itches. Special skin cleansing supplies for acne should be brought with you. Some other items you may wish to bring are hair curlers, tampons (very expensive where available), panty liners and hair dyes, along with anything you need to go with them if you want to maintain comparable tints.

SPECIAL FOODS

Before you leave, take stock of what particular processed things you really can't live without. For instance, one of the things I must have is Picante Sauce, which is not available in Egypt. On the other hand, all the things you need to make a really good salsa are there, so if you don't have to have the store-bought kind, you will do fine. A lot of foreign products are not likely to be found in Egypt. One of the things to consider stocking up on before you come are those handy little packets of sauce and seasoning mixes. Special ingredients for Mexican foods are not always available, so bring your favourite chilli mix.

Other things you cannot find (at the time of writing) include decaffeinated coffee and tea. The same goes for salt substitutes. Diet sodas are now widely available. There is one type of artificial sweetener but individual packets of that are rarely available in restaurants. If you are addicted to Koolaid, Gatorade and Crystal Light, try changing your taste to a local drink mix or bring a bunch with you. Instant coffees are stocked, but individual bags for brewing a cup of coffee are not. If you must have brown sugar, maple or corn syrup, shortening, chocolate chips, cream of tartar, pecans and mincemeat—bring them with you. Don't forget your favourite cookbook! Another tip: if you find a particular grocery product on the shelves one week, you might not find the same thing for some time. It appears to depend on what gets through customs and how often. It is sort of like shopping at Sam's Club in the US (except for the sizes)—you never know for sure what you will find from one time to the next. For example, I like a kind of canned soup. I was so excited one day to find it on the shelves at the Metro market where I usually shopped. So, I bought one or two cans (more than enough for what I would use that week or the next). I forgot that once that case of soup was gone, it might be some time before I could find some again. In fact, it was a couple of months before another shipment arrived on the shelves.

KITCHEN AND HOUSEHOLD SUPPLIES

Bring whatever favourite kitchen utensils you think will make you feel at home. There is nothing worse than not having your favourite things in the kitchen, especially if you have to cook every day. Now this doesn't mean you should transport your whole kitchen! In fact, the older I get, the more I am in favour of just getting everything there! It is easier and not terribly expensive; besides that way, everything works with the current. Many flats will come with minimal kitchen supplies and you can always supplement these in Egypt. I am now in favour of buying all small kitchen appliances when you get there unless your appliances are wired for 220 current. If you are coming from the US, remember that your appliances do not have the right current for Egypt. If you insist on bringing your own small appliances, such as toaster ovens, toasters, coffee grinders, coffee pots, microwave oven, mixer, food processor, blender, etc., from the US, remember to bring power strips. If you do this, then you will only need to buy a voltage transformer. You can buy one in Cairo.

Some people prefer to purchase everything in Egypt; use your judgement based on your budget and length of stay. Remember, if you import appliances under temporary admission in your air freight, you are supposed to take them out of Egypt at the end of your stay even if they no longer work. So don't throw away those broken appliances if you import them this way.

Bring lots and lots of plastic storage bags, ties and sandwich bags. Ziplock bags are not available many places. Measuring spoons and cups are not in cups or ounces, so if you cannot make the transition to metric, you should definitely bring these. The only things you really must bring are just your special kitchen things. Paper napkins, paper towels, waxed paper, aluminum foil, linens, utensils and tableware are available at local markets. Pesticides and cleaning supplies are also widely available.

ELECTRIC CURRENT AND EQUIPMENT

Certain adaptations are required for using American appliances in Egypt. Things to consider include voltage, cycles of alternating current, plugs and wall sockets, wattage and power surges. To use American appliances, you must have adapters, voltage converters, transformers and voltage regulators. If you plan to bring small American appliances to Egypt, you will need to know the following.

Egyptian current ranges between 220–240 volts (but can drop to well below 200) alternating at 50 cycles per second. Egypt's voltage can be brought down to 110–120 by using converters (for small appliances) and transformers (for large appliances). Voltage converters come in two sizes: one for appliances using up to 50 watts, and another for appliances using 50–1,600 watts. Converters do not work on appliances over 1,600 watts.

Egyptian outlets are the 'Continental' type, requiring plugs with two round prongs. These are different from British plugs that have two slightly shorter, slightly fatter, round prongs.

The difference between 50 and 60 cycles is not significant for most equipment—most simply run more slowly. Cyclical differences cause a problem with items that use alternating currents to produce a given speed of operation, e.g. clocks. Some modern appliances operate on direct current, thus have no problem. Others can operate on either 50 or 60 cycles. Check your appliances to see if they will work at 50 cycles before bringing them to find out.

Since Egyptian current varies between 200 and 240 volts, voltage regulators/stabilisers should be used to convert an uneven voltage input to a rather steady output. Voltage regulators/transformers are available in Egypt. These will also convert 220 volt current to 110 volt current. My experience is this: I have shot fire out of more than one hairdryer at my head and somehow managed to come out with my hair intact. Since then, I got wise and bought a cheap hairdryer in Egypt! It works without me trying to figure out what kind of transformer I need. I have also burned up a printer and several other things over the course of a few years.

A special note for those bringing computers. Prior to leaving, determine what you will need to operate your computer on 220 volts 50 cycles. You may only need to flip a switch on the back of the computer to change currents. If your computer doesn't have that, you will need a transformer to convert the current to 110/120 volts 50 cycles. A voltage regulator is definitely a necessity to protect the computer from current fluctuations. Blank CDs and diskettes can all be found easily in Egypt, though are probably much more expensive than bringing a large package from your home country.

TVs, Radios, and VCRs

US-made TVs (NTSC system) will not work in Egypt (which uses the PAL-SECAM system), but you can purchase colour or black and white sets in Egypt. VCRs are available in Egypt that adjust to all three systems, but they are expensive. You will need a shortwave radio receiver if you wish to get Voice of America or BBC radio. The best thing is to get satellite dish for TV—once it is installed, my experience is that the price is right and the service is good.

MONEY AND BANKS

There are over 100 banks in Egypt and numerous joint ventures and specialised banks. There are also more than 20 foreign banks represented in Egypt. To open a bank account in Egypt, you will need your passport. It is best if someone local goes with you who knows the bank's procedures; but if not, you can handle it yourself. In order to get a hard currency account, e.g. a US dollar account, you must deposit a minimum amount of money in that currency to open the account. Then, if deposits are made in that particular currency, you may withdraw funds in that currency. Otherwise, you may find that sometimes hard currencies are not available to purchase or are hard to find. For example, if you have Egyptian pounds and want to change them to US dollars, frequently there are no dollars to buy. I don't think I have ever been able to exchange my Egyptian money for US dollars or Euros when leaving the country, even though, you are supposed to be able to do this at the airport bank.

Most private transactions in Egypt seem to be by cash or credit card. The good news is, banks are seemingly everywhere in Egypt. Furthermore, in some of the larger hotels, you can find them open most hours of the day. Banks typically close on Fridays, Saturdays and often for several hours during the afternoon. Some exceptions to this rule are the banks located in major hotels, which may be open 24 hours per day, seven days per week. Other banks, such as at the airport, also operate special hours due to the high tourist traffic.

Exchanging foreign currency or cashing major brand traveller's cheques is rarely a problem. You will need your passport to exchange money or cash traveller's checks. ATM machines are now located in many of the larger hotels, so in an emergency (and assuming the system is working at both your home bank and in Egypt), it is possible to directly get funds from an account at your home bank.

For long-term residents, establishing a bank account at one of the larger international banks located in Egypt is probably easiest. Cashing foreign cheques, other than traveller's checks, can involve a quite lengthy procedure, often taking several weeks before you can get the money. I managed to withdraw money from my Check-Cash card at a local bank whenever I needed money, and only had a problem once or twice with the system being down somewhere. You cannot do this at every bank, but it is easy to find one that will get you cash with these cards.

Internationally recognised credit cards, such as American Express, Visa and MasterCard, are accepted in many places throughout Egypt. Some places that accept credit cards have different rates for credit cards and cash. When you plan to make a purchase, it is best to ask in advance if there is a difference in cost. Small shops, local services, local businesses and, of course, the multitude of private vendors on the street do not accept credit cards. For these you will need cash. When in doubt, just ask.

COMMUNICATION
Mail Services

Forget snail mail! If you actually want to send something by snail mail, the Central Post Office in Cairo, located in Midan el-Ataba, is open 24 hours a day. All other post offices are open from 8:30 am until 3:00 pm every day except on Friday when it is closed. Most major hotels have outgoing post boxes. Stamps are available at most hotels and you can post items from the hotels.

There are several ways to send packages overseas. An export certificate must first be obtained at the Central Post Office. Usually, the store from which an item was bought will take care of these formalities for you, for a small fee. Several express mail carriers, for example FedEx and DHL, also have offices in Cairo and Alexandria. They are expensive, but will also take care of all formalities. The best way to get things back-and-forth is through friends and relatives that are travelling. Seriously!

Phones

Forget everything else and just go straight to the nearest centre and get the latest and greatest in telephone communication— a mobile phone. (They are called cellular phones in the US and mobile phones in Egypt.) It is inexpensive and, for most people, a necessity in Egypt. If you truly do not want anyone to be able to find you easily by phone, skip this paragraph and see the information below on landline service. Practicially everywhere you go, mobile phones ring, beep or incessantly play tunes while people scramble to retrieve them from their pockets or bags. Don't be surprised to find your tour guide sporting the latest model and having an email address, something unheard just a few years ago! Pretty much all of the inhabited parts of the country are covered by mobile communication but, certainly, there are still areas off the beaten path that do not have cellular service. If you are planning on taking a mobile phone into Egypt, you need one that is of GSM (Global System for Mobile Communication) technology (900 mHz). Rate plans abound that include services for short- and long-term mobile users. I actually found that my international calls were no more expensive using my mobile phone that if I went to a phone centre. By the way, whenever you talk from a cellphone (calling or receiving), it is still considered a long distance call—even if you are calling a phone in the next room!

Egypt's landline telephone system has improved tremendously in the past few years, but is still far from perfect in outlying areas. Two new private telephone companies that own public phone booths may be found around stations, in main squares and hotel lobbies. Both have prepaid phone cards that can be bought almost anywhere and used throughout Egypt. Some store owners may permit limited calls to be made from their lines, but you should always offer to reimburse them for the service. Telephone offices also have a large number of phone booths for both local and overseas calls.

I used to go to one of the major hotels to make overseas calls. I now either use my mobile phone or go to one of the phone centres because it tends to be less expensive.

However, it is nice to know that most of the better hotels have telephone services that can connect you directly to major international telephone company operators such as AT&T, Sprint or other major international telephone companies. If you have a calling card from the company, your call can be charged directly to your bill. Otherwise, you may pay directly to the phone service at the hotel. In any case, there will be a small charge for using the hotel service. Most international telephone companies now allow collect calls to be placed from Egypt, but these have to be made through these international companies.

Many rented flats and houses come with telephone lines installed. If your flat does not have phone lines installed, it can take some time to get one without a rather large payment for immediate service. Even on home phones, calls are charged by the time used, not a flat user service rate.

Faxes

Commercial fax service is widely available throughout Egypt at business centres located in most 'better' hotels.

Internet

Wow! If you've been to Egypt before 1998, you won't believe the communication transition! Mobile phones and the Internet have changed the complexion of Egyptian communication with the rest of the world. Egyptian Internet usage is one of the fastest growing in the world. A few years ago, few outside the government or universities had webpages. Now, even the famous Khal-el-Khalili has a website for ordering via a secure webpage!

It was late in 1996 when Internet Café pioneered cybercafés in the Cairo area, opening two Internet cafés—one in Garden City and one in Maadi. Now, cybercafés and Internet services are available throughout the country. Cybercafés have popped up in most major cities (which is really great for an Internet junkie like me!) and are now on just about every corner (it seems!) in Cairo and the major cities. I don't believe you are more than a few minutes walk from an Internet café anywhere in Egypt; and it seems as if everyone you meet has

Communications: A Brief Recap

- Forget snail-mail—particularly for packages—as duty rates are astronomical for seemingly everything! The best way is ask friends who are travelling to Egypt to bring what you need!
- Get a mobile (cell) phone.
- Many flats and houses already have a landline installed. Landlines have improved over the years but are still lacking in outlying areas.
- You can buy prepaid phone cards which can be used all over the country.
- International calls can be made from mobile phones, phone centres or at most of the 'better' hotels.
- Commercial faxes can be sent from the business centres of 'major' hotels.
- Internet connection if free, but slow. Faster service is available for a reasonable price.

a hotmail or yahoo address. On top of that, Internet service is free in Egypt, so if you have your computer and a phone, you can get dial-up service free (let me warn you though, the free service is painfully slow!!!) Internet café providers offer email access, worldwide web access, Telnet and FTP, web design and hosting, and cybercafé and network solutions. Some will even let you hook your laptop up to their system to download/upload. Also, all major hotels (and some that are not so 'major') have business centres with Internet access.

Whether you pop into a cybercafé as a visitor to the country or have a long-term service contract (incidentally, rates are reasonable), you are never more that a few minutes from contacting friends around the globe! Just type 'Egypt' into any search engine to get a glimpse of what's new and a happening event within the country. To top off Egypt's movement into high technology, mobile email services became available as of October 2000.

PETS

From all accounts, taking a pet to Egypt presents no major problems. I have never tried it. Be sure to consult the airlines and a veterinarian about carrying cases, etc. The Prevention of Cruelty Society and some airlines offer pamphlets about preparing your animal for a long journey. Any animal brought in must have a veterinarian's certificate on the veterinarian's letterhead indicating the animal is healthy and has had an anti-rabies vaccination. This document must be certified by the authority under which the veterinarian operates. The pet must be examined within 14 days of departure. Even with this document, Egyptian agricultural officials may, if they see fit, hold the pet in quarantine for up to 15 days at a minimal cost per day, excluding food. All expenses for the animal must be borne by the pet owner. You should try to make arrangements through company officials in Egypt, a friend or your travel agent to make sure the Egyptian Veterinary Department at Cairo airport is alerted to the fact that you will be entering the country with a pet. There will be a minimal entry tax for dogs. Once this is paid, the animal will be issued an identity tag which should be attached to the collar for easy identification. Cairo has a well-equipped, excellent veterinary hospital, should one be needed.

Of more concern is repatriating the animal upon leaving Egypt. For the US, this is no problem. Again, it requires health and vaccination certificates. For the UK, animals are currently required to be placed in quarantine for a period of six months when they enter the country. The best thing to do if you are planning to take an animal is to check with the nearest Egyptian Consulate as well as with your local government authorities to check any restrictions that may be imposed.

Boarding facilities for pets are extremely limited in Egypt. So if you plan to travel within Egypt, you should consider that you will have to get a pet sitter or neighbour to look after your pet while you are gone. Imported pet food is available, but expensive and only a liminted number of brands are available, so many people make their own pet food. You can add pet vitamins and mineral supplements to the items that you bring with you. No prescription pet foods are available in Egypt.

Pets cannot run free due to the large number of loose animals with diseases. Rabies is fairly prevalent among the stray cats and dogs around Egypt. Given this, you might want to consider bringing baby gates for doors so you can keep the animal contained easily within a small space in your residence.

Many Egyptians do not like dogs. Some of this feeling relates to traditional roles of dogs and the number of strays running around loose in the cities. In addition, those with conservative interpretations of Islamic tradition tend to regard dogs as dirty. These people, especially, do not want to touch or be touched by a dog. This is something to keep in mind when hiring people to work in your home. Make sure anyone you hire knows there is a pet in residence and what rules apply regarding the pet's treatment. Unless you know a person likes dogs (and yours in particular), it is best to seclude the animal when friends come over. That way, no one is insulted or uncomfortable.

SERVANTS AND SERVICE PEOPLE

If you have never been able to afford a maid or a cook, this may be your chance. One good way to find a reliable and honest household servant is to ask among friends that already employ someone. You can also ask your building's *boheb*. You will likely find that whoever works for your friend will have a relative or friend that is just what you want. If your friend's employee is a good person, they are unlikely to suggest anyone of lesser character because to do so would look bad for them.

Once you have found the perfect person/s to work in your household, several etiquette factors come into play. People who have never had servants may actually find the situation uncomfortable. How do you treat a servant? Preconceived notions abound, from treating them like one of the family, to treating them 'equally' to anyone else who enters the household, to talking down to your servant. Certainly, it is never appropriate to talk down to a servant, either in private or in the presence of guests. To do so in front of guests would make you and them lose face, and cause you to lose the respect of your Egyptian friends. You can also count on any mistreatment on your part getting around through the local grapevine.

What if you are more inclined to treat your servant as a member of the family? Or, what if you have sincere notions about equality and are afraid any act that treats the servant differently implies unfairness? Well, there is definitely a middle ground that is appropriate in Egyptian society. The basic rule of thumb goes something like this: private and public behaviours are different.

You may well develop a warm and personal relationship with your employee, often sharing jokes and laughter together. In fact, it is quite appropriate for you to develop a feeling of responsibility, much like a family member would do. This includes being very generous with your employee, especially with things like surplus food, and clothing or other items you no longer need. Because they feel you are like family too, you may find them asking you for help with medical expenses or in a family emergency. This is normal and expected behaviour—it does not mean they are trying to take advantage of you. As their employer, you are in some ways responsible for them just as if they were members of your family. If you feel you cannot afford to give them all that they need or feel it is too much, at least give them something to show your concern for their well-being. Not to do so would be an insult. If you are concerned that the amount requested is too much, ask your friends to see what would be appropriate. Then, if need be, you can arrange to take some of it out of your servant's wages in the future. One of the thing I do is to always save my empty plastic water bottles to give to my maid because she recycles them.

This is the private side of your relationship with your servant. It is reserved for when outsiders are not around. When outsiders are around, especially other Egyptians, behaviour changes. In these situations, servants should be accorded the opportunity to show others how well they do their job and provide a service to you. For you to do any work in front of others that should be their job will embarrass them and your Egyptian guests. It is a matter of pride and respect for them to want to do all the work by themselves if others are present. For example, you and your cook may well have worked together making table arrangements or preparing the meal for a dinner party. This is all well and good. But when the guests arrive, you should not be seen doing any of the work. If you do, it implies that your server or cook is incapable of doing the job for which he or she was hired. It also shows you do not know how to behave properly.

Showing Respect

Never hesitate to say 'please' or 'thank you' when the situation warrants. Just like anyone else, servants appreciate the simple courtesies and actually expect to be treated with this type of respect by Westerners.

Making friends with shopkeepers, taxi drivers and other people you meet in your daily activities can provide one of the greatest ways to get to know about Egypt and Egyptian life. Don't be surprised if you are quickly invited for a dinner or to make social visits. In these cases, you should remember that they may not really be able to afford your company, to be able to receive you properly. Go, but remember that frequent social visits may place a financial hardship on the family. Since you may find you really enjoy the friendly company of someone who can't afford your visits and you would like to continue the relationship, take gifts or find some other way to compensate your host. You could do something as simple as asking them to do some little job for you so you could make sure they had extra money. For women, you might suggest that the wife give you cooking lessons or teach you how to go to market properly. You could always buy enough cooking ingredients for two families and share this with them. Or, you could buy them something in which they showed a special interest. Any little thing like this would give you the opportunity to give important, needed gifts and not take advantage of your friend's hospitality.

Making the Effort

Once, some friends of mine were going out of their way, spending money to be with me and my group that I knew they couldn't afford. I tried all sorts of ways to try to help with the financial responsibility I knew they could ill afford. I arranged for them to have a special dinner and cake for their anniversary; I took presents to their daughter—things that I knew might be outside their budget, but wanted or needed. Once, when the wife was taking us to the beach and had forgotten her sandals, I gave her mine, insisting I had another pair upstairs. When I left the country, I had all sorts of clothes, toiletries and things that I insisted she take, either for herself or to give to someone she thought might need or want them. Use your imagination and you can come up with all sorts of ways to relieve your friends from the financial burden of their culture's generosity without insulting their hospitality.

MISCELLANEOUS NECESSITIES

Things that drive me crazy are bathroom things I don't have or can't find. There never seem to be drain plugs that fit anywhere. Bring several of the wide, flat ones (rubber deteriorates very quickly in Egypt). In an emergency, I have actually used plastic bags, but this is definitely not the long range solution! Another handy thing to have around is a small household tool kit. Include things like picture hangers, hammer, small nails, etc.

Sometimes it gets pretty cold and a sleeping bag is a lifesaver during winter months. It is also handy for overnight trips to the desert. Remember, many places are not heated and it can definitely get quite cold during winter nights. I have been known to sleep under blankets, in a sleeping bag, while wearing a sweatsuit and long socks on the coldest nights. This makes it tolerable, but not necessarily cosy.

I think a small daypack is an absolute necessity for each person (except small babies, of course). The kind that is most comfortable has a foam rubber pad directly next to your back. I put little combination locks on zippered waist pouches and backpacks to insure that anyone trying to get stuff out of them has to cut them or slash them off me. At least, I am more likely to know it has happened than if they just have to unzip the bag. While I am thinking about it, in a really crowded place, you can wear your backpack on the front. Personally, though I hear there are pickpockets some places in Egypt, I have never had anything stolen. But I am more cautious when I am riding the underground railway or in a crowded train station. Other miscellaneous items to bring with you include: sewing items like buttons and pins, velcro, skirt hangers, mattress pads (haven't seen one in Egypt), a non-disposable flashlight, special holiday things, sheet music if you are a musician, extra guitar strings, etc., and hobby supplies. Definitely don't forget your children's favourite games and toys! Only some Fisher-Price and Lego toys and games are available in Egypt. Bring pictures to hang on the walls. Nothing can be more depressing than bare walls or nothing to remind you of home.

GETTING ABOUT
Trains
The Egyptian railway system covers over 7,000 km (4,350 miles). Principal routes connect Cairo with Aswan,

The Ramses train station in Cairo is the usual starting place for most trains heading out to other cities.

Port Said, the Suez and Alexandria. There are three classes of service offered. Third class is Spartan and rather uncomfortable. Second class is most useful for short distances. Neither third nor second class is air-conditioned.

First class trains provide air conditioning, meal service or dining cars, and some even have sleeping compartments for major routes. Refreshment services customarily offer sandwiches, sweets, pastries, coffee, tea and other beverages. Reservations may be made at the Midan Ramses Station in Cairo, the Central Station in Alexandria, or through any travel agency. Be sure to make reservations in advance, not only for sleeping berths, but also for seats on regular trips. Unless there is a breakdown, Egyptian trains operate on schedule.

Train Information

- You can find train schedules on the Tour Egypt! website at:
  http://www.touregypt.net/trains.htm
- Don't forget to see my article on Egyptian trains at:
  http://touregypt.net/magazine/mag07012001/magf1a.htm
- There is also a good article about the Abela sleeper trains at:
  http://www.sleepingtrains.com/

  You can contact them as follows:

  Tel: (02) 574-9474, 574-9274 (in Cairo)

  Email: reservation@sleepingtrains.com

Buses

Cairo buses used to scare me to death. Just the thought of trying to get on one seemed an impossible task, and the thought of getting on and never being able to get off flashed through my mind. Fact is, public buses in Egypt can be great fun and economical, but very uncomfortable and time-consuming. Local buses in Alexandria are much less troublesome and easier to use than those in Cairo. By the way, in Egypt, driving is on the right side of the street—American-style—so bus stops will be on the right as well.

Buses are definitely an economical way to get about. Buses and minibuses have numbers prominently displayed, usually in the front window and/or on the side of the bus. Unfortunately (if you are new to Egypt), many are printed only in Arabic numbers, but some also display English numbers. Unless you are getting on a bus at one of the main stations, you need to be able to read the numbers quickly because the buses may not come to a complete stop, but only slow down. Sometimes the buses are full when they pull into a station, and even fuller when they pull out the other side a few seconds later. You enter through the back door. Don't wait for people to queue or offer to let you go in front—they probably won't. You just have to push and shove your way onto the bus. You leave the bus through the front door, so if you aren't going far, better start squeezing your way forward as soon as you get on. At some point during your journey, a man will manage to find you to sell you a ticket, so have correct change handy. Buses are great places for pickpockets and the occasional pinch, with all those people squashed together. Therefore, take particular caution with your wallet, purse and money pouch.

There is a pamphlet, sold at newsstands, that lists all bus routes for Cairo's buses and minibuses. Unfortunately, it is only in Arabic, so may not be of much help. You will need to know what number bus or minibus will get you to your destination. Sometimes people are helpful, sometimes they are not. If the bus is stationary, the easiest way to find out where a bus is going is to simply yell your proposed destination. The driver (or passengers) will either wave you on or off to another bus. Another strategy, if you don't speak Arabic, is to have someone you know write your destination in Arabic on a small slip of paper. (By the way, this also works well with taxi drivers.) You can then hand the paper to the driver who will tell you if you have the right bus. Unfortunately, this only works with stationary buses. You probably want to make your first trip during off-peak hours when buses are a little less crowded.

Minibuses are definitely a little easier than regular buses. Supposedly, rules limit the number of passengers on minibuses, and people are not allowed to crowd each other

A rare sight—an uncrowded bus pulls into the bus station before it was moved from Midan Tahrir.

or stand. Like many rules in Cairo transportation, I have yet to see one where every inch of standing space wasn't taken, often with extra people hanging on the side steps of open buses.

Several other types of buses operate in Egypt. In smaller towns and villages, as well as in Cairo, private micro-buses (vans or trucks) meander through the streets. They do not have signs, so it is difficult to tell exactly where they are going or if they follow a specific route. If you think you want to get on one, yell out your destination as it passes. If the driver is going there, he will stop for you.

Everywhere you look, you will see tour buses prominently marked. These are private buses run by agencies, which operate package tours with stops at places of archaeological or other tourist interest. Many tourist (excursion) buses offer excellent services from Cairo to major destinations throughout Egypt. Inter-city buses provide an easy way to get from one major city to another, particularly from Cairo north and eastwards, to Alexandria, Port Said, Ismailia and the Suez. First class buses and jet buses have limited seats, usually 40. Your ticket will give you an assigned seat for these buses, which are air-conditioned and quite comfortable. Some provide a snack service and videos. You will have to pay for the snacks if you order.

Taxis

Taxis are everywhere. To get one, keep your eyes peeled for an empty one and simply wave your arm. In some cases, even a taxi with a fare will stop and you can share the taxi. There are two theories on figuring out how much a taxi should cost. When you are new to the area, negotiate the fare for your trip before you enter the taxi. Once you enter the taxi, they have you and the rate will surely be higher. Some taxis have meters, but they rarely work, so you are on your own to get a good rate. Plan on being ripped off until you get the feel for looking like you know what you are doing.

Things You Can Count On

- Taxi fares are higher around tourist areas.
- As a foreigner, taxi drivers will always try to charge you more than an Egyptian for the same service, no matter how good a negotiator you are.

  I do not negotiate taxi fares in and around Cairo anymore because I have pretty much figured out how much it should cost. However, I figure I always pay a pound or two more than an Egyptian would pay.

Still, taxi rates are reasonable and one of the most convenient ways to get around in Egypt. Once you begin to know your way around your favourite places, you will even be able to tell the driver the easiest way to get to where you want to go. You will also know reasonable fares and be able to state the price you are willing to pay up front, eliminating the bargaining.

Until then, be prepared for drivers pretending they do not know how to get to your destination (even major landmarks) and taking you for long drives through the city. Should you come across one of the few totally unscrupulous taxi drivers that refuses to take you where you want to go without unscheduled stops at an uncle's or brother's or sister's shop, simply refuse to get out of the taxi when he stops. If he says he won't go further unless you get out, get out and walk off yelling to try to get the attention from a nearby policeman or shop owner. In most cases, someone will come out and take your side. Egyptians do not like cheats either. If this doesn't work, take the taxi driver's number (listed on a plaque or paper in the taxi) and report him to the authorities. I honestly don't think reporting a taxi driver to the authorities does any good and is really more trouble than it could possibly be worth. I just put that in to satisfy anyone who really wants to follow that path.

The second strategy is to not negotiate the fare. If you look like you know what you are doing, you will be better able to get away with this strategy. It is difficult to give an accurate fare range because prices seem to change with the cost of petrol. As a starting point, a fair rate for going across Cairo (about a 30-minute ride) is about E£ 5, or a bit more. Very short rides should go for around E£ 3. Please remember that these prices depend heavily on the price of petrol. If petrol prices double, taxi fares should increase substantially. After all, taxi drivers need to make a living, too. Longer journeys will still need to be negotiated. Don't be surprised if the driver wants significantly more, but keep trying to negotiate a lower fare. Sometimes it works and sometimes it doesn't. Get out, say 'thank you' and walk off.

A strategy I learned from a long-term expatriate to ensure drivers don't demand more than the negotiated fare or more than you know is reasonable is this: always carry a large quantity of very small Egyptian bills—25 and 50 piastre notes are best. When you get to where you are going, do not pay the driver while you are sitting in the taxi. Get out of the taxi, making sure to take all of your belongings with you. Then hand the driver a wad (not neatly folded stack) of small denomination notes through the front window. Taxis are not air-conditioned, so the windows are always down and provide an excellent way to pay the driver. Then walk away. Unless you have tried to cheat the driver, by the time he has counted the money, you will be well on your way. Never try to cheat a taxi driver. They can, and do, yell loudly, attracting the attention of numerous police standing around with nothing better to do than settle the dispute. Even if you do not have piastre notes, small bills are always better than large ones. Some drivers may not have change, or at least say they don't have change.

By the way, a word of warning for women riding in taxis: do not ride in the front seat or next to the driver unless you are willing to run the risk of the driver's hands wandering a little. While they would never consider such affronts to an Egyptian or Muslim woman, foreign women are fair game. One reason for this is that no Muslim or Egyptian woman would place herself in the position of being accessible to such confrontations; therefore (according to their logic), if a woman places herself next to a man, it must be for a reason, so it is all right to touch her.

The Metro

The Metro in Cairo is exceptionally good, especially when compared to the time needed for the bus or a car. It provides the fastest and easiest way to get around Cairo if you are going near to the places it connects. The Metro system is modern, air-conditioned and clean throughout, and is getting a face lift. As of January 2001, the Metro provided rides to approximately 1.4 million passengers each day. To keep the system top-notch, construction of additional

The Cairo Metro line—currently running and planned lines.

lines and modernisation of the 13-year-old system was approved on an urgent basis. Old wagons and their air conditioning system will be refurbished, new wagons will be added, and new locomotives will be added. In addition, the line between Old El Marg and El Marg El Gedeeda will be doubled.

Station names can be confusing, so be sure to know the station name that takes you near to where you want to go. Line 1 runs from Helwan north-east to El Marg station. Only five stations in central Cairo are underground. Line 2 connects the Shobra to the Giza Suburbs station taking a tunnel under the Nile. It crosses Line 1 at the Mubarak and Sadat stations, so you can change lines here. Line 2 does not go all the way to the Pyramids, but comes close. If you take it to the Giza Suburbs stop, you will be very close to Giza Square where you can take a taxi, bus or micro-bus to the pyramids. Line 3 was originally planned to run from Embaba in the north-west to Salah Salem in the east crossing both existing lines in the city centre. Later the project was modified and the eastern leg will now end at the Airport. After Ataba (Line 2), it will continue towards the north-east through Abbasiya and Heliopolis. In the west, a branch from Kit Kat Square to Mohandiseen was added to the project. Line 3 will be 33 km (21 miles) long, with 29 stations, of which 27 will be underground. It will be built in four phases. (*See the Cairo Metro map on the facing page.*)

Finding stations is easy. Look for the signs with a big red 'M' in a blue star. The underground stations usually have several exits, so you need to know which one takes you where you are going above ground. If you go out the wrong one, you can end up a block or more from where you intended. By the way, the first car (two cars during peak hours) on each train is reserved for women only. You will occasionally see women in other cars, but women definitely prefer the women's cars (no pinches there).

About halfway down the steps to the Metro stations or outside the gates of the Metro station, posted signs indicate these are non-smoking areas. Believe the signs! If you do not, you are likely to have police pull you aside and issue a ticket on the spot that can be both expensive and time-consuming by the time you get it paid.

Traffic

Hang on to your hat, now you get to experience Egyptian traffic, Cairo-style! Traffic in Cairo is notoriously horrible! Most people tell you there is no logic to driving in Egypt. Egyptian traffic does not defy explanation, but it does take some understanding.

Cairo driving is extremely aggressive. The first rule is, if there is room for your car, take it. If there is not and you can bluff someone else, go for it. I have been in small buses whose driver bluffed out larger buses by sheer guts. Other drivers have bumped vehicles to get a space first. I have even had drivers pull bumpers off parked vehicles because 'they were parked too close to the corner (to make a turn) and should have known better'.

If you arrive at night, you may get a special treat. People drive with their lights off at night going as fast as room allows. Several explanations have been given for driving at night without lights such as 'I don't want to bother the driver in front of me'. Others think keeping lights on bothers oncoming traffic or runs the battery down.

Just find a spot and squeeze in on one of Egypt's crowded streets.

Another thrill is heading into oncoming traffic when you least expect it. If you are on a road and there is room in oncoming traffic, your driver may dart into oncoming traffic 'lanes'. I say 'lanes' because some major streets are actually divided. However, traffic lane markers and stripes are not painted on many roads. When lane markers are painted, it is usually on major motorways or thoroughfares. Even on motorways, lane markers are frequently ignored. There appears to be no such thing as a 'no-passing' zone.

Just to give you a feel for some of the situations you may encounter, I will relate a few of my own experiences. When out on a motorway, my driver saw nothing coming towards us, so took the oncoming traffic lanes to get around slower vehicles. Also, my drivers have plunged headlong onto crowded one-way streets in the opposite direction of the traffic to shorten the journey. Little bumps between cars are frequent and many of the vehicles you see in Egypt have numerous dents. Since traffic is slow much of the time, small bumps rarely cause major injury within Cairo (unless, of course, a pedestrian or similarly unprotected individual is struck). A basic tip is to expect anything—you will probably experience it sometime during your stay. If you are squeamish, definitely do not ride in the front seat of a bus or car.

Caution

Unless you are accustomed to extremely aggressive driving (neither the Los Angeles Freeway nor Houston traffic constitutes extremely aggressive driving to me), do not plan to drive in Egypt. Until you get accustomed to driving habits, it is probably best for you to use local taxis, buses or the Metro.

The principal branches of Egypt's motorway network are:
- Cairo to Alexandria (desert and Delta routes)
- Cairo to Port Said and Ismailia
- Cairo to Suez
- Cairo to el-Fayum

Bumper to bumper traffic along the Corniche el Nil.

- Cairo to Aswan
- Suez to Hurghada

These routes are kept in good condition. A new addition to Cairo's roads is the ring road or beltway designed to deflect traffic away from the downtown area. The ring road is the modern, divided, multi-laned motorway that facilitates getting from one side of the city to the other. Other main motorways are paved, but frequently in need of repair. Remaining roads are dirt. Desert tracks lead to the secondary oases, but are recommended for only highly skilled drivers with knowledge and experience in desert driving.

Travel Permits

Travel permits are not required for motorists using the major routes in Egypt. However, certain roads may be used only if you are in possession of permits. These routes include:

- the secondary roads of the delta
- the coastal road to Libya
- the track along the Suez Canal between Ismailia and Suez, the Sinai, Saint Catherine's Monastery
- some roads leading to the oases, especially those to Siwa and Bahariya.

Travel permits may be obtained from the Travel Permits Department, located at the corner of Sharia Sheikh Rihan and Sharia Nubar in Cairo.

You should also be aware of the dangers of off-road travel in Egypt. Old mines from previous conflicts remain buried in some areas of the country. Minefields are not easily recognisable because signs do not mark them. Instead, areas containing mines are enclosed by barbed wire, so you should definitely *not* drive into any such enclosed areas. Another clue that you may be in an area where old mines remain are deserted tank embankments. Also avoid driving through built-up sand on roads. These may hide land mines that have shifted due to flash flooding in desert areas.

Important New Traffic Regulations

'Bulletin! Egyptian driving patterns to change!' Sure, you say! Well, I don't believe it either, especially anywhere outside the downtown city areas or maybe near certain checkpoints. Egypt is a world leader in auto accidents. Consider road conditions hazardous anywhere outside the main cities. People drive fast at night with no headlights, through blowing sand, while weaving among the occasional donkey cart with no markings meandering down the motorway. In the past, going where you wanted, when you wanted, and how you wanted was normal Egyptian driving practice. To give credit where credit is due, the government recognises the magnitude of Egyptian traffic morbidity and mortality.

Responding to numerous horrific traffic accidents, the People's Assembly passed stringent new traffic laws in January 1999. Sounds like a good move that will make a difference. In fact, the new law did not seem to make much difference to traffic fatalities. About 5,000 people died from 22,000 traffic accidents in 1999, similar to the figures in 1998. Over two-thirds of accidents can be attributed to driver negligence, the remaining to mechanical failure and poor road conditions. Alcohol and drug abuse account for some of the worst accidents. Although the law has been in effect for several years, traffic deaths are still out of control because implementing the law is a problem. Egyptians' flagrant disregard for traffic laws and lack of respect for traffic police is the main reason why the law is ignored. Things are looking up though! Over 6,000 tickets were issued in Cairo in a two-day period during the first week of January 2001. In response, seat belt prices skyrocketed.

New Law Penalties

Under the new law, substantial penalties apply to the following:

- failure of drivers and front seat passengers to wear seat belts
- failure to wear a motorcycle helmet
- using mobile phones without a hands-free set while driving
- driving under the influence of alcohol or drugs.

Traffic Police

Numerous uniformed traffic police occupy small guardhouses and corners all along the streets of Cairo. Their precise purpose is a bit perplexing. Increasingly, traffic police actually do stop cars to allow pedestrians to cross, especially in the downtown and tourist areas. Although traffic police are located at most big intersections, they most frequently seem to be there for decoration or special circumstances. Traffic lights are typically ignored except in the central area of the city or at specific times in other areas. Only well versed Egyptian drivers can discern the hand signals given by traffic police indicating when it is actually time to obey them. Your best bet, as a newcomer, is to watch what other drivers do and follow suit. Most are at first overwhelmed by the traffic and see no logic in its pattern. This is especially true with horn-honking characteristic of Cairo. Note that traditional Cairo horn-honking will get you a fine in Alexandria, where the practice is now prohibited.

The Art of Horn Honking

In Cairo, horns seem to be honk incessantly all day and all night. There is some logic to the practice. Horns communicate a driver's intentions to other vehicles and pedestrians alike. As a general rule of thumb, one honk means 'I am here and coming' or is used to signal 'thanks' after passing a vehicle. Two honks mean 'I am passing you'. Three honks mean 'I am coming on fast—watch out!' It is actually a very efficient way of communicating in a city where lanes, lights and Western rules of right-of-way are non-existent. Automobile lights can serve the function of a horn at night, and are used mostly to let other drivers and pedestrians know you are coming. Sometimes lights and horns are used simultaneously.

Motorcycles, Bicycles, Donkeys and Donkey Carts

Interspersed among the mass of cars zig-zagging and honking are people using various other forms of transportation. Bicycles and motorcycles weave in and out among the cars. They often have either little horns or bells. Sometimes they have neither, and you will hear a hissing sound to warn you of their presence.

This donkey takes a break from pulling his cart along the streets of Esna and munches on some *berseem* (alfalfa) to replenish his strength.

Donkeys and donkey carts intermingle with car, truck and bus traffic on overpasses, main streets and alleys. People riding donkeys meander along through the traffic and are seemingly unaware of the pandemonium around them. Donkey carts are still a popular means of transporting goods throughout Egypt. The turmoil of Cairo traffic provides no exception. Drivers just go around these slower forms of transport. In many cases, donkeys and donkey carts seem to get the right of way, apparently because their movement is less flexible. Giza implemented an exception. In July 2000, by direction of the Governor, police began issuing fines of up to E£ 500 to owners of donkey and horse-drawn carts in certain parts of the governorate. This action, designed to rid the streets of the traditional cart (*caro*), should improve traffic flow and clean up tourist areas.

Except in the central business district of Cairo, you will also frequently see people (children or adults) walking or herding a water buffalo or goats on the roads or motorways. They do not stay on the side of the road, but instead take their place on the road or motorway along with the faster moving traffic. Camels are rarely seen on the streets of Cairo except around the area of the pyramids or near the camel *souk* (market). Other than for tourist purposes, camels are generally used on the farms to transport heavy agricultural products such as cane.

Motorcycles can be a particular hazard if you are not careful. They tend to go faster than most cars, and dart in and out at an alarming speed. I was actually hit by a motorcycle late one evening in an alley near Cairo's old medieval quarter. It happened because I froze when I heard the motorcyclist's incessant horn beeping. Unfortunately, when I heard the horn, I didn't know whether to move left or right or what, so I just stopped, thinking that would give the driver the best opportunity to go wherever he wanted. To my surprise, the driver was already committed and screeching to a stop. He didn't quite make it before he reached me. Angry shop owners immediately came out of shops yelling at the motorcycle driver. As far as I can tell, the best approach to avoiding collisions with motorcycles is to keep your ears perked and eyes constantly alert, especially when on smaller streets or alleys.

These traffic patterns hold throughout Egypt. However, in smaller cities, traffic certainly is not as congested as in

Cairo. Traffic in Alexandria is somewhat less troublesome than in Cairo, but faster. Lane markers occur more frequently on Alex's streets, but again are sometimes ignored. Some streets, for example the Corniche, become one-way during certain times of the day in Alexandria. One does not go against traffic in Alexandria.

Even with the abundance of automobile and truck traffic in Cairo, most people seem to be on foot. Egyptians walk everywhere. When going short distances, a mile or two, walking is the most practical means of getting anywhere because it is faster.

Survival on Foot

Positively the most important skill you must learn is pedestrian survival. The key words for pedestrian survival are 'situational awareness'. Egyptian drivers are alert not to hit pedestrians in case they might have a family member who would seek retribution. Do not count on their sharpness for your survival! Rural towns are considerably less congested than are the cities, but this only means the drivers are less alert to wayward walkers. Once you learn to cross the streets successfully in Cairo, and maintain your level of situational awareness when being a pedestrian in general, you will have the greatest probability of living in Egypt unscathed by bumps, hits and slam-dunks. While the same strategies work in all areas of Egypt, don't forget that traffic tends to move faster in Alexandria, so where you might walk in Cairo, you will need to run in Alexandria.

First, slippery-soled shoes are a hazard. Like streets in most places, Cairo's streets tend to slope downward from the centre. They also tend to be covered with a fine layer of the infamous dusty sand. Sand on sloping streets makes for bad traction. You never know when you are going to have to sprint the extra few feet to avoid an oncoming car picking up speed. Unless you want to end up lying under a parked car, or worse yet, the moving vehicle, shoes with soles that allow some kind of traction work best.

Second, don't worry about being at an intersection to cross a street. If you want to go across, head out into the traffic like the rest of the population. As previously mentioned, rarely do you find places where police or lights stop traffic for pedestrians to cross. Even when they do, there is usually someone coming around a corner right into crossing foot traffickers. So how do you get across? Well, the easiest way, when you first arrive, is to find some Egyptians who want to cross where you do and go with them. You must be careful not to lag behind them, however, because they are probably gauging their steps by not only what is coming in one 'lane', but what is coming in several. You may have just enough time to get across one line of cars, and stop as others in the next line speed past, only to quickly dart another lane's worth to stop again. It is frequently a zig-zag process. Whatever you do, don't try carrying on a conversation while crossing the street. This tends to slow people down and diverts their attention from oncoming cars, buses, trucks, bicycles, donkeys, donkey carts and motorcycles. Not only must you keep your eyes peeled for movement from every direction, but you must also keep your ears attuned to the sound of hisses, horns and bells. Don't forget—two-wheeled vehicles tend to dart in and out among the bigger varieties and may not be visible when you start between two cars. Also, do not wait for cars to stop before crossing the street (they likely never will, although the occasional Cairene may take pity on a foreigner). In really congested areas, slowed or non-moving traffic makes your progress easier.

Third, pedestrian traffic is not limited to sidewalks. Nor is wheeled traffic necessarily limited to streets. People walk anywhere and everywhere there is room to move (just like cars go anywhere there is space, so do people on foot). Bicycles and motorcycles weave through pedestrians whether on the sidewalk or in the streets. They often appear as if by magic out of some little nook or alley between buildings which may be hardly perceptible to the newcomer. Again, keep your eyes and ears open.

Asking Directions

If you ask someone for directions, be prepared to get an answer. Almost all people are willing to try to help you.

A street in Alexandria. Traffic is not as troublesome although the pace is faster. This applies to foot traffic as well.

However, they may not know where you want to go. It is a typical Egyptian trait to always have an answer to a question, whether or not the respondent knows where you want to go. It is simply not considered appropriate for most Egyptians to say, 'I don't know'. Alternatively, a person may indicate they do not understand what you are asking rather than admit to not knowing what you are looking for. More likely, they will point you in some direction whether it is the right one or not. The result, of course, is you may find yourself wandering in circles when where you wanted to go was only a short distance from where you began. Arm yourself with an accurate street address if you want to get good directions. Getting to the general area of town and simply asking for a place name results in many a wild goose chase.

SIGHTS, SMELLS AND SOUNDS
Air Pollution
With massive traffic jams and no quality control on exhaust systems, Cairo air pollution at certain times of the year gives you the feeling of wandering London during a heavy fog—one that smells like exhaust fumes. Cairo's air pollution is the worst in Egypt. Especially in summer, when heat inversions are common and winds from the Nile are least, the air becomes laden with smog. From a distance, Cairo takes on a reddish glow. Smog is distinctly less in winter than in summer. It seems that bringing the Metro underground railway system online has reduced the air pollution somewhat, though smog still remains a serious problem in Cairo.

Smoking
The attitude of Egyptians towards smoking is best depicted at a place called the 'Piano Bar' in the World Trade Centre. The so labelled 'non-smoking' area is a chair nailed to the wall at the edge of the ceiling. Egypt is a land of smokers. If you cannot tolerate cigarette smoke, you had best change your ways, take plenty of antihistamines or stay out of Egypt. There are some non-smoking areas in Egypt but few in restaurants or most public places. A few of the better

hotels are now advertising non-smoking rooms. Most cruise boats prohibit smoking in the cabins. Other than that, the only non-smoking zones are the Metro, some museum areas, the occasional elevator (not all) and a few other special sites.

A Favourite Pastime

Unless there are overriding reasons for not smoking in a particular place, for example sensitive equipment that might malfunction with too much smoke (such as computers) or explosive chemicals, people smoke. The best efforts of health officials are making only a minimal impact toward stopping or limiting one of the favourite Egyptian pastimes.

Smoking etiquette requires anyone who is smoking in a meeting or group to offer everyone else in the group a cigarette. Foreign cigarettes are particularly preferred, so be prepared. If you do not smoke, do not feel compelled to accept a cigarette when offered. Egyptians do not mind if you don't smoke; however, they expect to be able to smoke in your presence in any event. Expect your guests to smoke, whether in a business meeting or when visiting your home. Your personal preference for non-smoking may not count.

Smoking is a man's prerogative in Egypt. Egyptian women who smoke rarely do so in public. Other than cigarette smoking, which is done everywhere, the preferred method is the water pipe. Water pipes are smoked in restaurants, at home, and in the myriad of small street cafés where men congregate, drinking coffee or tea while playing table games. Water pipes are called *shisha* pipes in Egypt, a word derived from the Arabic term meaning 'hashish'. The tobacco smoked in these pipes is not hashish. It is a gummy mixture of molasses and tobacco, sometimes with a flavour, such as apple, added.

Noise

Many people find the high noise level in Egypt to be quite bothersome. To me, Cairo seems to be much quieter than it used to be. I remember seeing a video once where the person was asking for a 'quiet room' at an Egyptian hotel. Laugh and forget it! If you are looking for silence and solitude, I recommend going to the desert alone or another country, although suburbs are much quieter than central Cairo. The only places in central Cairo that are reasonably quiet are some of the interior rooms in the large five-star hotels. Even then, traffic noise may filter through the walls.

What kinds of sounds can you expect? Well, I have already alluded to the traffic sounds—horns, cars, trucks, donkey carts. Even without these urban noises, Egypt is alive with sound. Beginning before sunrise, there are the calls to prayer that echo from the minarets of mosques all over the country five times a day. The first time the 4:30 am call to prayer startles you from a sound sleep, you may shake your head trying to figure out what is happening. After a few days, the calls to prayer promote a peaceful and stabilising feeling, letting you know that all is right in the world.

Another aspect of Egyptian culture is the seeming need to have music all the time. Every shop and café, especially in the tourist areas, has music playing constantly. And it is loud! At first, Egyptian music sounds sharp to the Western ear because it is a quarter tone out from Western music. Eventually Egyptian music weaves its magic of romance, often soulfully singing of unrequited love. Lively belly dancing songs incite movement in the most sedate guests.

The noises of Egypt may be disruptive for the first couple of weeks but in no time, it will feel normal. After you have been there for a while, you will only notice when the sounds are out of the ordinary. At this point, silence may become deafening.

Colours of Egypt

Egypt is a country of stark colour contrasts. It is almost inconceivable—until you have seen it—to visualise the drastic contrast between the desert and the 'green'. The 'green' refers to the areas irrigated from the Nile throughout the country. Green areas tend to be a mile wide or less along either side of the river. Literally, where the irrigation stops, the desert begins. The 'green' is often very tropically lush with much shade and waving palms. The desert is stark with few immediately visible lifeforms.

Except for small areas along the Nile and parks, Cairo is a palette in monochrome. Buildings made of native stone or

There is a sharp contrast between the rich vegetation of the flood plain and the stark environment of the desert.

concrete match the surrounding desert environment. The basic colour of the city is a slightly greyer shade of tan than the desert proper, which tends to be a light golden tan with a very slight reddish hue. In winter, the sky may be bright blue, especially in the mornings. However, even in winter, the afternoon sky fades to a lighter shade of blue. Up and down the Nile, morning winter skies are clouded with smoke from open cooking and heating fires. The smoke settles along the river due to the high population density at the river's edge.

During summer months, the sky tends to be a greyish light blue that fades into white. The pale sky against the desert tan increases the stark contrast between green and desert. It also adds to the monochrome effect in cities. Egyptians seem to delight in adding colour at every opportunity. Brightly coloured household decorations, rugs and even clothing sparkle against the sandy coloured world. The style of furniture most popular in middle and upper class homes is rather baroque with intricately carved heavy pieces of wood. Couches and chairs are frequently covered in decorative brocade fabrics.

Dirt
What commonly passes for dirt in Egypt is really very finely powdered sand. It is everywhere! Sand blows in the air, seeps

through doors and windows, and even lodges itself under the fingernails and toenails. The sand is so finely grained that when you rub it between your fingers, it does not feel particularly harsh. Sand blows in from the desert and cannot be eliminated or controlled, even with the most zealous attempts by Egyptians. Shopkeepers and hotel attendants constantly wash pavements, foyers and any other surface on which dust can collect. Floors are almost constantly being swept or washed with soapy water and a squeegee. Pavements are frequently hosed down and swept to control the dust.

Truly, nothing works for long. The climate is so arid that within minutes, the dust dries, starting its cycle of collecting everywhere once again. Most stores, homes and hotels have one or two bristle mats for wiping your feet when you enter. It is a common courtesy to wipe your feet carefully when entering any establishment or home.

In some cases, when you enter some homes you may even be expected to remove your shoes. I have always heard of this custom, but have never actually seen it practisd. So the best advice is, do not remove your shoes unless everyone else has removed theirs. Do what your host or others guests do. Removing shoes is particularly unwieldy to Westerners because they usually wear socks or some type of hose to protect their feet from direct contact with their shoes. You will find that, except when dressed in Western business attire (males and females), most Egyptians do not usually wear hose or socks. The most common shoes are open, sandal-type shoes. On the street, especially among the working class, flip-flops are the shoes of choice.

Waste Material

Initial perceptions of the streets of Egypt definitely shock the most experienced of travellers. Everything looks dirty. Part of this is due to the monochrome colour of Cairo. Another contributing factor is the result of constant building and renovation throughout Egypt. Unused building materials and numerous piles of debris are usually left wherever they fall, whether on streets, pavements or roofs. Once left, construction litter tends to stay. Clearing debris away is clearly a low priority. As a result, much of Egypt looks perpetually under construction or as a friend pointed out, 'like a war zone'.

Rubbish collection is a totally different issue. Household rubbish is collected regularly. Cairo's 'unofficial' refuse collectors, the Zabbaleen, collect two-thirds of the garbage. 'Official' collectors collect the remaining refuse. The largest Zabbaleen settlement is Manshiet Nasser. Their entrepreneurial expertise has resulted in an intricate social structure surrounding refuse recycling. Here, different families specialise in different materials. Families sort through rubbish, dividing it into plastics, metals, paper, rags, bones and organic matter.

Trucks are rapidly replacing the customary donkey-pulled carts for transporting rubbish through the city. Most flats and villas have back entrances where rubbish is collected.

Refuse and litter present unique problems for most cities throughout the country. People drop refuse and litter just about everywhere in Egypt. In fact, finding a waste bin is almost impossible in most cities. Waste collects on the pavements and on the edges of streets—anywhere it can find a place to settle. No amount of picking up by people employed for that purpose controls the rubbish appearing on the streets daily.

A major exception to the litter problem is the Metro system and some newer areas of the city. Waste bins are strategically placed at Metro stations. Serious fines and a side visit to the local police station can result from failure to use these bins.

Public Toilets

Go before you leave home! Always take toilet or tissue paper with you—just in case (if you use them). You might also want to carry a plastic, disposable bag for discarding toilet paper in case you have to use a local toilet that doesn't have a place to dispose of it. If you plan to be out all day around town and need facilities, the best bet is to find a friendly restaurant, order something, and use the facilities there. Public toilets are few and far between in most Egyptian cities. They do exist although may be overlooked by the casual observer. In the older parts of the city, entrances to public toilets often look like an entrance to a Metro station (without the prominent signs).

If you have not used a traditional toilet, be prepared for a shock. The typical, traditional toilet is a hole in the ground with two footplates on either side. Usually, there is a hose with a handle to turn on the water for cleaning yourself. The hose should be on the left side for easy access by the left hand, the one appropriate to use for these functions. If you prefer toilet paper, bring your own. Women will find tights, leotards and other clothing that must be totally removed to be a real problem in traditional toilets.

Most modern flats, villas, restaurants and hotels have facilities with modern flush toilets. Since the system isn't geared to handle large quantities of toilet paper, if you see a bucket on the side, place the paper there. If there is an attendant, it is appropriate to tip the attendant upon departure.

FACILITIES FOR THE HANDICAPPED

Do not plan to find mobility ramps for the handicapped in Egypt. Some larger tourist hotels have sloped walks useful to wheelchairs; however, most hotels, restaurants, shops and flats require people to be able to walk and climb some stairs. Once into buildings, even though many have lifts, some are quite small, designed to hold only two or three individuals. Many lifts, especially in older buildings, require the passenger to physically be able to close outside doors and interior gates as well as run the contraption. Older lifts also have a tendency to stop slightly out of line with the floor, thereby making your entry or exit hazardous. Access to underground Metro stations requires stair mobility. Visits to most antiquities and tourist sites also require people to be able to climb stairs and walk substantial distances. In general, getting around for mobility handicapped individuals is all but impossible without hired assistance.

ANIMALS

In a society with little mechanised equipment such as Egypt, many animals serve as beasts of burden. Bony-looking donkeys carry heavy loads and people. Camels are laden with loads larger than could be carried in the bed of a small pick-up truck. People from societies where the major association with animals is through pets and where stringent laws regulate animal treatment often find the sight of working animals in Egypt upsetting. These animals are necessary to ease the human burden in a country that is heavily labour intensive.

Other animals seen frequently in and around the streets include stray cats and dogs. It is easy to figure out which cats and dogs belong to the streets. They look scruffy, scraggly and gnarly. Stray animals hang around docks, hotel entrances, alleys and restaurant—anywhere they might find food. Cats serve a good purpose by keeping the rodent population down. They can frequently be seen wandering around tables or on rafters in some outdoor restaurants.

Expatriates who are not thrilled with their assignments in Egypt sometimes refer to stray dogs as 'tickets'. Many of these animals carry fleas, ticks and diseases, including rabies.

Never feed stray animals as this tourist is doing. Rabies is common among strays.

An expatriate who has been bitten by a stray dog can frequently get his company to send him home for medical treatment or even reassignment, since it is not likely the animal had been vaccinated against rabies and it is usually unlikely a specific animal could be identified. Therefore, stray animals can be the expatriate's 'ticket' out of an unhappy situation.

The compulsion to cuddle animals and aid weak, helpless animals inclines some people to feed or pet stray animals. Most of the strays are around people enough that they are quite docile. Many will even come up to you and rub against your leg. Not all of them are docile, and one never knows which is which. Try not to let your compassion for the strays overcome your common sense.

Unusual Behaviour

There was a female dog that wandered the street where I used to live in Garden City. I passed her day after day and nothing happened. Then one night, I was walking to the market and she came from across the street and snapped at me. Fortunately for me, I saw that her behaviour was unusual and jumped away just as she leaped for my leg. She got a small bite of my pants leg, but none of me.

SHOPPING
Shop 'Til You Drop!

There are more and more great shopping areas in and around Cairo! The highest concentration of shopping malls is in Nasr City, where seven shopping centres are open to the public, including Tiba Mall, Genena Mall, Wonderland, City Centre, Al-Aqqad Mall, Serag Mall and the newly-inaugurated City Stars. Check out the new City Stars Centre Mall located in Nasr City. The seven-storey facility has most of Egypt's local brand names (including Dalydress, Mobaco, BTM and Concrete) along with major international brands—some for the first time in Egypt—including Virgin Megastore, Mango and Esprit. The mall also offers a wide variety of coffee shops

'I have never been in a mall of this size, over seven levels and the finest designs.'
—An American visiting the new City Stars Centre Mall in Nasr City.

and restaurants, and a vast food court with 12 outlets. City Stars has a multiplex cinema equipped with 13 screens and an indoor theme park built on a total area of 6,000 sq m (64,583 sq ft). As you would expect, high rents in the malls mean higher prices; but, you can get things you couldn't even think about getting in Egypt only a few years ago!

Shopping is, at the same time, one of the most fun things and one of the most frustrating things you can do in Egypt. There are has two kinds of shopping areas: modern and traditional. In the better parts of Cairo and Alexandria, modern boutiques and stores abound with the newest European fashions and Western goods.

The rest of Egypt is full of traditional small shops and fairly big department-type stores that sell everything from toothpaste to coffee pots and batteries. They are in every nook and cranny. Omar Effendi's (government-owned), located in most big cities, is the Egyptian counterpart to a Western department store.

As mentioned previously, markets or *souks* are easily accessible in all towns and cities. In stores and markets where you see printed price signs, for example in the windows, prices are set. You don't bargain in these places. Of course, you don't bargain at any of the modern malls either! If you are in doubt as to whether a place you are shopping in has fixed prices or bargaining, just ask. Sometimes shops have both fixed price items and bargaining.

Bargaining

Egyptians love to shop and bargaining is a national art form! Bargaining is a challenge that makes shopping really fun. It also gives you a great opportunity to get to know local people and their ways. Egyptians will bargain for everything from carpets to gold to trinkets to bottled water, cigarettes, and popsicles. I will briefly describe a typical process, but remember, this is only a general guideline. Develop your own negotiating style and get into the spirit of Egyptian shopping.

First, you will, of course, see something you want. So you ask the price. The shopkeeper gives you a price that is the 'first price'. Depending on the product, this may be as much as 500 per cent what the shopkeeper expects to get. More expensive items tend to have a lower mark-up.

Next, you can try telling the vendor you were 'just looking'. At this point, he will typically either ask you what you are willing to pay or give you a second or 'good price'. If you really don't want the product, tell him so. If, after several attempts, the shopkeeper won't take 'no' for an answer, you can offer an 'insult' price. This is a price so ridiculously low that you know and he knows you do not expect to get the item.

If, on the other hand, you actually would like to purchase the item, offer a price of, say, 20 per cent of what the 'first price' was. This process can have several iterations, so that before you finally agree on a price you may go through second and third or more prices before you get to a 'best price'. Some sellers will go directly to a 'best price' after the first price if they feel you are a seasoned bargainer. Others just like the game.

Local, neighbourhood bargaining or bargaining with a shopkeeper or owner of the store with whom you have an established relationship is one thing. Any time you shop in tourist areas is quite another and may present the problems outlined below.

A vendor at a typical tourist gauntlet. If you show interest, be prepared for some insistent attention.

Shopping in tourist areas can be traumatic. Unfortunately, you will probably shop in these areas at some time or other since tourism pervades so much of the Egyptian economy. Even if you are an expatriate living in Egypt, in tourist areas, you are just another 'foreign tourist' who is fair game. This is where you will typically run the gauntlet of vendors accosting you with all kinds of come-on statements and queries. They can be terrible pests! It is extremely frustrating when you say no and the hawker refuses to accept your answer, then proceeds to follow you or grab your arm to 'escort' you into his shop. If a vendor grabs your arm, feel free to pull it away and tell him, very firmly, not to touch you. Vendors know they should not touch you and would never consider it proper to grab an Egyptian, especially a woman.

The best way to walk through tourist areas, such as the famous Khan el-Khalili Bazaar, relatively unassailed or unhassled, is to develop a posture that gives the appearance you know where you are going and what you are doing. Impossible at first, but easy to distinguish by shopkeepers after you have been there a few times. Also, they probably recognise you after a few times (even years later). I don't know how they do it, but shopkeepers seem to have the most amazing memories for faces and sometimes names!

Don't answer queries or respond to statements made as you walk among the alleys (unless, of course, you actually want to go in to price or purchase merchandise). Foreign women often hear comments such as, 'Darling, I've been looking for you all my life' or 'Darling, I'm what you have been looking for all your life'. There is a compelling tendency to make a curt or snippy response. Do not give in to the temptation. If you give any acknowledgement, you will be followed for ages, with the vendor sometimes increasing the suggestiveness of comments.

If you want to somehow politely acknowledge a 'nice' shopkeeper's plea to look at his goods, you can refuse to make eye contact or speak, but, with your arm by your side and hand facing the ground, wave the hand back-and-forth keeping the palm facing the ground. I sometimes say 'la' shukran' which translates to 'No, thank you'. Most will leave you alone after that. It is only the rudest person who will harass you after that.

Gold

Shopping for gold requires a special comment. Egypt is known for its gold shops. Gold sold is usually 18, 21 or 24 carats. Only rarely will you ever find anything of less quality. You should see a little scratch or nick on each piece of jewellery made with Egyptian gold. This is actually a government tax stamp. The stamp is used to certify the quality of the gold and that appropriate government tax has been paid on the gold used in the jewellery.

Finding a good gold merchant is not difficult if you know a little about how to shop for gold. The most reputable gold merchants are always willing to weigh the gold and show you the scale to verify the weight. If a merchant tells you all of their gold is sold by the piece, not weight, theirs may or may not be a good place to buy. Tell them that you want them to weigh the piece anyway because you want to know how much gold is in the piece. Then you can gauge their price by what you feel is an appropriate amount to pay per gram. Some very small pieces are sold only by the piece and are only rarely negotiable.

Current gold prices are printed daily in most newspapers. The price you should pay revolves around this rate even though the gold in the jewellery you are buying may have been purchased at another rate. The real negotiating area of gold prices revolves around the cost of workmanship in the piece. The following is just an example because the price of gold fluctuates, but should give you a general feel for how to bargain for gold.

If the published price for 18 carat gold is, for example, E£ 50 per gram with the tax stamp, you should expect to pay somewhere in the range of E£ 60–65 per gram for a finished piece of jewellery. Unless the piece has very intricate workmanship, you should never pay more than about E£ 10–20 per gram over the going rate for Egyptian gold—usually many times less. Italian gold is also popular in Egypt, but the cost is generally higher per gram than Egyptian gold.

The purity of gold articles is generally described in three ways: by percentage, in fineness and in karats. The following table shows how one compares with the others.

Percentage (Parts of Gold per 100)	Fineness (Parts of Gold per 1,000)	Karats (Parts of Gold per 24)
100 per cent	999 Fine	24 Karats
91.70 per cent	917 Fine	22 Karats
75.00 per cent	750 Fine	18 Karats
58.50 per cent	583 Fine	14 Karats
41.60 per cent	416 Fine	10 Karats

Gold Conversion

Avoirdupois Weight (American)

- 1 grain (gr) = 64.79891 mg
- 1 dram (dr) = 27.34375 gr = $\frac{1}{16}$ oz ≈ 1.772 g
- 1 ounce (oz) = 16 dr = 437.5 gr ≈ 28.35 g
- 1 pound (lb) = 16 oz = 7,000 gr = 453.59237 g
- 1 hundredweight (cwt) = 100 lb = 45.359 kg
- 1 ton (t) = 20 cwt = 2,000 lb = 907.18474 kg ≈ 0.907 t

Troy Weight

The grain has the same definition as for Avoirdupois weight.

- 1 pennyweight (dwt) = 24 gr ≈ 1.555 g
- 1 ounce troy (oz t) = 20 dwt = 480 gr ≈ 31.103 g
- 1 pound troy (lb t) = 12 oz t = 5760 gr ≈ 373.242 g

Duty-free Shopping

Before leaving the airport, most people stop in the duty-free shops for last minute purchases. A less well-known aspect of duty-free shopping in Egypt is that there are several branches of Egypt Free Shops in the country. People entering the country are allowed to purchase products at these shops for up to one month after entering Egypt. Some items are good value and others can be bought less expensively at many of the local shops. It just depends on what you are looking for.

You will need your passport and maybe your air or ferry post ticket to purchase items in these shops.

Additionally, Port Said is a duty-free zone and many Egyptians go there to purchase products that would be more expensive elsewhere. Port Said shopping is not as good as it was in the past, so unless you are planning on making some major purchases, it may not be worth going there just for shopping. It is, on the other hand, a delightful city and worth the visit if you have time. Buses run from Cairo several times per day and a daily excursion to Port Said, for whatever reason, is quite reasonable.

Alcohol

A word on alcohol is pertinent at this point for one very good reason—duty-free stores are the easiest and least expensive place to buy imported liquor. Like many other Muslim countries, Egypt does allow alcohol purchase and consumption within its borders, but public drunkenness is not acceptable behaviour under any circumstances in Egypt.

Most Muslims do not drink alcohol. Seasoned foreign business professionals neither drink alcohol in the presence of their Muslim associates nor serve alcohol in their homes when entertaining locals unless they know the person drinks alcohol. If you know your Egyptian friend or colleague drinks alcohol, then it is like everyone else, you offer. If you drink alcohol, it is most prudent to do so in the confines of your home, hotel room or in a cabaret in the absence of your non-drinking Egyptian colleagues and friends. You will gain more respect from your Egyptian colleagues if you follow this behaviour (even though it is certainly not required in all situations) due to your perceived understanding and respect for their religion and ways.

Sometimes my Egyptian friends who have travelled outside the Middle East think all Westerners drink alcohol and wish to show their knowledge of Western behaviour and cultural practices. To make visitors feel welcome, a few Egyptians will offer you alcohol or even serve it with dinner. Again, although it is not required, you will gain more respect if you politely decline—unless the host partakes also.

Some of the oldest known beer recipes come from the hieroglyphics of ancient Egypt. Contemporary Egyptian beer—Stella Local and Stella Export—are readily available at many restaurants, as are some imported beers. Egyptian wines, some of which are quite tasty and others not very good, are also available at many places in Egypt.

Buying imported liquor is easiest and cheapest at duty-free shops. Otherwise, count on it being very expensive. Imported liquor is served by the glass at better hotels and restaurants throughout Egypt, where drinks are typically quite expensive. You can also buy imported liquor from the few major liquor stores, but be sure to ask specifically for imported liquor and check the label carefully.

There are a few small stores located throughout Cairo that sell liquor. Many of the local liquors have labels that look just like those of imported liquors with the exception that one word on the label may be different. An example is the substitution of the word 'Waller' on the local variety for the word 'Walker' on one famous brand of imported liquor. Avoid purchasing these imitations, as the contents bear no resemblance to their famous imported counterparts.

Although I have never confirmed the rumour, local folklore suggests that the imitation liquors can cause blindness. Confirmed deaths and severe illness have occurred as a result of alcohol poisoning from these products. This was because the principal component of the bottles' contents was rubbing alcohol. Some of the local, cheap liquors have very unusual smells and tastes, reminiscent of what could be a combination of perfume and formaldehyde. Since people scrounge through garbage for empty used foreign liquor bottles, which are then recycled to bottle local mixtures, you might consider breaking all old liquor bottles before you dispose of them to help eliminate this hazard.

FOOD AND ENTERTAINING

'Like any crossroads culture, Egyptian cuisine has picked and chosen those ingredients and food that grow best as well as best meet the flavor and nutritional needs of their people.'
—Joyce Carna, *Egyptian Food*

DINING ETIQUETTE

Food is definitely part of the Egyptian expression of hospitality and generosity. Now is a good time to think about how you personally perceive food and what is appropriate social eating behaviour. Where I was raised, it was impolite to eat a lot when visiting. If this meant you had to eat before you went, OK; but you should certainly not appear gluttonous when in public. On the other hand, not far from where I was brought up, the customs for eating in public differed radically. There, it was considered bad taste to leave food on the table. In other words, you might have to eat yourself nearly to death, but you must eat all that was prepared or risk insulting your host. These are polar examples, and your traditions probably fall somewhere in the middle. I tell you this because certain social rules apply to visiting in Egypt if you want to be a good guest.

First, being a good guest requires you to show appreciation for the food offered to you. How do you do this? By eating. Being a good Egyptian guest is not a put-everything-you-expect-to-eat-on-your-plate-for-the-whole-meal-at-one-time event. If you do this, you may find you insult your host when you refuse to take seconds or thirds. You greatly compliment your host by returning for more food, so plan ahead to go back for more food. Refilling your plate once is an almost absolute necessity. Going back twice shows even greater appreciation, but once is certainly enough if you can't possibly hold any more food. More than twice is definitely too much, however. I finally figured out that putting a little food on my plate (for example, by not trying all dishes at once), and spreading the food out a little to make the plate look full, meant I had more room for seconds or thirds. This works particularly well when food is served buffet style.

What happens if your host serves you a food that you absolutely hate and cannot tolerate to even think of eating? In my case, this happens whenever I face internal organs or seafood. Seafood is easy—I have a medical allergy excuse and this is always understood. But what do you do if you just absolutely deplore the taste of something being served and have no medical excuse? Probably the easiest thing to do in order not to insult your host, is to take just a little of whatever it is you do not want, then kind of move it around with your fork or in some way 'pretend' to eat it. Never say something like, 'Oh, I'll pass on that— I don't like it'.

Taking some of the food offered is especially important if the meal is rather formally served by servants to each individual. In this case, do not pass on a course or dish when it is being served, just deal with it after it is on your plate. Rarely will a servant refuse to remove your plate when the next course is served just because you haven't eaten all of the previous course. Many informal dinners at the home of a friend are served family style. In this case, many of the dishes will be passed around. For other dishes, you will pass your plate for the person closest to the dish to place some on your plate. In this case, you can say something like, 'I'll get some of that in a minute, but first I want to try such and such'. With luck, they won't notice that you do not ask for some later. Alternatively, of course, just take some. Of course, with buffets, less attention will be drawn to the fact that you simply 'skip' a particular item.

I seem to consistently have vegetarians travelling with me. They can run into a particular problem. Many Egyptians do not eat meat with every meal, but do serve it when guests are present as a sign of respect and/or generosity. If you are vegetarian and meat is served to you, again it is probably best to take a little and then just don't eat it. If, for some reason, you are asked why you are not eating it (highly unlikely), then just indicate that for medical (or religious) reasons you do not eat meat.

If you are the host of Egyptian friends or colleagues, there is one principal rule for good etiquette—never, ever run out of food or appear to be stingy with what you offer! Make many dishes and more than you ever expect to be eaten. If you are having four people for dinner, cook enough of each dish for six or eight. There should always be a lot of food left after the meal. Once, when explaining to a friend about a wedding I attended, I commented that I had never seen so much food at one place in my life. She told me categorically that 'there should be as much food left as was eaten after the wedding party was over'. This was 'to show that you had enough for the occasion'. Of course, leftover food will not go to waste. You can always eat some of it the next day. Besides, if you happen to have servants, it is expected that you would offer some of the excess to them.

If you plan to serve food items that essentially are served in one-serving (for example, baked potatoes or hamburgers), be sure to have plenty of extras. For example, the concept of the backyard barbecue, where one steak per person is fixed, is totally incomprehensible. "Why," the Egyptians wonder, "would anyone be so stingy as to fix each person only one piece of meat?" Of course, one of the most important things for a host is to be generous, so having a meal such as this definitely makes you look selfish! Does it mean you cannot have a barbecue? Of course not. It just means you need to cook extra.

RESTAURANTS AND TAKEAWAY

My favourite restaurant is La Bodega's in Zamalek. My favourite coffee house is Cilantro's, also in Zamalek. My favourite thing to do when I don't want to cook is go to the Otlob.com website (http://www.otlob.com) and order dinner to be delivered. Truly, this is a blessing for me. All I have to do is decide what I want to eat, go to the Otlob site, select it, and it's magic! Thirty minutes later, my doorbell rings and there is my dinner—delivered with a smile and I didn't even have to dirty the kitchen. Yes, it's totally decadent, but oh, so nice! If I need to have Texas food (and there are those days), I can go to Chili's or Johnny Carino's (either in person or via Otlob.com). There are so many American fast food chains in Egypt, I won't even bother to mention them. However, they are principally located in either Cairo or Alexandria. If it exists in the US, as a rule, you can find it in Egypt.

MEALS AND FOOD

Except for a few distinctly Egyptian dishes, Egyptian cuisine tends to be a combination of Mediterranean cuisines, typically Turkish, Greek, Palestinian, Lebanese and Syrian. Over the years, Egyptians have modified the ingredients and cooking methods to suit local palettes. While a number of spices are customarily used, they seem to be used in moderation. This gives the food a rather bland taste when compared, for example, to Mexican, Cajun or Indian food. Added to the standard middle-class diet, you can also find many restaurants that serve sophisticated recipes copied and adapted from Western cuisine.

Typical Dishes

- *Fuul*: boiled broad or fava beans
- *Labne*: yoghurt-based cheese
- *Felafel*: bean cakes; also known as *ta'miya*
- *Roz* (rice) with Nuts
- Stuffed Vine Leaves
- *Baba Ghanou*: dip made from aubergines, *tahina*, garlic and lemon
- *Moussaka*: casserole of aubergine, minced meat and tomatoes
- *Omm 'Ali*: bread and butter pudding
- Rice Pudding

  For more information on recipes and English/Egyptian food names, go to Cairo Dining at:

  http://www.cairodining.com.

Breakfast

A typical Egyptian breakfast consists of beans, bean cakes, eggs and/or pickles, along with bread and *nawashef* (dry foods) or *fuul*. *Nawashef* complements the basic breakfast and includes dry food items like olives, cheeses (such as *labne* which is a yoghurt-based cheese), jams and perhaps slices of cake. Hard-boiled eggs (never soft-boiled), omelettes or fried eggs, onions soaked in vinegar and mixed pickles usually accompany *fuul*.

'Eish baladi, *fuul* and *ta'miya* constitute the unofficial staples of the Egyptian diet. The word *'eish* (sometimes spelled *aysh*) means bread and 'life' in Egyptian—'life without *'eish* is not life'. *'Eish baladi* is a pitta bread, but you can also find *'eish fransawi* or French bread throughout much of Egypt.

Fuul (sounds like the American word 'fool') is boiled broad or fava beans. There are three main types of broad beans, the basic ingredient in *fuul* and *ta'miya*. *Fuul roomy* are large, flat and whitish; *fuul baladi sa'idi*, or local Upper Egyptian broad beans are whitish and middle-sized; *fuul hamam* are small, round and dark brown in colour. All of these types of beans taste essentially the same, but require different cooking times. When making *fuul*, beans are boiled whole for six to nine hours over a slow fire, then mashed with oil, lemon, salt and other flavourings such as crushed garlic, graded onions, chopped tomatoes and cumin.

Ta'miya (also called *felafel*) are bean cakes. These are deep-fried flat discs made from skinned white broad beans or chickpeas. *Felafel* is as much a modern day dish as it is an ancient one, although today's versions tend to use chickpeas instead of the traditional broad beans. After the legumes are soaked overnight, they are drained and minced with dill, coriander, onions, garlic, parsley, leek and other spices. In addition to being delightful by themselves, *ta'miya* are great as sandwiches with either *fuul* or *tahina* sauce (a sauce made from sesame seeds) and salad (chopped lettuce and tomatoes). If you buy these on the street, be sure to tell the vendor whether you want hot peppers added.

Lunch and Dinner

Lunch is the main meal of the day for most Egyptians and is served sometime between two and five in the afternoon. Dinner is usually more non-specific. Typically, dinner constitutes eating leftovers from lunch or is similar to the *nawashef* of breakfast. Starches, mainly rice and bread, form the mainstay of the Egyptian lunch and dinner. These are usually moistened with vegetables cooked with meat, chicken or fish. Lunch and dinner may be accompanied by sweets, which are puddings, desserts or ices. Beverages served with all meals may be hot or cold. All are non-alcoholic. By the way, most of the time, if you ask about a meat dish, the response will be that it is 'meat'. On several occasions, I have observed people seeking a more definitive explanation at a restaurant or buffet line regarding what animal or what part of the animal was being served. Frequently, the answer was simply 'we are having meat'. Usually lamb will be identified separately from beef.

Meats are largely grilled or roasted, whole or minced (ground), with lamb and chicken predominating. You see a lot of cows but they seem to serve more as farm equipment than beef. The *shish kebab* style is extremely popular and is served either with or without the skewers but always with traditional accompaniments: greens and tomato salad, *tahini* sauce and pitta bread. Bread is always whole wheat pitta, coated with coarse ground wheat.

Egyptians love tomatoes that always seem to burst with colour and flavour. The traditional salad is chopped tomato, coriander, mint, little hot green peppers (not the distinct flavour of jalapenos but closer to serranos) and onions, coated with garlic oil. Great for flavour, but you definitely will need mouthwash at the end of the meal. Aubergines, mashed as the main ingredient in *baba ghanou* (a dip), is also used in Egyptian *moussaka* with a mild white cheese. Okra, cabbage, cauliflower and potatoes show up frequently, stewed with tomatoes, garlic and seven spices (allspice).

Rice is universal! The grains mix short basmati-like rice with longer brown, nutty-tasting rice. I think the fruits in

Egypt taste better than any I have tasted in years, especially the different varieties of oranges, lemons, peaches, strawberries and melons. However, many of the apples are imported and seem to be mealy by the time you get them. Egyptian bazaars display staggering amounts of spices, sculptured into colourful spice pyramids, from yellows of saffron and ochres of curries to deep blues of powdered indigo dye.

Recipes To Try

Here are two of my favourite recipes, kindly given to me by my friend, Amany.

Meatless Stuffed Vine Leaves

Ingredients:

- ¼ cup olive oil
- 2 medium onions, minced
- 1 cup short grain rice
- ½ cup pine nuts
- ¼ cup raisins
- 50–60 preserved vine (grape) leaves
- 1 tablespoon fresh dill, chopped
- ½ teaspoon ground allspice
- salt and pepper to taste
- 2 lemons, thinly sliced
- (in Egypt, lemons are like key limes in the US)
- 3 tablespoons lemon juice
- 1 tablespoon olive oil
- Boiling water

Method:

Heat ¼ cup olive oil in a large skillet. Add onions and sauté until translucent. Add rice then sauté until rice is glazed. Add pine nuts, raisins, dill, allspice, salt and pepper. Mix well and set aside. Cut stems from grape leaves and place in a large bowl. Pour boiling water over the leaves. Drain and rinse then leave to cool. Line the bottom of a large saucepan with 2–3 large vine leaves. Set aside.

(Continued on the next page)

(Continued from previous page)

Place each leaf, shiny side down, on a flat surface. Spoon about 1 teaspoon of the rice mixture onto the centre of each leaf. Roll the leaf with the mixure inside, tucking the ends in as you go. Place the roll into the saucepan. Continue making more little rolls and placing them into the pan until you have one layer of rolls. Place lemons slices on top of this layer.

Repeat layering rolls and lemon slices. Invert a heat-proof plate on top of the stuffed leaves to prevent the rolls from sliding while cooking. Press the plate down gently. Pour in the boiling water until it is about 1 inch from the saucepan rim. Cover and simmer over low heat for 30 minutes or until the rice is tender. The leaves should be tender but a bit chewy. Cool slightly. Arrange the stuffed leaves on a platter. Sprinkle with lemon juice and 1 tablespoon of olive oil.

ಶಶಶ

Bechamel Sauce

Ingredients:
- 4 tablespoons butter
- ½ cup flour
- 4 cups milk
- white pepper
- a pinch of ground nutmeg
- ½ cup shredded gouda cheese
- ½ cup shredded Gebna Roumi (Romano) cheese
- 2 eggs

Method:
Melt the butter in saucepan, then add flour and brown. Slowly add the milk, stirring constantly with a whisk until it becomes creamy. Add the white pepper, nutmeg and cheeses, and continue cooking until all the cheese is melted. Leave to cool. Beat the eggs and add to the cooled mixture.

You can pour this mixture onto cooked macaroni, zucchini, artichokes or browned aubergine before baking the dish.

SHOPPING FOR FOOD
Butchers, Street Vendors and Food Hygiene

Egyptians are by tradition quite concerned with cleanliness. Part of this is due to the teachings in the Qur'an (the Islamic Holy Book). This is evident not only in attempts to control nature's sandy penetrations, but in the concern with hygiene associated with religious practices. All exposed parts of the body (for example, face, hands and feet) must be washed before entering the mosque for prayer.

A lot of outsiders don't know that desert sand is considered to be a cleansing agent under some circumstances. For example, if a Muslim is in the desert and unable to 'wash' with water before prayer, he may ritually 'wash' with sand.

Concerns for prayer hygiene do not seem to transcend to food preparation habits among many lower- and middle-class Egyptians. Open-air markets predominate. Food is sold, butchered and prepared amid the street clutter. Street vendors, small walk-up shops for prepared food and drinks and open-air markets abound throughout Egypt. Animal carcasses hang in the open air without refrigeration. Dinner 'on the hoof' stands around waiting to be slaughtered or sold for home preparation. Look on any street and you are likely to see a woman walking with a basket full of live geese or chickens on her head returning from the market to prepare dinner.

If you plan to buy your own meat, it is important to identify a good, reputable butcher whose meats are slaughtered at government butchering facilities to ensure the least likelihood of getting tainted meat. Meat slaughtered at government butcheries will be marked by big red stripes painted on the sides of the carcass. Probably, the best way to find a good butcher is to ask around among your friends or acquaintances that have been in Egypt for some time. They will be in the best position to tell you the safest places to purchase meat and fowl. I admit that I am partial to the Western-styled grocery markets where the meat is usually shrink-wrapped, such as Metro Markets or Seoudi.

As mentioned previously, food prepared by street vendors or in small local cafes is everywhere in Egypt. In many

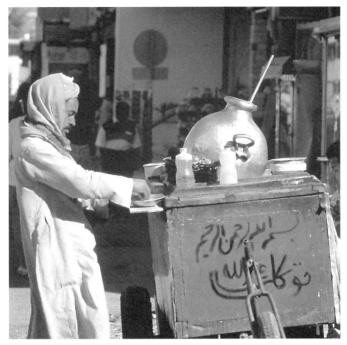

One of the many street vendors seen throughout Egypt.

of the smaller cities, these are the only places, except restaurants associated with hotels, to get prepared food. Since many, many eating places in Egypt are open-air or in buildings with doors and windows open, again you may not find the shiny, disinfected cooking surfaces people have come to expect in many parts of the world. Only the bigger cities have chain restaurants or four- and five-star dining facilities.

Better restaurants and hotel kitchens are usually quite clean and sanitary. Great care is taken, especially due to concern for tourists, to maintain safe food handling and preparation in these establishments. If you are particularly nervous about 'getting germs', it is probably best to limit your eating out to these types of places, at least at first. Egyptians everywhere pride themselves on hospitality and high quality service. Special care is taken to ensure table settings and foods are attractive, clean and pleasant to the senses. Courtesy is a given.

Bacterial Remedy

Personally, I tend to 'eat like an Egyptian'. If Egyptians eat the food, I eat the food. But like anyone else, I have particular likes and dislikes, so some types of food I avoid. There are a couple of little tricks that help avoid some of the most common sources of bacteria that can result in diarrhoea, or 'Pharaoh's curse', as it is referred to by tourists. Most of the time Pharaoh's curse is not serious, just uncomfortable. One neat trick I learned from my Egyptian friends to avoid getting bacteria from salads is to top them with freshly squeezed lemon juice or a little vinegar. Whereas cooking kills bacteria, fresh salad ingredients harbour the little culprits. Anything with a lot of acid will often take care of the squiggly bacteria that can hide on freshly washed lettuce, cucumbers and tomato skins. One of the greatest street dining delights are *felafel* (fried chickpea or broad bean) sandwiches. They are usually served with shredded lettuce and chopped tomatoes on top of the *felafel* in a piece of Egyptian bread. Just ask the vendor for a piece of lemon and most will gladly accommodate you. I even follow the Egyptian style and squeeze lemon on salads at five-star restaurants or at home—just in case.

Frankly, if you are going to stay in Egypt for any time, you must throw aside some ingrained notions of what constitutes cleanliness about food. Eat only well done meat, fowl, fish or eggs no matter who cooks them.

Fruits, Vegetables, Breads and Sweets

Fruit and vegetable stalls along Cairo streets provide you with not only some of the best tasting products anywhere, but with a visual smorgasbord.

In stall after stall or in small shops, proud shopkeepers display fruits and vegetables at the peak of ripeness. Fruits and vegetables are not picked green and stored for days or weeks before being transported to market as they are in many Western societies. Produce you see at Egyptian *souks* may well have been picked the day before and brought by truck or donkey cart to the market overnight. Fresh warm bread and sweet pastries make your mouth water as you walk among the stalls of *souks* or meander into the corner bakery. Try them. They taste as good as they smell!

Fresh fruits and vegetables (above) can be found at many shops in the city. These have been picked at the peak of ripeness not before so you get only the best. Also to be found are roadside stalls selling fresh bread (below). They are delicious so give them a try.

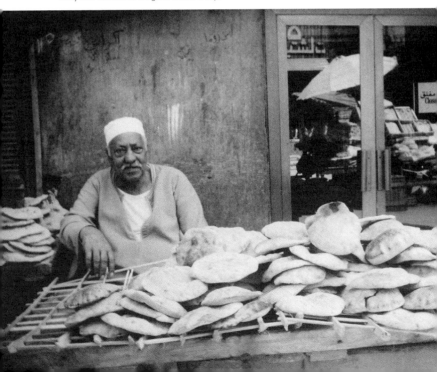

Fruit and Vegetable Shopping Hints

- Unless you know the the market person will select good fruit and vegetables for you (you only learn this by experience), insist that you select the fruits and vegetables yourself.
- Watch carefully to ensure that no rotten commodities are slipped into the bottom of your bag or additional items added to increase your purchase.

DRINKING WATER

Most guidebooks warn visitors not to drink the local water, eat food on the street or partake of fruits and vegetables that cannot be peeled and/or cooked. Only you know your own constitution and body's immune system. I would point out that if you are going to be in Egypt for some time and plan to follow Western standards of hygiene, you will have to sequester yourself in a hermetically sealed room (there are none that I know of in Egypt). It is impossible to maintain practices foreign to the land for extended periods of time.

You can buy drinks from these shops but if you are buying bottled water, make sure that the seal is unbroken.

Until you can get used to a little dirt and some germs in your system, you will have to follow precautions without a doubt, but I suspect that this cannot continue for long periods of time. Besides, it will not be long before you forget to brush your teeth with bottled water (and you will probably find you do not get a major case of diarrhoea doing this).

Most major Egyptian cities state their tap water is potable. Cleanliness of rural water supplies is considerably more problematic. Usually in small towns and villages, water is drawn from wells or piped in, but cannot be considered potable. Many people get slight diarrhoea when drinking water in rural places. *Giardia*, one of those bad little parasites which lodges in the intestinal tract, is more likely to be found in rural rather than big city water supplies.

One of the habits I find most interesting among some foreigners revolves around their obsession for ice in drinks. People who religiously carry bottled water so as not to get germs from tap water—the same ones who even brush their teeth with bottled water—turn right around and order ice for their drinks. They never once ask themselves where the water comes from that makes the ice. Ice is made from tap water.

A word of caution: if you are buying bottled water, make sure the seal is not broken when you get the water. There is little concern in big hotels and restaurants. At these places, waiters delight in presenting the chilled water bottle, pointing out the unbroken seal, and ceremoniously breaking the seal for you. On the other hand, some street vendors take old

Safety Tips

- Be careful of eating food bought from street vendors.
- Ice is usually made from tap water.
- Squeezing some fresh lemon juice on fruits and salads can help kill harmful bacteria.
- Wash your lettuce with just a tiny bit of chlorine bleach to kill harmful germs.

bottles, fill them with tap water and sell them to customers as bottled water. If someone tries to sell you a bottle of water with the seal broken, politely request another bottle with the seal intact. If they say this is all they have, thank them and go to another vendor.

After a while, you will begin to slack off on the bottled water and 'germ-free' imperative. This is particularly true if you are integrating into Egyptian society. When you are invited to someone's home, it is extremely rude to refuse your host's hospitality and not eat their food, whether it is a tomato and cucumber salad or fresh grapes. Usually, you will be offered a variety of drinks such as colas or fruit juice as well as water. If you are still on a strict regimen of bottled water, and water is what you want to drink with your meal, just take your water with you. Everyone understands the newcomer's concern with drinking water. So, it will not seem rude or even unnecessarily strange for you to be cuddling a bottle of water when you appear (unless, of course, you have been living there for six months or a year, in which case you will be perceived to be very strange indeed).

You will not find chilled, public drinking fountains in Egypt, except perhaps in better hotels. Instead, you will notice large pottery jugs full of water located at various fairly inconspicuous places along the streets. The jugs keep the water cool and are there for all to drink. These are public drinking fountains, Egyptian-style. You will notice that people walk along, stop, say a few words (perhaps), maybe give the storekeeper a small tip, pour water into the community cup, take a drink of water and continue on their way. Unless you are well adapted to Egyptian life, it is probably best to avoid drinking from public water jugs.

ENGLISH/EGYPTIAN SPICE GLOSSARY

English	Egyptian Arabic
allspice	*boharaat, bohar*
ammonia (powdered)	*nashader*
anise	*yansoun*

English	Egyptian Arabic
basil (fresh)	*rihan*
bay leaf, laurel	*wara' el laura*
capers	*qobbar, abu khanger*
caraway	*karawya*
cardamom	*habbahaan*
cayenne pepper	*shatta*
chicory	*chicoria*
chilli	*felfel ahmar amrikani, shatta*
chives	*korraat baladi*
cinnamon	*erfah*
cloves	*oronfel*
coriander (dry or seeds)	*kozbara nashfa*
coriander (fresh)	*kozbara khadra*
coriander (powdered)	*kozbara matthoona*
cumin	*kammun*
cumin (black)	*habbet el baraka*
curry	*kari hindi*
dill (fresh)	*shabat*
fennel	*shammar*
fenugreek	*helba*
garlic	*toom*
ginger	*ganzabeel*
hibiscus	*karkade*
juniper	*habb el aaraar*
licorice	*erq souss*
mace	*bisbassa*
marjoram	*mardagoush, bardakosh*
mastic	*mesteka*
mint	*naanaa*

English	Egyptian Arabic
nutmeg	*gozet et tib*
paprika	*felfel roumi, mish harra*
parsley (fresh)	*ba'duunes*
pepper (black)	*felfel eswed*
pepper (red)	*felfel ahmar*
pepper (white)	*felfel abyad*
rosebuds	*zir el ward*
rosemary	*hassa el baan*
saffron	*zaafaran*
sage	*marmareya, akbdar chey*
salt (for cooking)	*malh kheshen*
salt (table)	*malh na'em*
savory	*zaatar el bar*
sesame	*semsem*
sorrel	*hummad*
sumac	*soumak*
tarragon	*targhun*
thyme, oregano	*zaatar*
turmeric	*kurkom*

ENJOYING EGYPT

CHAPTER 7

'I read the inscriptions on the walls, and cried;
for this was the proof I have lived for... that the Egyptians
were indeed the builders of the Great Pyramids.'
—Egyptologist Dr Zahi Hawas upon discovering the tombs of
the workers and artisans believed to be the builders of the
Giza pyramids (from an article in Arabic in the local press)

THE CALENDARS USED

Business and the secular community operate under the Gregorian calendar. However, other calendars have official status in Egypt. The Islamic calendar is based on a lunar cycle of 12 months of 29–30 days. Thus, the Islamic year is 11 days shorter than a Gregorian year. As a result, Islamic holidays and feasts occur some 10–12 days earlier each year.

The Islamic Calendar

The Islamic calendar was first introduced, in AD 638. The reference point of the calendar system is the Hejira in AD 622, and Hejira years are usually denoted by 'AH' (from the latin 'Anno Hegirae') in Western languages. The Islamic year begins on the first day of the first month (1 MuHarram). Therefore, the starting date for the Islamic calendar, which is 1 MuHarram, AH 1, corresponds to 16 July 622 AD. Among the Muslim holidays observed in Egypt are:

- Ras as-Sana (celebrated at the beginning of the Islamic calendar, the Hejira)
- Mouled el-Nabi (the birth of the Prophet Muhammad)
- Eid al Fitr/el-Fitr (end of Ramadan, *see the next section*)
- Waaf el Arafa (eve of Adha)
- Eid el-Adha (the Bairam celebrating the end of the annual pilgrimage to Mecca)

Note that the Islamic calendar, like any based on calculation, comprises only estimated dates. The calendar is not based on the actual sighting of the moon, which marks the start and end of the month of Ramadan.

The Coptic Calendar

The Coptic calendar is based on a solar cycle and consists of 12 months of 30 days and one month of five days. The first day of the Coptic year (month of Toot) begins on 11 or 12 September each year. Several Coptic Christian holidays are observed by the population. These are:

- Epiphany (celebrating the baptism of Jesus on 19 January)
- Annunciation (on 23 March)
- Easter (celebrated on different dates each year and preceded by 55 days of fasting)

RAMADAN

Ramadan is a particularly important month in any Muslim country. Egypt is no exception. During Ramadan, many shifts occur in daily schedules due to the requirement to fast during this month. Instead of staying open all day, many businesses and shops shorten daytime working hours. In fact, during the month of Ramadan, things essentially shut down during the day throughout Egypt.

Egyptians do not starve themselves during Ramadan. Basically, the fast simply requires a shifting of schedule from primary activity during daylight to night-time activity. Each day, the fast is broken by a large meal served shortly after sunset. During Ramadan, Egyptians who observe the fast arise before sunrise. It is customary to consume a fairly large meal before the daily fast begins. As a result of eating pattern shifts, activity patterns also shift during Ramadan. Egyptians, always prone to night-time activity, increase their nightly activity significantly during this period. Nights are used for visiting, shopping and some business activities. Ramadan is followed by the Eid of el-Fitr, a multi-day celebration during which families gather for feasting and prayer.

During summer months, activity also picks up significantly during the evenings. Postponing activity until night avoids the worst heat of the day, but does not necessarily involve

STOP TELLING THE TOURISTS IT'S RAMADAN WHEN IT'S NOT!

TRIGG.

a consequent shift in eating patterns. Obviously, observing the Ramadan fast during the summer increases the length of time between meals.

As a visitor to or foreign resident in the country, you may choose not to follow the Ramadan fast. If so, you should not eat in public if it can be avoided. The major general exception to this rule revolves around tourists and some tourist establishments. Egyptians in and around the tourism industry acknowledge that many tourists to their land are not Muslim. Therefore, many seek to accommodate tourists by providing daytime meals to them throughout this period. Most commonly, only the larger hotels and tour ships accommodate tourists in this way. Even in tourist areas, access to everything is limited during the day. If you can, buy food supplies you think you will need for the next day during the preceding evening. You should count on finding restaurants, cafés and most business establishments closed during most of the daylight hours of Ramadan.

FESTIVALS

Several major festivals occur in Egypt. January marks the Cairo International Book Fair and the International Documentary and Short Film Festival. March heralds the Annual Flower show at the Orman Gardens and the International Children's Film Festival. One of the most fascinating festivals, the Sham el-Nessim (literally the 'Scent of Spring'), actually traces its history back to the time of the Pharaohs. In ancient days, Egyptian men gave a lotus flower to their ladies, and families took leisurely cruises down the Nile in flower-decorated *feluccas*. Now, almost everyone celebrates the Sham el-Nessim by having family picnics in gardens and parks along the Nile. This traditional festival takes place on Monday following the Coptic Easter. For horse enthusiasts, check out the Egyptian Arabian Horse show.

Calendar of Festivals and Holidays	
Coptic Christmas	7 January
Union Day	22 February
Sinai Liberation Day	25 April
Labour Day	1 May
Evacuation Day	18 June
Bank Holiday	1 July
Revolution Day	23 July
Coptic New Year	11 September
Armed Forces Day	6 October
Suez Victory Day	24 October
Victory Day	23 December

ENTERTAINMENT
Cultural Activities

Lots of cultural activities exist in and around Egypt! You can choose from theatre, dance, opera, symphony and cinema (foreign and domestic).

There is something absolutely surreal about going to the opera or symphony in Cairo. Walking through the streets of Gezira, with a soft evening breeze blowing off the Nile never ceases to impress me. The new Cairo Opera House (the old one burned) is truly the National Cultural Center, with good acoustics and several venues for enjoying the arts. As such, it has a full calendar of international and national events, both from local artistes as well as visiting companies from Europe and the United States. To view the calendar of events, see:

http://www.cairooperahouse.org/
opera_home_english.aspx?lang = en-US.

One of the Opera House's regular acts is the Cairo Symphony Orchestra which performs from September through June. Their Christmas concerts are fantastic! To find out more about the orchestra and their performance schedule, visit:

http://www.cairo-symphony.com/

Cultural Centres

Foreign and local cultural centres also offer a variety of activities such as language classes, films, exhibits and recitals. In Cairo, some of the more active are the British Council, the Goethe Institute, and the American, Austrian, Canadian, French, Italian, Japanese and Spanish cultural centres. In Alexandria, check out the American, British, French, German, Italian, Russian, and Spanish cultural centres.

Among the other options in Cairo are the Archaeology Club of the American Research Centre in Egypt (ARCE), which offers field trips and a series of lectures. You can find information about an ARCE chapter near you at:

http://www.arce.org/

The Egypt Exploration Society in Agouza organises a programme of lectures on a wide variety of topics, given by prominent Egyptologists from all over the world. These are held in London, Manchester and Cairo. Membership costs to both archaeological societies is reasonable. You can find information about the Egypt Exploration Society in Agouza at:

http://www.ees.ac.uk/membership/benefits.htm

If you are interested in drama, the Maadi Community Players is an option. Several Christian churches and religious groups around Cairo offer religious and social programmes (*see a partial listing of this in the* Resource Guide*, page 310*). Among these are representatives of the Anglican, Protestant, Catholic, Christian Science, Quaker and Mormon groups.

There are also several women's groups that generally welcome new members and especially those with interests they would like to share. Women should check on the Maadi Women's Guild. This group arranges get-togethers and lectures, and offers opportunities for volunteers to help several Egyptian charities. The Women's Association of Cairo also offers many opportunities. The Community Services Association is a gem, offering lots of classes on a large variety of subjects.

Cinemas

Egypt's cinemas are relatively inexpensive by Western standards except during the International Film Festival. There are numerous places to see films and you can always find the latest Western films in Cairo close to when they open overseas.

It has been my experience that almost all of the seats are good for seeing the films (except the seats at the very front) and are quite comfortable. Some of the cinemas, for example Genena I–VI and Wonderland I–VI, are in huge malls that provide lots of additional entertainment for before or after the show. And, don't forget the MGM at the Maadi Grand Mall. These are just a sampling for cinemas in Egypt. If you want to see films in Arabic, go to Cinema Rivoli on 26 July Street in Azbekiya.

You can find the mainstays of Western cinemas here in Cairo too: popcorn, food and soda pops! One thing that may be a little different from the US is that when you buy a ticket for a show, you purchase an assigned seat.

Libraries and Bookstores

Freed from Persian control in 331 BC by Alexander the Great, the Egyptian city now known as Alexandria became home to the world's most famous library and the world's first university. The Alexandria Library housed the largest collection of world's greatest, most notable works (some 700,000 catalogued manuscripts from the 3rd century BC). There were actually two sites of the ancient library: the Royal Library (located close to the harbour within the royal palace) and the Daughter Library, south of the city at the Serapeum. The Royal Library was destroyed by war in 48 BC when fire spread from the dockyards to the city. The Daughter Library appears to have lasted until Emperor Theodisius ordered the destruction of all pagan temples in AD 391.

An ambitious international effort to efface the ancient loss brought together plans for the new Biblioteca Alexandrina. Built near the site of the ancient Royal Library, the 40,000-sq-m (430,556-sq-ft) facility houses 4–8 million volumes, 50,000 maps, 100,000 manuscripts and numerous other materials. The Biblioteca functions as a convention centre and tourist attraction as well as a place of learning, dialogue and tolerance. The complex includes a Library for the Blind, a Young People's Library and four other specialised libraries; the Alexandria Conference Center; three museums including

Ergonomically designed chairs and tables at the Biblioteca Alexandrina encourage people to use the library more often.

Viewing the mummy exhibits at the Biblioteca Alexandrina which has, besides its specialised libraries, three museums, a conference centre, a planetarium and a host of other tourist attractions.

one focusing on science; a planetarium; seven research centres; a calligraphy institute, and the International School of Information Studies.

I was fortunate enough to explore the facility shortly before it officially opened. It is incredible! One thing I find most amazing are the tables and chairs—all ergonomically engineered for ease of reading and comfort. However, annual library cards are relatively expensive unless you plan to utilise the library frequently.

Public libraries exist throughout Egypt, for example the new library in the Zamalek neighbourhood of Cairo (the Greater Cairo Library). Many Egyptian libraries are affiliated with universities, schools or private associations. Even if you are allowed access, you may not find the variety of materials you are accustomed to in your home country's libraries, especially in the way of fiction. Some universities allow the general public to use their resources as reference materials, but do not allow individuals to check materials out from the library. The American University in Cairo (located at Midan Tahrir) has one of the better libraries and their

These ladies are doing some research at the Biblioteca Alexandrina.

bookshop is a treasure trove. The library is down the street and across from the main entrance to the University. You will need to check with the University regarding access to the library and hours of operation. Also, check with the various embassies to determine what resources they may have available to the public. Other than that, a few small private libraries exist, but access to them is generally quite limited and very hard to find. Definitely check out the Community Services Association library. They have a large lending library of English-language paperbacks donated by members of the community.

If you are addicted to reading and need a new novel each week to keep you going, bring a good supply with you. It will be cheaper and significantly easier; besides, you can always trade with someone who has totally different books. On the other hand, numerous bookshops exist throughout Egypt. Most, quite naturally, carry predominantly Arabic publications. However, several carry rather extensive selections in English, French and German. Bookshops range from small, hole-in-the-wall places that are musty, dusty and confusing, to well-arranged, spacious stores with staff members that seemingly know every book in the place. You will not find the huge, mega-selection discount book stores typical of the United States and Europe anywhere in Egypt. Some books are simply not available in Egypt. Relatively speaking, books of any type are actually quite expensive in Egypt. An event to look for is the Cairo International Book Market that occurs in early winter in Nasr City.

Almost all major hotels have kiosks that carry a limited selection of English, French and German reading materials, including some fiction. Typically, their selections may include a few bestseller selections, one or two classics and, perhaps, some biographies. Mostly, these hotel kiosks carry coffee-table books, tourist books and publications related to Egyptian antiquities since tourists represent their principal market.

Television and Radio

A lifesaver to television junkies has been the arrival of satellite TV. It has truly revolutionised access to the outside world and television viewing. The government does not censor programmes that come in over satellite. For example, you can now get CNN and the NBC Super Channel. However, don't expect news programmes like the ones you might get in the United States. They are not the same and you get the international version of the news programmes, which may well have very little local US coverage.

Local TV is definitely dreadful for the foreigner, though it has gotten significantly better with the new Nile TV station broadcast in English and French to serve the expatriate population. The eight local TV stations remain government controlled. Two of them (Channels 1 and 3) are mostly Arabic offerings. Channel 2 has daily English language programming, but much of this is censored. Most English programmes are either subtitled in Arabic or dubbed.

Local radio stations are similarly rough on the foreigner. English language news can be heard on FM 95 at 7:30 am, 2:30 pm and 8:00 pm. This is the foreign-language station, which broadcasts from 7:00 am until midnight. Besides English-language programming, French, German, Greek and Italian programmes are offered. As mentioned earlier, a good option is a short-wave radio receiver. Other options include tape players, boom boxes and portable CD players. A word of caution with these: bring a good supply of tapes and CDs with you. The ones you find in Egypt are great for local music, but the quality is often inferior. Many are several generations away from any original recording.

Newspapers and Magazines

Several options exist for getting printed news in English. Egyptian newspapers definitely slant coverage towards what the government wants to see printed, although some lively debates do appear. Censorship in Egypt is considerably less than in other countries in the Middle East. More than that, there is substantially less censorship in Egypt than 15 years ago. Is censorship gone? Absolutely not! Many books are still deemed anti-Islamic and not available. President Mubarak loosened the reigns on the press considerably, but, if you are expecting all-out freedom of the press, it simply is not there yet.

The *Egyptian Gazette* is Egypt's daily English-language newspaper. Finding the *Gazette* outside of Cairo or Alexandria is problematic. On Saturdays, the edition is called the *Egyptian Mail*. For the past few years, *Al-Ahram* (the Arabic-language daily) has published a weekly English summary on Thursday (also available on the Internet; *see the* Resource Guide *for more details*). Similarly, a French version is published on Wednesday. The *Middle East Times* is a weekly English-language newspaper published on Sunday. Most newspapers can also be found on the Internet—just search for them by name!

Many major Western newspapers and news magazines can be found in Cairo and Alexandria. Some can even be found in other good-sized cities, but they may be a bit dated. Among the English-language publications available are *USA Today*, *Newsweek* and *Time*. These publications are not censored as they are in some other Middle Eastern countries (and used to be in Egypt 15 years ago). You can find them at the major hotels, a few news-stands and bookshops.

Magazines Published in Egypt

Here are several other magazines, which are published in Egypt, that are rather good.

- *Egypt Today*
  A monthly, local English-language publication that covers a range of topics.
- *The Middle East Times*
  A bi-monthly publication published in the United Kingdom.
- *Egypt Magazine*
  A bi-monthly magazine which covers cultural items and contemporary issues.
- *Sports and Fitness Egypt*
  Provides monthly highlights of sporting events.
- *Business Today*
  A good magazine for business related topics on Egypt and the world.
- *Business Monthly*
  The monthly journal of the American Chamber of Commerce (AmCham) in Egypt.

Cabarets and Discotheques

Dancing lights, clinking glasses and loud music hit you squarely as you step through the doors into the sanctum of Egypt's response to the Western nightclub. Coloured lights playing on silver balls bounce kaleidoscope sparkles throughout the room. These are the discotheques frequented by Egyptians.

Everywhere you turn, smiling couples move to the tantalising tempos of Western disco and rock music. The sounds of the 1970s and 1980s reverberate through powerful amps blasting from every corner. Hot spots for unmarried Egyptian couples (almost totally upper-class), discos provide a haven for the Western-style singles' life. You can get imported alcoholic drinks at many clubs, as well as local beer and wine. Dancing is openly flirtatious, though not really suggestive.

Foreigners more frequently patronise another category of nightclub referred to locally as cabarets. These are usually fairly expensive and often include belly dancers, folklore performances, Arabic music and a lavish food spread. All the major hotels have floor shows and you can usually combine this with an excellent dinner. You will often find that cabarets have a cover charge and/ or a minimum charge, usually with a tax added on at the end.

Casinos

Casinos operate in only a few of the five-star hotels in Cairo. Egyptian nationals are prohibited by law from gambling in casinos, but all foreigners are permitted. If you plan to gamble, be sure to make it when you are not out with your Egyptian friends so they won't have to remind you they are not allowed. The casinos have everything from inexpensive slot machines to large-stake gaming tables. You will have to show your passport to get in.

PROSTITUTION, HOMOSEXUALITY AND EXTRA-MARITAL RELATIONSHIPS

Prostitution is definitely one of those topics most Egyptians do not want to talk about. When pushed, most will simply tell you prostitution is illegal. Some will tell you that they think prostitution used to be legal; others simply tell you there has never been legal prostitution in Egypt. In any event, prostitutes do work in Egypt. Historically, prostitution used to be associated with being out late at night and with the arts, particularly musicians and belly dancers, in other words, those who were outside the mainstream of traditional Egyptian society. The most famous area, 40–50 years ago, used to be around Mohamed Ali Street. Now, there is no organised district, per se, such as in Amsterdam. How do you recognise a prostitute? Again, answers are elusive. Most people answer, 'Well, you just know'. You probably will, too.

Gay rights do not exist in Egypt. There is no movement, no public acknowledgement for a very simple reason: homosexuality is illegal in Egypt. Homosexual acts leave a person open to being punished for committing the crime of 'disgraceful impudent acts'. Under this law, a convicted person can be imprisoned for up to one year and fined up to E£ 300. Usually, this law has not been used against Westerners—they are just deported instead of imprisoned. This does not mean you definitely will be deported rather than imprisoned, however. Recognise this: homosexuality is not welcome in Egypt.

Does this mean there are no gay hangouts in Egypt? No, it does not. As mentioned in other sections, friends of the same sex may hold hands casually in public without this being interpreted as homosexual behaviour. But anything that looks like public gestures of affection between persons of the same sex (things that are perceived to be homosexual) provokes strong negative reactions. Men wearing earrings are assumed to be homosexuals! For more information, check: http://www.gayegypt.com

Messing around with extra-marital heterosexual affairs can also result in dealing with the force of the law. A lot of this relates to divorce laws, but laws nevertheless. Does this mean Egyptians don't mess around? No, but be assured that discretion is definitely a must! In point of fact, they just don't care about foreigners as long as they do not flaunt unacceptable (by Egyptian standards) behaviour.

The subject of extra-marital affairs brings up another topic of interest. What about mixed-gender couples who travel together or live together? This gets a little tricky and there is definitely a double standard. An Egyptian man and woman who are not married to each other cannot register in a hotel room together under the law. On the other hand, usually (though not at all hotels), a foreign unmarried man and woman can register to stay in the same room. But a foreigner cannot register to be in the same room with an Egyptian of the opposite sex if they are not married. So, what do people do? They get separate rooms and carry on as before.

TRAVEL AND TOURISM

'Experience Egypt as a guest, not as a tourist'—this phrase is from Maryanne Stroud's website describing her riding facilities at Recoub Al Sorat, or Riding the Righteous Path (http://www.alsorat.com/index.html). She and Tracy Karbus, who has the riding facility at Abu Sir, Giza, have experienced Egypt as tourists and also as residents. As they say, "We know the difference... Visiting Egypt in buses that never leave the main roads misses the rich cultural diversity here."

'It is our pleasure to receive every tourist in Egypt as an honoured guest and a VIP.'
  —Minister of Tourism at a recent German tourist trade show

Tour Guides
Medhat: 'Value Added Guide'

A chance to experience the rich culture that is really Egypt inextricably pulled me toward Medhat when I first met him in 1994. I had a group of 14 university students with me, and had booked all of our travel and tours through an agency in the US. As our good luck would have it, Medhat turned out to be our boat Egyptologist. Medhat was (and continues to be) a breath of fresh air—his English is GREAT! You can understand him and he understands you—even most of the subtleties of colloquial American English. He actually listens to what you want (instead of giving canned speeches), never rushes you (unless you are about to miss the boat), and helps

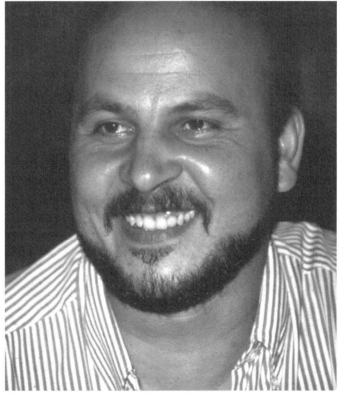

If you are looking for customised, personally designed added value to your Egyptian experience, Medhat is your man!

Watching and listening to Medhat as he expounds on the wonders of Philae.

Transportation to the Valley of the Kings.

tailor a visit to Egypt that will exactly fit your needs. He put the whole trip (including hotels, boats, transfers, donkeys and tips) together for me when I returned a year or so later with the next group of university students anxious to learn about the real Egypt. The second group had strange (for the time) requests—like wanting to ride horses between the Great Pyramids and Saqqara at sunrise or taking donkeys at sunrise to the Valley of the Kings by going up the mountain behind Queen Hatshepsut's temple. (The donkey rides have actually caught on, along with balloon rides on the Western bank in Luxor.)

I have just returned from a traditional classical tour I arranged through Medhat, designed to introduce my sister to the classical sites (and more of them than any standard tourist ever gets!), as well as to give her an opportunity to get to know real Egyptian culture and people. Medhat came through again! He can organise penny-pinching tours such as the ones I needed with my students or grand elegance that includes five-star hotels and boat cruises and a private minibus or Mercedes for getting you to and from sites, and shopping. The trick is to know what you want, convey it specifically to Medhat, then sit back and enjoy a totally personalised Egyptian experience. Through Medhat, I have

The author taking some time to pose for a shot while visiting the necropolis of Saqqara.

come to love his wife and children and the many new friends I have made because he was willing to share the real Egypt with me.

Ayman

Ayman, whom I met through Medhat, first told me about the Exodus tours he was doing in the Sinai in the mid-1990s. He now specialises in ecotourism, principally in the Western Desert. Although there may be a really neat hotel at the oasis, Ayman's adventure tours are personally designed for two-legged desert foxes. The tours are rough going for the meek. If you like the adventure of going behind a sand dune for a bathroom, cooking out over an open fire, and sleeping under the stars—in general, being with nature in the desert—this is the place to go. If you really want to do a Sinai tour, he still does that as well.

Arabi

Arabi (I also met him through Medhat) is the only person I know who actually had a crocodile on his roof (yes, a real, live one). The crocodile is now dead, but the memory lingers. Arabi knows an incredible amount about the flora and fauna

Take a tour with Arabi and be introduced to the rural side of Egypt like these water buffalo taking a cool dip in the river.

of Upper Egypt. He will happily take you on a tour of a Nubian village; name every kind of bird you see in the nature reserve in Aswan; and even show you a banana farm and water buffalo (up close and personal). If you watch closely, you will probably see him dip his cup in the cold, rushing river for a quick drink while you are out skirting between the rocks and reeds of the Nile.

Touring Egypt

I suppose if there is any place on earth where going to tourist sites is one of the most exhilarating experiences you can have, it must be Egypt. I try to think of something that competes with it, but sheer size and number of meaningful sites in Egypt boggles the mind. On the down side, it can be very hot, sticky and dirty. Blowing sand and sweaty tourists crammed together at almost all of the sights continues to detract from the sheer magnitude of the antiquities. I have yet to find a good time to visit the Egyptian Museum. There is no traffic pattern and too many people at any given

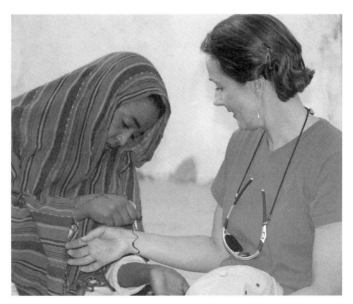

Jackie, the author's sister, getting a henna design painted onto her hands by a Nubian lady when she visited Egypt for the first time.

time, but, you absolutely must see Tut's mask and funerary objects. Fortunately, a new museum is being constructed though I don't anticipate seeing it for at least ten more years. Hopefully, I am pessimistic in this estimate. Of course, if you are not interested in antiquities and the growth of human civilisation, you should probably go somewhere else instead of Egypt. If it is your first time to travel around the country, you might as well start with doing the classical tours. Go to the pyramids—yes, all of them. I fully admit to being a total sop when I first saw the Great Pyramids of Giza—yes, I started crying. I couldn't help myself.

So what is the best way to go about touring Egypt? The answer depends entirely on how much money you plan to spend, how long you have to tour, and where you choose to go and stay. Do you need a tour guide? Well, sometimes 'yes' and sometimes 'no'—it depends, for the most part, on where you are going as well as how comfortable you are with Arabic and dealing with the people on-site that are going to undoubtedly try to sell you things, including their services. To

Vendors at the pyramids, like the one above, sell all sorts of souvenirs but you should not allow them to harrass you.

get the most out of the adventure (especially when you are new to Egypt) and to ease your way in and out of sites, be sure to hire a legitimate tour guide! It is critically important to hire a reputable, licensed tour guide. People are not legally allowed to approach you on the street or at the tourist sites and try to drag you off to their brother's or uncle's or some other relative's shop. This was common ten or 15 years ago, but definitely should not be happening today. HOWEVER, it does still happen, especially when there are no tourist police in sight!

In fact, it happened to me before I got through customs. A man (who must be licensed because he was in a restricted area) approached me. I heard from a friend that some of their foreign friends fell for this and the person doubled the rate on everything (including the hotels). You should never go with people nor hire them until and unless you can confirm that they are legitimate! Repeat: do not go with anyone nor hire them until and unless you can confirm, independently, that they are legitimate! In fact, if people will not stop harassing you at a site or store after you have politely told them to leave you alone, don't hesitate to call a Tourist Policeman over. Pushy hecklers know they are not supposed to be harassing you!

Good Tour Guides

Need a good tour guide? Want to ride donkeys or horses? Here are my recommendations:

- Medhat A'Monem
  Tel: 012-367-6574
- Ayman Mohamed
  Tel: 012-354-6491; fax: (02) 525-0886
- Mohamed Arabi
  Tel: 012-324-0132
- Ibrahim Amin
  Tel: 012-347-6343
- Maryanne Stroud
  Tel: 012-211-8386

If you live in Egypt or are there for an extended time, there are many tourist sites that are good for day or weekend trips. Just hop on a train or hire a driver and head out. Others require a long weekend or more to enjoy fully. And, of course, some are so far away that a weekend get-away requires you to fly.

Enjoying the Trains

Personally, I like the trains! Whenever I get the chance, I take a train because it lets me 'see' and 'feel' Egypt and her people. For more about my train experiences, see the article I wrote with Medhat at:
http://touregypt.net/magazine/mag07012001/magf1a.htm)!
Unfortunately, trains don't go everywhere. Some of the trains are getting to be a little run-down now. The Spanish trains continue to be the best.

From Cairo, you can take the train north to Alexandria and west to Mersa Matruh, or you can go south to Aswan. If you want to scuba dive or snorkel, you will want to go to the east coast, for example to Hurghada, or to the Sinai, perhaps at Sharm el Sheikh. The east coast requires either going by road or flying. The Sinai can be reached by road, but it is simply too far to make it feasible, so flying is the best way to get there. Absolutely, positively, sometime take a Nile Cruise! We all have our favourites and I have been on several exquisite boats. My preference is clear: I want to be on one of the Abercrombie and Kent boats. A&K boats offer top-of-the-line facilities, food and staff. I also like them because the number of people assigned to an individual guide is smaller. However, I have also had a wonderful time on other boats such as the Star Sapphire. There are so many good boats from which to choose, that you can hardly go wrong.

Wherever you decide to go and however you get there, enjoy the beauty and diversity that is Egypt.

COMMUNICATING EGYPTIAN STYLE

CHAPTER 8

'I'm re-reading it with a slow deliberate carelessness.'
—T E Lawrence

Arabic, the official language of Egypt, sounds strange to the native English speaker. At once it rings with a lilting melodic intonation accompanied by an alien series of guttural sounds difficult for the English-speaking palate to form.

Eleven distinct languages or dialects ring out in the cacophony of sounds throughout Egypt. Cairene Arabic is the most widely understood dialect used for non-print media, both in Egypt and throughout the Arab world. It is an amalgam of Delta Arabic and Middle Egypt Arabic with borrowings from literary Arabic. Saidi or Upper Egyptian Arabic follows as the second most common dialect in Egypt. Egyptian Spoken Arabic distinguishes itself from Arabic spoken in other parts of the Arab world principally through a few consonant sounds and local colloquial phrases. Most highly educated Egyptians speak English and/or French.

Classical or Modern Standard Arabic (MSA), which is not a mother tongue, is the language of the Qur'an, the Islamic holy book. It is also used in most textbooks for learning written Arabic. This form of Arabic finds its greatest utility in written materials and formal speeches. Learning Classical Arabic provides an excellent basis from which to read Arabic newspapers or documents. It also forms a good platform to develop spoken Arabic, though words in spoken dialects differ as much as 50 per cent from MSA, according to some sources.

Many tapes for learning Arabic phrases use Egyptian Arabic because it is a widely understood dialect. Since Egyptian cinema and recordings are popular throughout the Arabic-speaking world, most people who speak the language understand the normalised Egyptian Spoken Arabic (based on Cairo speech) established through the media.

Coptic, one very important language you will not hear spoken, reportedly comes from Ancient Egypt. This extinct language lives on through the liturgical language of the Coptic Christian Church. No first language speakers of Coptic exist, since the language went extinct apparently in the 16th century.

The large numbers of foreign tourists throughout Egypt introduce an interesting effect on communication styles. Anywhere that you find a significant tourist penetration, you will also find people able to communicate at least minimally in English, French, German, Italian, Spanish, Japanese and probably several other languages. In tourist areas, people constantly approach the unwary stranger in a language Egyptians guess, based on the foreigner's appearance, will be understood. If you don't respond to entreaties in one language, tourism entrepreneurs simply switch languages until they find one you understand. However, in the more traditional parts of cities or in the rural areas, few people speak any language other than their native tongue.

SIMPLIFIED ARABIC PRONUNCIATION AND ALPHABET

- The Arabic alphabet contains 28 letters. Some additional letters are used in Arabic when writing placenames or foreign words containing sounds which do not occur in Standard Arabic, such as /p/ or /g/.
- Words are written in horizontal lines from right to left, numerals are written from left to right
- Most letters change form depending on whether they appear at the beginning, middle or end of a word, or on their own (see tables).
- Letters that can be joined are always joined in both handwritten and printed Arabic. The only exceptions to

this rule are crossword puzzles and signs in which the script is written vertically.

- The long vowels /a:/, /i:/ and /u:/ are represented by the letters **'alif**, **yā'** and **wāw** respectively.
- Vowel diacritics, which are used to mark short vowels, and other special symbols appear only in the Qur'an. They are also used, though with less consistency, in other religious texts, in classical poetry, in textbooks children and foreign learners, and occasionally in complex texts to avoid ambiguity. Sometimes the diacritics are used for decorative purposes in book titles, letterheads, nameplates, etc.
- The letter [jeem] is pronounced as a hard [g] in most Egyptian dialects (see [ğīm] in the table), e.g., [gabal] for [jabal] (mountain) or [gamil] for [jamil] (beautiful), and so forth. This pronunciation is considered typically Egyptian.
- The letter [qāf] is pronounced as a glottal stop [?] in Cairo and the Delta, but as a hard [g] in Upper Egypt (the Sa'id), which is perhaps due to the Bedouin influence. It does, however, confuse things because the same spoken sound [g] corresponds to different Arabic letters depending on whether you are in Upper or Lower Egypt.

Latin	Name		Final	Medial	Initial	Isolated
'(a)	'alif	ألف	ﺎ	—	—	ا
b	bā'	باء	ﺐ	ﺒ	ﺑ	ب
t	tā'	تاء	ﺖ	ﺘ	ﺗ	ت
ṯ	ṯā'	ثاء	ﺚ	ﺜ	ﺛ	ث
ğ	ğīm	جيم	ﺞ	ﺠ	ﺟ	ج
ḥ	ḥā'	حاء	ﺢ	ﺤ	ﺣ	ح
ḫ	ḫā'	خاء	ﺦ	ﺨ	ﺧ	خ
d	dāl	دال	ﺪ	—	—	د
ḍ	ḍāl	ذال	ﺬ	—	—	ذ
r	rā'	راء	ﺮ	—	—	ر

Latin	Name	Final	Medial	Initial	Isolated
z	zāy	ز	—	—	ز
s	sīn	س	ـس	ـس	س
š	shin	ش	ـش	ش	ش
ṣ	ṣād	ص	ـص	ـص	ص
ḍ	ḍād	ض	ـض	ـض	ض
ṭ	ṭā'	ط	ط	ط	ط
ẓ	ẓā'	ظ	ظ	ظ	ظ
'	'ayn	ع	ـع	ـع	ع
ġ	ġayn	غ	ـغ	ـغ	غ
f	fā'	ف	ـف	ـف	ف
q	qāf	ق	ـق	ـق	ق
k	kāf	ك	ـك	ـك	ك
l	lām	ل	ـل	ـل	ل
m	mīm	م	ـم	ـم	م
n	nūn	ن	ـن	ـن	ن
h	hā'	ه	ـه	ـه	ه
w	wāw	و	—	—	و
y	yā'	ي	ـي	ـي	ي
	hamza	ء	—	—	—

Arabic Vowel Diacritics and Other Symbols

Arabic	Transliteration
لا	lām 'alif lā
بُّ	bbu
بِّ	bbi
بَّ	bba
بّ	šadda bb
بْ	sukūn b

Arabic	Transliteration
بُو	bū
بِي	bī
بَا	bā
بُ	ḍamma bu
بِ	kasra bi
بَ	fatḥa ba

Arabic Numerals and Numbers

English	Arabic Numerals	English Transliteration
zero	٠	ṣifr
one	١	wāḥid
two	٢	iṯnān
three	٣	ṯalāṯah
four	٤	'arba'ah
five	٥	ḥamsah
six	٦	sittah
seven	٧	sab'ah
eight	٨	ṯamāniyyah
nine	٩	tis'ah
ten	١٠	'ašarah

GREETINGS AND COMMON PHRASES

Do you have to learn Arabic to get along in Egypt? Yes and no—it depends on where you are, what you are doing, who you are with, as well as how long you intend to stay. In some instances, it may prove more beneficial to understand how many Egyptians perceive some aspects of communication rather than concern yourself with total proficiency in the Arabic language.

Words possess power. As such, conversations contain frequent blessings to keep things going well. Blessings are also used to demonstrate that the speaker harbours no envy toward a person or object. Westerners commonly attribute this speaking pattern to concepts of fatalism—that one cannot control one's fate. However, another perspective is that frequent blessings actually represent efforts to control future events to some extent. For example, envy or perceived envy toward something relates to belief in the 'evil eye', a belief shared by many Europeans and some North Americans. Belief in the evil eye (or just 'the eye'), though common, is less pronounced among educated Egyptians. The evil eye is feared because it can bring harm to a person or thing if looked at (consciously or unconsciously) with envy. To prevent harm, and therefore the perception of envy, one should offer blessings or other statements of goodwill. Amulets, used in conjunction with religious phrases, most frequently depict drawings of eyes, open palm prints and the colour blue.

To avoid making a bad situation worse, euphemisms replace explicit references to an illness, death or disaster. Until you can learn the local euphemism code, it is probably best to try to avoid conversations related to these types of sensitive subjects. The principal exception is describing symptoms to a doctor, which should always be explicit.

How you say something is often perceived to be as important as what you say. Egyptians speak and write with a flowery eloquence unlike English verbal or written patterns. What appears to be long-winded, repetitious dialogue should be viewed as a demonstration of the speaker's high educational level and refinement. Don't be put off by threats, promises, exaggerations or nationalistic slogans that pepper dialogues. These are meant for effect, and again represent the speaker's language proficiency.

Certainly, command of the local language gives you an advantage in daily life or business. On the other hand, since so many people in Egypt speak English, native English speakers find simple daily survival easy without fluent Arabic, especially in the major cities. If you plan to stray away from the beaten path, you will likely need a minimal command of Arabic or a translator. The respect you receive and your acceptance in the country improves considerably once you command knowledge of elementary greetings and responses. Listed below are some key everyday greetings and phrases

- *Shukran*
  Literally, 'thank you'. Probably *shukran* will be the first Arabic word you learn.
- *'Afwan* or *el 'afw*
  Literally, 'you're welcome', 'not at all', or 'don't mention it'. Either the long or short form is an appropriate response to 'thank you'.
- *Iwa* (*Aywa*) or *naîam*
  Literally, 'yes'. *Iwa* (pronounced like the mid-western state of Iowa) seems to be used more frequently in Egypt than *naîam*, although both are understood and accepted.
- *La'*
  Literally, 'no'. Used alone or in a series—*la'*, *la'*, *la'* is the common way to say no.

- *Assalamu'alaykum* and *wa 'alaykum assalam*
  Literally, *assalamu'alaykum* means 'peace be upon you'. It is the more formal greeting for meeting new people. Literally, *wa 'alaykum assalam*, translates to 'and upon you peace'. It is the appropriate response to the formal hello. This greeting seems to be used less frequently as a greeting in Egypt than other parts of the Middle East.

- *Marhaba*
  Marhaba is a more informal 'hello' greeting used either between friends or when greeting a stranger, for instance in a store.

- *Ahlan* and *ahlan wa sahlan*
  Literally, *ahlan* and its response *ahlan wa sahlan* mean 'nice to meet you' or 'welcome'. This is the most common greeting used among friends and strangers alike in Egypt.

- *Ma'a ssalama* and *Allah yisallimak*
  Literally, 'go with safety' and 'may God make you safe'. *Ma'a ssalama* is a common goodbye phrase used when leaving someone's home or business premises.

- *Inshallah* (*Insha'Allah*)
  Literally, 'God willing'. *Inshallah* is used frequently in conversations. For example, when confirming that they will be at a meeting, it is common to hear the other person say something like, 'I will be there at ten, *Inshallah*' or '*Bukra, Inshallah*'. ('Tomorrow, God willing.')

- *Izzayak?* (to a man) or *Izzayik?* (to a woman)
  Literally, 'How are you?' Notice the different form used for men and women.

- *Alhamdu lillah*
  Literally, 'Thanks be to God'. Although there are many phrases used to say 'I'm fine', this is one of the most frequently used.

- *Hamdillah 'ala ssalama*
  Literally, 'thanks be to God for your safety'. This phrase is used when someone recovers from an illness or returns from a trip.

- *Mashallah (Ma sha' Allah)*
  Literally, 'what God wills'. This phrase is used when seeing a child or complimenting someone's health.
- *Ma'alish*
  Literally, 'never mind' or 'it doesn't matter'. When Egyptians translate this phrase into English, they most often say, 'No problem!' *Ma'alish* is much more than a casual phrase, it actually represents a total way of looking at life's trials and tribulations. The phrase provides a whole range of responses to disappointments, frustrations and acceptance of adversity.

THE VERBAL DIMENSION

In Egypt, conversations frequently involve close contact and low tones, sometimes almost at the level of a whisper. Just as frequently, conversations suddenly erupt into loud shouting matches with everyone talking at once accompanied by arm waving, table pounding, threatening gestures and generous punctuating oaths. Boisterous dramatisations more commonly occur among males of the same age and social status who know each other well, but can also occur among total strangers.

Getting Into the Swing of Things

Once when I was taking a group of Americans to a market in old Alexandria, we had an unanticipated police escort. Much to our surprise, our escort took us through traffic to the wrong place. When I began exclaiming loudly to our interpreter that we did not want to go to this place but another, the bus screeched to a halt, my colleague departed, a crowd gathered, and there ensued a loud screaming match replete with vociferous arm waving and pointing. Next thing my group knew, I was out yelling at our interpreter who then relayed my complaints in a loud voice to the escort. People sat mesmerised in their seats, shrinking at the idea that some or all of us were going to be hauled off to jail for fighting in public. Of course, it was simply normal conversation to the Egyptians involved.

THE NON-VERBAL DIMENSION

Successful communication in Egypt requires not only the ability to communicate verbally, but also an understanding of the non-verbal aspects of communication that accompany speech. Sometimes called the silent language, paralanguage, or body language, it comprises all those hidden means of communication we convey with our presence. Non-verbal communication among Egyptians is intense and very much a sensory experience. Talking is often accompanied by gestures, touching, mutual enjoyment of warm, moist breath and smells, and piercing looks with the eyes.

Gestures

Especially when excited, Egyptians make liberal use of gestures when talking. If you watch people closely, you will also begin to notice head and facial gestures that are commonly part of communication. Since foreigners often use gestures in the wrong place or situation, it is advisable that you do not use these gestures until you are very familiar with Egyptian culture, but it is important to recognise them in order to get the full meaning of what is going on around you. You should note that the most common hand gestures should be made with the right hand only, never the left.

Here are some of the more common do's and don'ts concerning gestures.

- Most Western lewd hand or arm gestures are well understood throughout Egypt, and should not be used under any circumstances.
- Probably every tourist book in the world written about travelling in the Middle East reminds people not to cross their feet exposing the soles to people. This is an extreme insult.
- A common gesture used in the United States is to raise one's hand and make a circle with the thumb and forefinger to mean 'good' or 'OK'. The same symbol may mean 'zero' to the French, 'money' to the Japanese, or 'male homosexual' in Malta. Do not use this gesture in Egypt. If you want to indicate something is OK or very good or that you are winning, it is a better bet to use the old 'thumbs up' gesture by making a fist with the right hand with the thumb extending upwards.

- Pointing at people is equally insulting in Egypt, as it is in the United States and Europe.
- Beckoning someone to come to you by holding the hand palm up, curling the forefinger several times, is considered rude and commanding. If you want someone to come over to you or to indicate that you want to talk with someone, hold the right hand up, palm facing outward, and close all four fingers back and forth to the palm.
- If you want someone to go away, hold the right hand out, palm downward, and either move it laterally back and forth or move it as if scooping something away from you. It will also be understood if you use this gesture with the right arm hanging down by your side or just slightly in front of the leg.
- If you want someone to wait, calm down, go slowly or be patient, hold the right hand out, palm upward, touch the thumb and fingers together, and them move the hand up and down.

Space

Personal space is really a Western concept that is foreign to most Egyptians, especially in public. Much of this probably relates to differing concepts of the 'self' as interpreted through alternative cultural perceptions. To the Westerner, 'self' means all of the body, the shell of the individual, i.e., the tangible person. To the Egyptian, the 'self' resides somewhere deep within the core of the shell, closely tying the individual with the more representative meanings of honour, morality and character, i.e. the symbolic person. The way this translates into behaviour is quite simple: Westerners prefer a minimum communication distance of about 46 cm (18 inches), whereas Egyptians prefer 23–25 cm (9–10 inches).

Don't be surprised if you find yourself backing up when talking with an Egyptian. I have watched conversations proceed down a hall or across a room when a Westerner could not adjust to very close proximity when talking. Closeness when talking in the United States or Great Britain is reserved for intimacy or secrets. Even when stuck in an elevator, Europeans and Americans often back as far away

Bargaining over the price of a camel—personal space takes a back seat in Egypt but eye contact is important to show trust and sincerity.

as possible and stop talking, petrified they may actually have to touch another person or smell their breath. Adjusting to close proximity with others requires time. You will probably never be completely comfortable with the typical personal space distance in Egypt, but you will adjust.

Smiles

As mentioned before, it is quite acceptable to smile and make limited eye contact in mixed-gender social circumstances among friends and acquaintances or to smile through the course of normal conversation. Of course, men should be extremely cautious to avoid smiling beyond a casual greeting smile at Egyptian women under all circumstances. Directed smiling at women you don't know may be interpreted as rude, a sexual approach and/or as an insult because it shows a lack of respect and compromises an Egyptian woman's reputation. In extreme situations, making this type of inappropriate approach could result in her male relatives' retribution for their family honuor or their approach to you to establish a marriage contract (which was probably not your intent). Remember, among more conservative single Egyptians, mixed-gender contact other than with close relatives rarely occurs, so smiling is a way they indicate prospective interest in a marriage.

Since foreign men's exposure to Egyptian women is likely to be more limited than foreign women's exposure to men (there are simply more Egyptian men out and about), the remainder of this section will consider women's smiling behaviour. Social rules are different for women. There are certain circumstances where it is totally inappropriate for women to smile warmly at men—most especially, in public places with strangers. As much as I hate categorising, establishing 'types' of smiles is probably the easiest way to explain consequences of unwitting smiles from foreign women. Although there are huge ranges of smiles, for the sake of simplicity, I am going to categorise smiles into three types which are fairly easy to recognise: formal or polite (e.g. for business or shopping interchanges), social and informal.

When a woman smiles warmly (with or without eye contact) at a male stranger, this means 'she is interested', so a warm smile is frequently interpreted as a come-on. Coupled with the not uncommon Egyptian man's perception that Western women are 'loose' or 'on the make', unwary smiles can place you in an extremely awkward position. Rarely is this type of smile interpreted as a prelude to marriage. In fact, though I often advise women to be cautious in making eye contact with Egyptian men, a smile can be even more suggestive and, thus, more problematic. There is something between a full-blown smile and a frown. If you are a woman going to Egypt, practise it.

Now I am not suggesting that if you are a female you should walk around with a scowl or frown on your face. Certainly, 'polite' or 'distant' smiles, especially when thanking someone or asking directions with strangers is all right. But you should be careful of the 'casual' smile, because casual in Egypt is not the same as casual in the West.

Broad differences in smiling behaviour among cultures tend to break down as follows. People ignore strangers in public in some cultures while others do not. For example, it is rare for people to acknowledge each other at a train station, a lift or generally in public in the United Kingdom. In parts of the United States, this is also not uncommon, for example in east coast subways. However, people from many parts of the United States tend to smile, nod, and/or say 'hello, how are you?' to strangers as they walk down the street, enter a lift, or in any situation when they are in direct proximity with another person regardless of gender. To them, it means nothing, but is simply considered a common courtesy and polite behaviour. If you happen to be from an area where this latter practice is common, it will be difficult to break this habit, but break it you must if you don't want misunderstandings on a regular basis.

Misunderstanding on the Train

Since I happen to come from an area where it is considered rude to pass a stranger without some sort of greeting, I speak from considerable experience on how difficult this trait is to break. To show how important it is to curb this particular habit, however, let me give you an example of what happened to a friend on an Egyptian train. A happy, friendly beautiful American woman enjoying the thrill of being in Egypt, entered a train. In doing so, she smiled brightly (with little eye contact) and politely said, "Excuse me" to a man standing close to the door as she passed. Totally innocent and appropriate behaviour from her perspective (perhaps even required for politeness in her culture), her actions were totally misinterpreted by the man. He followed her into the car, tried to start a conversation, and asked her to sit with him. She, of course, became distressed by the attention, not understanding why he was following her. According to her normal rules of behaviour, she had done nothing wrong. When a colleague quickly tried to come to her rescue by telling the man to leave and that she was his daughter, the man simply asked her 'father' if he could sit with her. Profuse no's were not accepted and the man proceeded to stand at the end of the car and stare at the woman, making her even more uncomfortable. Finally, a couple of our Egyptian male friends had to intervene to get the man to leave her alone.

Eye Contact

In Egypt, reading eyes is a non-verbal art form. Americans and especially northern Europeans find the intense level of gaze common in Egypt to be disconcerting and uncomfortable. Why? Because long, deep, penetrating gazing in the West generally means intimacy. In fact, depending on where you are from, direct eye contact connotes honesty, respect, disrespect, flirtation or a sexual come-on. Among some subcultures, direct, non-prolonged eye contact means sincerity and truth. Among other groups, it is a sign of disrespect. Typically, northern Europeans are among the least comfortable with high levels of gaze during conversations. This is true for either male or female, whether in mixed or same sex groups.

Direct, semi-prolonged or intense eye contact between same or mixed sex individuals in a business meeting implies honesty and sincerity among Egyptians. This gets back to reading eyes. Most people cannot control pupil dilation when their interest is aroused. It doesn't have to be sexual interest between a man and a woman. Any kind of interest will do, for example, a comment made in a business meeting which triggers interest in pursuing the business deal. Therefore, to the Egyptian, much can be learned about the honour and integrity of a person by gazing intently into the eyes.

In a society such as Egypt, where men and women do not customarily have a great deal of social or verbal interaction except in school, within the family or in conducting business transactions, eyes tell much about the character of the individual. Inadvertent, frequent eye contact can be particularly hazardous for the Western woman in non-business related settings. Even relatively brief eye contacts, especially when repeated a few times, denotes interest and might be considered coquettish, flirtatious or an open sexual invitation. Certainly, the more educated or Westernised Egyptians accept greater latitude in eye contact than do others due to the simple fact that they have more frequent contact with outsiders and are more able to judge behaviour on non-ethnocentric guidelines.

Touching

As mentioned above, same sex interactions are replete with touches and gestures. Keep your hands to yourself in mixed company! Unmarried males and females simply do not touch one another, especially in public. Married people often walk arm-in-arm or occasionally hold hands when walking. Regardless of whether you are with Egyptians or other foreigners, kissing, fondling or other public displays of intimacy are strictly taboo throughout Egypt.

Except when shaking hands, men should be careful never to touch Egyptian women except in an emergency. If she falls on the street, it is probably all right to pick her up, but remove your hands as quickly as possible. Women—if a man falls, let him get up on his own or let other men assist him as necessary. Do not intervene unless you are a doctor and the person's life or safety is at stake.

EGYPTIAN TIME

The clock reads the same in Egypt, but responses and expectations differ significantly from those in the West. Working on Egyptian time boggles the mind. Things happen when they happen, no sooner. If you are on a tight schedule, you are probably destined to suffer severe frustration. Your best bet is to simply learn to work in approximate time schedules.

I have occasionally asked friends how long it would take to walk or drive to some place nearby. Invariably the answer seems to be the same. Except on rare occasions, every place is ten minutes' walk or drive. My usual response is, "Ten Egyptian minutes or American minutes?"

I view Egyptian time as a process of '*Yalla*! *Yalla*!—Wait.' *Yalla*! simply means 'Let's go!' or 'Hurry up!' No matter how much you hurry, inevitably interminable waits follow your haste. Expect delays and adjust—it is the norm.

QUEUING

Forget you ever knew the concept, it does not happen in Egypt! Just like driving, people traffic in Egypt knows no lane markers. Only a forced queue could possibly persuade Egyptians to 'wait in line'.

Once I watched a number of Americans dutifully form what they perceived to be a line while waiting to get a ticket for the Metro. Totally confounded by people slipping outstretched arms with money in front of them, the Americans still waited in line. They just kept standing, unsure of what to do next. Finally, a sympathetic toll taker noticed the Americans standing there and waved them forward to sell them their ticket.

So, be assertive. Get into the spirit of how to get that burger or Metro ticket. Otherwise, you may wait a considerable time before someone takes sympathy on your plight.

PHOTOGRAPHY

You should always ask permission before taking a picture of someone you don't know. You can do this verbally, or as I often do, by getting their attention, pointing to the camera and shrugging the shoulders as if asking, 'Is this OK?' Asking before snapping the shutter applies specifically when you focus in on an individual or small group of people. Of course, when taking street scene pictures, it is impossible to ask permission of all the people. In this case, use your posture to make sure no particular person feels threatened by the camera. After all, most people are quite used to seeing hundreds of tourists running around the country snapping pictures everywhere.

Women are particularly sensitive about having their pictures taken by strangers. If a woman sees you aiming a camera lens at her and does not want her picture taken, usually she will turn away. An alternative way to let the shutterbug know a picture should not be taken involves raising the hand over the face or holding the arm up towards the photographer. Some men also do not want their pictures taken. They use the same non-verbal signals, and also will occasionally shout out at you. Especially in tourist areas, people allow you to take their picture for a small tip. Again, ask. Do not offer a gratuity to a friend when taking pictures among a group, but it never hurts to ask if it is OK to take the pictures.

Photography is allowed at all antiquities, but sometimes photography tickets are required. Other areas allow photography, but no flash pictures. Still other places require special tickets for the use of video cameras.

It is against the law to take some pictures, usually politically sensitive buildings, embassies or military installations. Also, there is still a prohibition against taking pictures of bridges, but this seems to be less enforced now than in the past. If you are in a locality where pictures are not allowed, usually there is a policeman or military person around who will tell you not to take pictures. Signs indicate a few areas where photography is banned, such as the airport.

Finally, and this is very important, never tell someone you will send them copies of the pictures unless you absolutely, positively can do so. Many people in rural areas or even at tourist sites ask if you will send them copies. Most tourists are insensitive, usually saying, 'Yes, I will send them as soon as I get home.' Then they go home and never communicate with anyone again. On the other hand, do not tell them, 'No, I cannot send you a copy.' Instead, tell them, '*Inshallah*' or 'I will send you a picture if I can.' This will be understood. It allows you to answer positively, which is appropriate, but not to feel as though you committed to action you cannot reasonably accomplish.

BUSINESS

CHAPTER 9

'True wisdom is less presuming than folly.
The wise man doubteth often, and changeth his mind;
the fool is obstinate, and doubteth not;
he knoweth all things but his own ignorance.'
—Akhenaton, Pharaoh, 14th century BCE

BUSINESS STYLE

People often describe the Egyptian business style as being personal. This concept interweaves a level of formality into personal relationships built on trust. Who you know definitely carries more weight than what you know in terms of facilitating business deals in Egypt. You can always pull in the technical expertise you need, but without the personal network to make things happen, you are most likely destined to failure. This is why building personal relationships becomes so critical to success. The hallmark of Egyptian business revolves around formality and personal relationships. Formality typically enters the picture through protocol (who sits where, who is involved, etc.) and dress. However, personal relationships built on trust mark the cornerstone of who succeeds and who does not.

Do not be surprised when, upon introduction to an important person, the conversation quickly turns to a 'who do you know' kind of scenario. When a person introduces himself at a meeting or someone is introducing you, you will often get a long list of comments like, 'I was with so-and-so at such-and-such' or 'My cousin so-and-so has been very instrumental in accomplishing this, that, or the other'. Do not view this as bragging or name-dropping. That is not the purpose. What the person is doing is letting you know that he has the contacts necessary to fulfil his end of the bargain.

The conversation may follow many forms, but eventually both participants or groups must somehow establish their bona fides in order for the dealings to go forward.

Always, always, always, start business negotiations with the highest ranking person you possibly can. Manoeuvring through the system becomes exponentially easier the higher up you start. It is easy to work down a system, but often much more difficult to work up one. However, don't forget the just beginning son of an important businessman, politician or leader either. Once he is convinced, he may well be able to get his father or uncle interested in your business proposal.

BUSINESS DRESS

Fairly formal is the custom. Remember Egyptians tend to dress a little more formally for most occasions than do Westerners anyway. Dress for men should most often include a jacket and tie, especially for the first meeting. You may find that your Egyptian counterpart is dressed a little more casually during the summer months, but again, it is better to be a bit overdressed than underdressed. You can always remove your jacket if the situation warrants. Women's dress should either be a conservative dressy sort of dress (not after-five or cocktail type) or a business suit. Definitely do not wear short skirts—the hemline should be at least below the knees.

BUSINESS CARDS

Come armed with lots of business cards! It is customary to exchange cards with people you meet, especially all people attending business meetings. Even if you are not working (male or female), you should have some cards printed to give to people when you meet them.

If you can, have them printed on both sides—one side in English and the other in Arabic. If not, one side in English is acceptable. Many people in Egypt have several phone numbers printed on their cards. Typically, these will include home phone numbers as well as email addresses and business and fax numbers. So if you want to impress your Egyptian colleagues with your sincerity and knowledge of customs (and don't mind them calling you at home), get cards printed with your home phone number included. It looks so much better than scrawling the number on the back of the card.

BUSINESS MEETINGS

Two things come to mind when thinking about business meetings in Egypt. The first is time and the other relates to how a meeting is typically conducted. The best recommendation I can offer is practise patience and build flexibility into your schedule.

Some people think Egyptians are chronically late because business meetings never seem to begin 'on time' according to foreign practices. This actually is not always true, just a matter of perspective. Whether you arrive at the precise moment your appointment is scheduled, or before, or a few minutes late, you will not be shown into your appointment until host hospitality formalities have been shown. As a general rule, the higher up the official is in an organisation or government, the greater the likelihood a subordinate will escort you to a reception room for some time to have coffee, tea or a cold drink. Of course, as soon as I say that is the standard, an exception occurs. This appears to be a function of the perceived rank of the visitor. The more equal in terms of social, political or business position, the more likely you will be escorted to your appointment and then served refreshments. In any event, Egyptians build hospitality time into appointments and you are expected to adhere to this protocol before business can be discussed.

Egyptians seem to build in a hospitality time in all of their schedules, not just their meetings. Depending on the circumstances, some business people actually operate rather punctually, but this is often the exception. Nonetheless, you are expected to show up for business meetings on time; however, you will probably find yourself waiting for some time to actually begin the meeting. Even if you are late, do not expect to just walk into the meeting. Most probably, regardless of when you arrive, you will usually be shown to a receiving area and served coffee, tea or a cold drink, to ensure

Appropriate Venue

Conducting business meetings in your hotel room may be fine in your native country, but you should not do so in Egypt. It is usually best to schedule a separate sitting room for these situations to give the appearance of the seriousness the matter warrants.

you are given the hospitality you, as a guest, deserve. I say 'most probably' because just about the time you have this all figured out, you will come upon a situation where you are shown directly into your meeting and then served refreshments. This seems to be a practice reserved for some types of situations which are not altogether predictable. The times I have experienced this seem to be when I have had meetings with very highly placed government officials, such as a governor or minister.

As an American, I learned long ago to be a bit sceptical of business dealings with colleagues and to couch business concerns in legalistic, contractual arrangements. In American business transactions, trust goes only so far (and definitely not very far at that). Then one must have the backing of a legal document to bind the commitments. Even when someone gives you their word and shakes on a deal, final negotiations are left to the lawyers. For many kinds of transactions, lawyers may well be required in Egypt as well. Certainly, at some point, legal contracts become necessary. However, at a more informal level of negotiation, when an Egyptian tells you, on his or her word, that something will be done or is agreeable, it becomes a matter of personal honour and the deal will usually be honoured. Before you run off to the bank with the deal, however, make sure you actually know what it is you and the other party have agreed on.

An area of common misinterpretation relates to the subtleties of answers given by Egyptians. This is especially true when asking something of a person who considers you a friend (and if you are doing business with them, they probably have put you in the category of friend). As a rule of thumb, when a friend asks you to do something, it is never appropriate (by Egyptian standards) to say no. If an Egyptian answers a request with a non-committal yes or something like 'we must look into this', then the comment actually means 'probably no'. By the way, this is not to say that Egyptians will not try to get the better of a negotiation—but then, that is all just part of being a good businessman. Does this mean you will never hear 'no' uttered in a business negotiation? Probably not, but then it is easy to understand a direct no. The subtleties of the different kinds of 'yes' will more likely cause the most misunderstandings.

I have heard Westerners say they were cheated when there was really a misunderstanding as to what was agreed to in the first place. This can lead Westerners to believe that their Egyptian counterparts 'lied' to them, when in point of fact, the Egyptians had behaved honourably and honestly according to their own understanding of the agreement. I cannot tell you the number of times when trying to arrange things for my students that I thought there was total understanding as to who was to pay for or arrange what—only to find out later that my counterpart's understanding of the agreement was different from mine. This does not mean that my counterpart acted in a dishonourable or dishonest way—he did not. Rather, it meant that we simply did not communicate our respective expectations quite accurately. My only suggestion to avoid this kind of situation is to spell out in minute detail just what you expect. This won't eliminate all misunderstanding but can certainly reduce the frustration level and number of misunderstandings.

How meetings are conducted requires the development of flexibility and patience as well. If you expect to have the

Do's and Don'ts in the Workplace

- Do dress conservatively and well.
- Do offer guests coffee, tea and/or other refreshments.
- Don't be late for meetings (even though you may sit for an hour or more before you are called).
- Don't get irritated at waiting for a guest or to go into a meeting.
- Do bring business or personal cards for all meetings and guests.

undivided attention of your business host during a meeting, you will probably be disappointed or possibly confused.

Typically, during Western business meetings, all calls are stopped or some comment is made to let you know that some terribly important overseas or long-distance call may come in during your visit. You also expect, under most circumstances, that other individuals either leave or not interrupt the meeting. If you are expecting privacy and undivided attention, you may well need to forget this tradition for most meetings. Once you are ushered into your meeting, you may well find you are among five or ten other persons all sitting in the room at various places. Each is also trying to conduct business with the same person. Phones ring and are answered. Long conversations may ensue. People run in and out, catch the host's attention, and conduct their business just as though you were not sitting or standing there. You may find your temper swelling while thinking, 'What am I doing here? This person is not taking this seriously. Doesn't this person realise that time is money, and my time is valuable too?' Actually, conducting meetings in this way is common practice, not a personal statement or action against you.

The times I have experienced exceptions to this type of meeting seem to have occurred most commonly when I have met with ministers or other very high level officials. These individuals seem to follow a more customary Western-style business meeting approach, giving you more or less undivided attention. However, it is still not uncommon for a subordinate to come in and interrupt the discussion with pressing issues that simply cannot wait until your meeting is finished.

BUSINESS HOURS

Those accustomed to working from eight to five or, for that matter, seven in the morning to late evening, will find Egyptian business hours difficult to understand. The custom of working for eight hours straight is practically unheard of in most of Egypt. I have alluded to the fact that many shops and *souks* are usually open until late at night. Sometimes these establishments close for some time in the afternoon. Other times they do not close (for example in tourist areas), but you will notice a change in who is working. The reason this happens is the tradition of the afternoon nap.

Bureaucrats do not follow typical Western business hours either. As a rule, bureaucrats seem to work more or less between the hours of nine or ten in the morning through about two in the afternoon. Again, the custom is to leave for lunch around two and follow this with a nap. Usually people are still around in the building until a little later in the afternoon, but it seems impossible to get anything done except during the earlier hours.

Of course, if you are working with higher level ministerial people, you may find the hours somewhat different. Some higher ranking officials and other businessmen accustomed to working with Westerners tend to follow a schedule slightly more reminiscent of Western business hours, but do not expect this to be the norm. Count on not doing your work between approximately two and four, with possibly evening meetings as a supplement.

TOPICS TO AVOID

Nearly every book you read gives you hints on topics you should avoid in business meetings or with Egyptians in general. Usually, the well-meaning author reminds you not to ask any in-depth questions about a man's family, particularly his wife or daughters. On the other hand, if you know your colleague has a wife, three daughters and an ailing mother-in-law, it would seem cold not to make a casual comment roughly stating that you hope all is well with his family (or getting better as in the case of the sick mother-in-law). This shows your friendship and caring for him as a person. Certainly on a first meeting, you should not be the first to bring up the topic of his wife and daughters (most especially if you have never met them). Use good judgement and you probably won't go wrong.

The second topic usually listed to avoid is religion. This can be tricky since many Egyptians may well bring up the subject and you are left trying to figure out how to get out of discussing the topic. And, yes, this can even happen in a business meeting, particularly when you are going through some of the 'get-to-know-each-other' protocol. Interestingly, many Egyptians are fascinated about Western Christianity. This is another one of those cases where the media introduces some preconceived notions that might not be accurate from your point of view. For example, some have viewed American televangelists via cable or satellite and assume that all American Christians (maybe even Christians throughout the world) have similar views. Your best bet, should you get stuck in an awkward situation, is to try to shift the topic around to having them explain Islam to you. That way you can avoid making any statements that could be viewed as hostile or inappropriate, and you are showing an interest in them.

The third topic to avoid is politics, the government or government policy (unless of course you are asking questions about how these things affect your proposed business deal). This is another one of those topics that seem to fascinate Egyptians. Since you are a foreigner of presumed high ranking (or else you wouldn't be there), anything you say may be open to misinterpretation. In a worst case scenario, you could be perceived to be talking for your government. Unless you are a government representative there for that specific purpose (in which case you will have specific instructions), comments on your government's policies or their government's policies could have serious unfortunate repercussions. Egyptians will rarely express a personal opinion about their government or officials that is, in any way, negative if there are more than two people present (unless, of course, that is their business). They expect you to follow a similar stance.

Discussing sex or telling dirty jokes is not in the best taste either. Once I prepared a briefing sheet for some American university officials and duly reminded them to avoid dirty jokes and discussions of sex. After the meeting (all the participants were men), one of my colleagues quickly came up to me and said, "We didn't know what to do. They started telling us dirty jokes." There are a couple of ways to view this type of behaviour. First, your counterparts may well be trying to show you how cosmopolitan they are, thinking that you expect this type of conversation. Second, they may really like dirty jokes. In either event, you may very well lose respect if you start chiming in with, "Have you heard the one about...?" In any event, whether you find the conversation distasteful or just in bad form, not reacting at all or responding with only the very slightest smile will usually get you out of an awkward situation. This is not the place to ask where you can find a prostitute.

NEPOTISM
I hate using the word nepotism—it has such negative connotations in so many countries. Nepotism is defined as favouritism shown to relatives or close friends. Well, in Egypt—where so much is based on personal knowledge and trust—logically, you find a great deal of favouritism or patronage to family and close friends. It is accepted, expected, and the appropriate way to conduct business affairs. This is how business has been conducted for millennia. You would never consider doing business with someone you don't know or whose reputation cannot be

checked through friends and relatives! And, almost all new jobs are found by networking!

No matter how you personally feel about nepotism as a custom, from a pragmatic perspective, Egypt's nepotistic practices can work to your benefit in business. Once you have established the trust needed with one person, other doors seem to open magically. It seems that everyone you talk to has a relative doing exactly what you need. Not uncommonly, members of a family will have a brother or cousin or father or uncle or in-law in just the position desperately needed to help with your project.

BRIBES

Only a very fine line of distinction separates bribes from gifts from *baksheesh*. Is a little 'tip' given to an official who has helped you get some paper signed a bribe or *baksheesh*? Depends on your perspective, doesn't it? (*See the section on 'Baksheesh and Tipping' in* Chapter Four: Social Interactions, *page 111.*) Some refer to it as the informal cost of doing business in Egypt. Payment of bribes is illegal under many foreign laws. In higher level negotiations, certainly direct payment of a cash supplement to an official would seem inappropriate in Egypt as well as elsewhere. It would not, however, seem inappropriate to engage someone (or their son or brother, etc.) who has a separate business (but is also in an influential position) as a consultant or agent on your project by Egyptian standards.

On a more pragmatic level, sometimes a little *baksheesh* can assist getting a needed signature in a timely fashion. One situation I observed related to the need for a police report for purposes of an insurance claim on goods stolen from a hotel room. The question of retrieving the goods was never a real issue since it was assumed that they were long gone. Rather than calling the police at the time of the alleged theft (which would have involved all kinds of hassles, inquiries and searches), the person was advised that 'it would be easier' to wait until later and simply get a police report in another city, for a cos of E£ 20. Indeed, it took about an hour, several weeks later, to acquire an appropriate police report for insurance purposes. There was no delay and no hassle, and everyone left satisfied (except, of course, for the fact that the goods were still missing).

SETTING UP A BUSINESS
Several types of business organisations exist in Egypt, generally in the form of incorporated companies, partnerships and sole proprietorships. Foreigners are rarely interested in the unincorporated forms used by Egyptian traders.

Most foreign investors choose the Limited Liability Company, known as a WLL (with limited liability). The Joint Stock Company (Shareholder Company) is the most commonly used form of corporate business entity in Egypt. Foreign investors may carry on business in Egypt through a branch office. However, this provides no tax advantage. Companies whose sole interest is the exportation of goods to Egypt must generally appoint a local agent who must be an Egyptian national or company. Labour requirements apply to all companies whose capital exceeds E£ 50,000.

Business Information

A good source of information on how to establish a business in Egypt is the National Trade Data Bank, available over the Internet for a fee. Go to:

http://www.stat-usa.gov/tradtest.nsf

and click under 'Commercial Guide'. Note that you have to be a subscriber to access the information.

Alternatively, you can check out the American Chamber of Commerce in Egypt website at:

(http://www.amcham.org.eg) for business news.

DEALING WITH THE BUREAUCRACY

Bureaucracies anywhere can be a definite pain! Unfortunately, to establish a business or conduct many business transactions in Egypt requires working with the bureaucratic infrastructure. Rarely can you simply go to the local office, pick up and fill out the papers, and expect things to get done in a timely fashion. It always appears to involve a lengthy process which can try one's patience. True, the Egyptian government is making significant changes to facilitate movement through the bureaucracy, especially for the development of new businesses, but reality changes slowly—very, very slowly, no matter how good it looks in the press.

Why is working with the Egyptian bureaucracy so problematic? Of course, part of the problem is the massive paperwork and permits needed to get anything done. But there is one other more perplexing problem. What happened to all those forms you so dutifully submitted to the person at the desk? How could they just disappear into the bottomless chasm of Egyptian bureaucracy? Easy! Everyone must have his input.

Now don't forget that every Egyptian who has a job (especially one of the valued white-collar jobs) feels pride and honour with the job. This means they must show how important they are (and that they actually do have a role in the process). Overlaying this need to show personal importance is that old bugaboo deference. Each person must filter every action to the person next in line above them and, no matter what, it seems difficult to jump layers in the deference scale unless—and this is important—unless you have the personal contacts to get straight through to the person you need. This is where having an Egyptian agent (required for some kinds of enterprises) or business partner who is well connected can come in very useful.

Bottom line: getting permissions or permits that should take only pro forma approval may well involve going through many, many lower officials to finally get to the one person who actually has the authority to put the required signature on the needed form.

EGYPT AT A GLANCE

CHAPTER 10

'There can be hope only for a society which
acts as one big family, not as many separate ones.'
—Anwar el-Sadat

Official Name
Arab Republic of Egypt

Capital
Cairo

Flag
Three equal horizontal stripes of red, white and black (from top to bottom) with the national emblem, the Golden Eagle of Saladin, in the centre, within the white stripe.

National Anthem
Bilady, Bilady, Bilady (My Homeland, My Homeland, My Homeland)

Time
Greenwich Mean Time plus 2 hours (GMT +0200) with daylight savings of an extra hour.

Telephone Country Code
20

Land
Located in North Africa, Egypt has the Mediterranean Sea to its north, Sudan to its south and Libya to its west. Its eastern

neighbour, separated by the Red Sea, is Saudi Arabia, while Israel and Jordan are to its north-east.

Area
total: 1,001,450 sq km (386,662 sq miles)
land: 995,450 sq km (384,345.4 sq miles)
water: 6,000 sq km (2,316.6 sq miles)

Highest Point
Mount Catherine (2,629 m / 8,625.3 ft)

Climate
Mainly desert weather where the summers are hot and dry but winters are moderate.

Natural Resources
Asbestos, gypsum, iron ore, lead, limestone, manganese, natural gas, petroleum, phosphates, talc and zinc.

Population
77,505,756 (July 2005 est)

Ethnic Groups
99 per cent of the people of are Eastern Hamitic stock (i.e. Egyptian, Bedouin or Berber backgrounds) while the remaining 1 per cent are either Greek, Nubian, Armenian or other European.

Religion
Predominantly Muslim with about 6 per cent Coptic Christian and other religions.

Official Language
Arabic

Government Structure
Republic

Adminstrative Divisions
26 governates: Ad Daqahliyah, Al Bahr al Ahmar, Al Buhayrah, Al Fayyum, Al Gharbiyah, Al Iskandariyah, Al Isma'iliyah, Al Jizah, Al Minufiyah, Al Minya, Al Qahirah, Al Qalyubiyah, Al Wadi al Jadid, Ash Sharqiyah, As Suways, Aswan, Asyut, Bani Suwayf, Bur Sa'id, Dumyat, Janub Sina', Kafr ash Shaykh, Matruh, Qina, Shamal Sina', Suhaj

Currency
Egyptian pound (EGP or E£)

Gross Domestic Product (GDP)
US$ 316.3 billion (2004 est)

Agricultural Products
Beans, corn, cotton, fruits, rice, vegetables and wheat.

Other Products
Cattle, goats, sheep and water buffalo.

Industries
Cement, chemicals, construction, food processing, hydrocarbons, metals, textiles and tourism.

Exports
Chemicals, cotton, crude oil, metal products, petroleum products and textiles.

Imports
Chemicals, foodstuffs, fuels, machinery and equipment as well as wood products.

Airports
Estimated total of 87, of which 72 have paved runways. The main international airport is in Cairo.

Weights and Measures
Egypt operates on the metric system, European-sized clothes and shoes, and the Centigrade/ Celsius temperature

scale. This poses no problem for people from Europe or the UK, but throws Americans into a tizzy trying to figure out what is what. Below are listed a few of the most common conversions.

Temperature

Centigrade/ Celsius	Farenheit
0	32
5	41
10	50
15	59
20	68
25	77
30	86
35	95
40	104
45	113

Length

1 metre	is	39.4 inches 3.28 feet 1.09 yards 0.001 kilometres
1 foot	is	12 inches 0.305 metres 1 yard 0.000305 kilometres
1 mile	is	1.61 kilometres 5,280 feet
1 kilometre	is	0.621 miles 3,280 feet

Weight

1 pound	is	0.454 kilogrammes 16 ounces (avoirdupois)

1 ounce	is	0.0283 kilogrammes 28.3 grams
1 kilogramme	is	2.2 pounds 35.3 ounces
1 gramme	is	0.0022 pounds 0.0353 ounces

Women's Shoe Sizes

American	6	6.5	7	7.5	8	8.5	9
UK	4.5	5	5.5	6	6.5	7	7.5
Continental	36	37	38	38	38	39	40

Men's Shoe Sizes

American	5.5	6.5	7.5	8.5	9.5	10.5	11.5
UK	5	6	7	8	9	10	11
Continental	39	40	41	42	43	44	45

Women's Clothing

American	10	12	14	16	18	20	22
UK	32	34	36	38	40	42	44
Continental	38	40	42	44	46	48	50

Suits, Overcoats, and Sweaters

American	34	36	38	40	42	44	46
UK	34	36	38	40	42	44	46
Continental	44	46	48	50	52	54	56

Collar Sizes

American	14	14.5	15	15.5	16	16.5	17
UK	14	14.5	15	15.5	16	16.6	17
Continental	36	37	38	39	40	41	42

FAMOUS PEOPLE

Ramses II

The son of Seti I and Queen Tuya, Ramses II was the third king (1279–1213 BC) of the 19th Dynasty. Called Ramesses the Great, he lived to be 96 years old, had 200 wives and concubines, 96 sons and 60 daughters. His favourite wife was apparently Nefertari for whom he built a temple in Abu Simbel. In addition to his great tomb (KV 7), Ramses II built a great tomb for his sons, KV 5, which is currently being excavated.

Hatshepsut

The fifth ruler (1473–1458 BC) of the 18th Dynasty, she was the daughter of Thutmose I and Queen Ahmose. As was common in royal families, she married her half-brother, Thutmose II, who had a son, Thutmose III, by a minor wife. When Thutmose II died in 1479 BC, his son, Thutmose III, was appointed heir. However, Hatshepsut was appointed regent due to the boy's young age. They ruled jointly until 1473 BC when she declared herself pharaoh. Dressed in men's attire, Hatshepsut administered affairs of the nation. Hatshepsut disappeared from the historical record in 1458 BC when Thutmose III, wishing to reclaim the throne, led a revolt. Thutmose III then had her shrines, statues and reliefs mutilated.

Tutankhamun

'King Tut', aka 'the Boy King' probably ruled Egypt between 1334–1325 BC, possibly the 12th ruler of Egypt's 18th Dynasty. Not considered to be an important pharaoh, prior to Howard Carter's discovery of his tomb, almost nothing was known of him. One disappointment in Carter's discovery was that there was little in the way of documentation found within his tomb. Akhenaten, the heretic pharaoh, was most likely his father. His mother was probably Kiya, though this too is in question.

Cleopatra

In the springtime of 51 BC, Ptolemy Auletes died and left his kingdom in his will to his 18-year-old daughter, Cleopatra, and her younger brother Ptolemy XIII who was 12 at the time. Cleopatra was born in 69 BC in Alexandria. Her death on 12 August 30 BC at the age of 39 marked the end of the Egyptian Monarchs as it coincided with the Roman Emperors coming in to rule in Egypt. The Ptolemies were Macedonian in descent, but ruled as Egyptians, as Pharaohs. Cleopatra was the last Pharaoh of Egypt.

Naguib Mahfouz (1911–)

Egyptian writer who was awarded the Nobel Prize for Literature in 1988, and was the first Arabic writer to be so honored. Born in Cairo, Naguib Mahfouz began writing when he was 17 and until 1972, was employed as a civil servant. Mahfouz's major work in the 1950s was *The Cairo Trilogy*, which the author completed before the July Revolution. The individual novels were titled with the street names *Palace Walk*, *Palace of Desire* and *Sugar Street*. Mahfouz set the tri-generational story on a ficticious, tiny winding street named Zuqaq al-Midaq in the neighborhoods of Cairo where he grew up.

Gamal Abdel Nasser (1918–1970)

Born in Alexandria to a family that comes from the Assiut Governorate, Nasser was brought up and educated in Alexandria and Cairo. He led a nationalist movement in 1952 that ousted the Egyptian monarchy and transformed Egypt into a republic. Nasser became Prime Minister of Egypt in 1954 and subsequently negotiated an end to Britain's 72-year occupation of Egypt. Nasser was elected president of Egypt in 1956 and remained in office until his death in 1970. His accomplishments included the construction of the Aswan High Dam, the institution of land reforms and a programme of industrialisation, and the restoration of Egyptian self-government.

Anwar el-Sadat (1918–1981)

Muhammad Anwar el-Sadat succeeded Gamal Abdel Nasser as the president of Egypt in 1970, and retained the office until he was assassinated in 1981. He shared the 1978 Nobel Prize for Peace with Israeli prime minister Menachem Begin. In 1979, Egypt and Israel signed a peace treaty. As a result, Sadat's popularity fell dramatically in Egypt due to internal opposition to the treaty, worsening economic conditions, and his suppression of resulting public dissent. He was assassinated by Muslim extremists while reviewing a military parade commemorating the Arab-Israeli war of October 1973.

Hosni Mubarak (1928–)

Mubarak succeeded Anwar el-Sadat as president of Egypt on 14 October 1981. He was re-elected in 1987, 1993 and 1999. President Hosni Mubarak was born in the Al-Menoufiyah governorate, located in the heart of Egypt, in the Delta area.

CULTURE QUIZ

SITUATION 1

You and your family have been in Cairo for a few months. In a conversation with one of your new Egyptian friends, you express interest in taking your family to visit the beach in Ismailia over the weekend. Your contact tells you, "Oh, I have a lovely villa there which is yours to use. I will arrange everything." On the assigned date, a driver arrives to take you to Ismailia. When you get there, you find that arrangements have been made for a grand meal at a local restaurant. The driver stays in Ismailia to drive you anywhere you want to go while there and then take you back to Cairo the next evening. When you get back to Cairo, you pay the driver for his services and also give him what can be considered a good tip. Next day, you visit your friend to tell him how wonderful the trip was and express your thanks for all the hospitality and use of the villa in Ismailia. He tells you, it was "No problem. You are welcome." Then he tells you that the cost for the trip is E£ 420. Your response is:

ⓐ "I already paid the driver. Give me a detailed list of the other costs and I will be happy to pay you for that."

ⓑ React with annoyance and shock, and refuse to pay, saying, "Well, where I come from when we invite someone to visit, we don't ask them to pay."

ⓒ Thank him for his gracious hospitality, telling him that this is so little to pay for such a wonderful weekend.

Comments

Well, if you never want to see this friend again, choose either **ⓐ** or **ⓑ**. If the friend means something to you, choose **ⓒ** and write it off to experience. Even though with **ⓐ**, you already paid the driver according to your way of thinking, your friend arranged for the driver. Therefore, any money you gave the driver was considered a 'tip' by him. **ⓑ** is just blatantly insulting to your Egyptian friend.

It is easy to fall into this kind of situation. Your Egyptian friend is not misleading you by offering to arrange everything. They may even suggest you be their guest at their villa, but this still may not mean you would not be expected to pay for the costs. In other situations, especially if your Egyptian friend is quite wealthy, they would not ask you to compensate them for any expenses incurred. In this situation, your friend would assume you would reciprocate on another occasion.

When in doubt, ask. There are a couple of ways to handle this situation beforehand. First, when something like this happens, you could easily tell your friend something like, "Wow, it is great of you to offer. How much do you think it will cost for transportation and everything?" Another way you might want to handle an offer that seems too good to be true or when you don't want to be obligated for a future reciprocation is to say something like, "Oh, I would never presume to impose on you. We would expect to pay for all costs associated with such generosity. How much will that be?"

Most of the time, if your friends actually expect you to pay for something, they will be straightforward and treat it as a business deal—especially if you ask. But, don't forget the 'rule of threes'. Your hosts may first protest that you shouldn't pay. If they do this, be sure to say something like, "Oh, no. I couldn't let you do that much." You should go through this kind of banter until they insist the third time, at which point you can feel free to accept because it means they actually mean you should not pay. Just remember to try to give them an opportunity for a way out since they may feel obligated to offer even if they cannot afford to.

SITUATION 2

You are responsible for arranging seating for a luncheon meeting for some visiting foreign business people and some Egyptians. Among the 12 Egyptians attending will be the Minister of Important Affairs (fictitious ministry), a distinguished scholar, three prominent business representatives, a university dean, a retired ambassador who advises the prime minister, the consul general assigned to your country and various other persons. Your home country's delegation will be 12 people, among whom will be: the president and CEO of Conglomerate International, a corporate vice president from another company, the project developer (the person who actually did all the work to make the business deal possible and the person who actually knows the answers to any questions that might be raised), a representative from your country's embassy in Cairo, yourself, and various other persons involved in the deal. How do you seat the people?

Ⓐ Have four tables for six so everyone can sit with their own country's people. They will want to sit with their friends anyway and catch up on the gossip.

Ⓑ Have one long table with seats on each side and let people choose their own seat or assign seats.

Ⓒ Place six or eight people from your country at a head table, with the Egyptian contingency down each side along with the others from your country.

Ⓓ Arrange for a horseshoe-styled table. Seat the three most prominent Egyptians and three most senior people from your country at the head table; alternate the remaining seating between country representatives according to ranking (senior-most ranked persons closest to the head table).

Comments

Well, this one can be difficult because there might be some hidden relative status factors of which you are not aware. **A** is not good because it undermines your intent which is to foster an opportunity for cross-communication between Egyptian and home country people. **C** is equally inappropriate, but for a different reason. Choosing this option suggests that people from your home country are in some way superior to your Egyptian hosts—not the impression you want to give, assuming you want to do business in the country.

B is a possibility, but better if you direct people to seats either across from or next to a person of similar status. The hazard of letting people choose their own seats is not with the Egyptians (they will undoubtedly assort according to rank), but with your home country participants. Your home country colleagues may well not recognise the importance of status in seating or how their position among the group is perceived. This could easily lead to a low-ranking person sitting next to a very high-ranking Egyptian; after all, who wouldn't want to sit next to a minister, for example.

D gives you the best opportunity to recognise important persons from both groups. The tricky part then becomes determining who should sit at the head table. If there is a doubt about who should be recognised in this manner, ask a trusted Egyptian friend. In the example given, the Egyptians you would probably choose to sit at the head table would most likely be the minister, the retired ambassador and the visiting consul general. Among the visitors, you would probably choose the CEO, the embassy representative, and either the project director or the visiting company vice president, depending on how you perceive their importance. Since you are the organiser, you might also seat yourself at the head table, next to the podium so you can easily introduce your speakers.

SITUATION 3

You decide you want to have a few people over to your house for an informal gathering—just sitting around and talking. One of your favourite friends is a local taxi driver and entrepreneur (on the side). But you really want to have some of your Egyptian business acquaintances, some of whom are professors, over as well to meet some of your home country friends. Who do you invite?

Ⓐ Invite them all over at once. They can all mingle around the punch bowl and buffet. It will be good for your Egyptian friends to meet people from different social strata.

Ⓑ Invite the taxi driver and his family at one time, your business acquaintances at another.

Ⓒ Forget it, just invite foreign friends, it is easier.

Comments

It would not be socially appropriate to invite the taxi driver and business acquaintances at the same time. Choosing **Ⓐ** would place all of your Egyptian friends in an awkward position and would not change the existing social structure one iota. Choosing **Ⓑ** is the best choice for being able to share an evening with all of your Egyptian friends. **Ⓒ** would certainly not insult anyone, but would definitely limit your social circle.

SITUATION 4

You are a man doing business in Egypt. Your colleague, Mr Moustafa, invites you to a meeting at his house for six o'clock on Wednesday evening. When you get there (you are 15 minutes early), you hear scuffling behind the door and a small voice tells you, "No one is at home.".

Ⓐ You scream, "Of course you are home, I hear you."

Ⓑ You try to explain that you have a meeting with Mr Moustafa at six, but that you are a little early, and insist that you be allowed to come in.

Ⓒ You try reason, explaining that your taxi just left and that it is too hot to wait on the porch.

D You tell them who you are and that you will wait on the porch for Mr Moustafa to come home.

E You tell your taxi driver to wait before you go to the door, just in case no one is at home. After being told no one is there, you leave, go have a coffee or tea, and return in 30 minutes to an hour later.

Comments

A, **B** and **C** are definitely bad choices. Responses **D** or **E** are acceptable, but probably **E** is preferable under the circumstances. The reason you got the response you did was because there were only women at home when you called; or possibly it was a servant answering the door. In this case, it would be inappropriate for you to be allowed into the house. The first mistake was coming early. For one thing, because of the problems with Cairo traffic, Mr Moustafa may have been delayed in traffic. Alternatively, even though Mr. Moustafa told you to be there at six, he may not really expect you to be exactly on time, much less early. To avoid this kind of situation, a couple of things could be done. First, don't come early. Second, you could stop somewhere close to Mr Moustafa's house and use a public phone to determine if he is there or you could call before you leave just to reconfirm that Mr Moustafa will be there when you arrive. In any event, give Mr Moustafa a little extra time and never challenge the word of the woman answering the door.

SITUATION 5

You (a woman) and three of your women friends are out shopping and need a taxi to take you back home. It is a busy time of day and taxis are hard to find.

A You all decide to get into one small taxi which will hold only three in the back so that one of you must sit in the front seat with the driver.

B Even though it will cost more and may take more time, you get two taxis, so two can sit comfortably in each one.

C You decide to wait until you see one of the station wagon-sized taxis. Although you may have to wait for some time and it will cost a little more than one small taxi, a station wagon will allow all of the women to travel together while sitting in a back seat.

Comments

Either **B** or **C** is appropriate. Although each of these options is inconvenient and will cost more, they are the better choice because a good Egyptian woman (unless she is very old) would not consider sitting in the front seat with a taxi driver. To do so might invite the driver to make advances to you and could be seen as a sexual come-on.

DO'S AND DON'TS

I have made so many cultural blunders that I struggle to determine which belong to the 'most common' category. Here are some you should keep in mind.

DO'S

- Ask when you don't understand something
  No one will be insulted or think you are dumb if you say, "Should I think of this like an American or Egyptian?" If you don't know what is expected of you, ask, "What am I expected to do?" or "What am I expected to wear?" or "What is the proper way to address him/her?" If you don't know what something means, just ask. Most Egyptians will be all too willing to assist you.
- Respect your Egyptian hosts and you are more likely to be respected in return
  I feel almost foolish stating something this obvious. But I have seen many expatriates who look down their noses at their Egyptian hosts and regard them as somehow inferior. If you do that, it is little wonder why your hosts view you with contempt.
- Attend to your own personal cultural needs
  You can't, nor should you, renounce your own cultural values in an effort to fit into the Egyptian milieu. Sure, you should respect your host's values, but also remember to respect your own. In every day practice, you will probably find some sort of middle ground that accommodates both world views.
- Women, do sit next to women on public transportation. You are much less likely to get unwanted attention if you, for example, take the front car on the undergound train.
- Do be sensitive when discussing the Egyptian government, religion, culture and law.
- Do wear sunscreen and keep insect repellent available.
- Do avoid off-road travel. Unless you are travelling with a guide or someone who knows the area, you should not be there. Remember, there are still some unspent

landmines in some parts of Egypt. It is my understanding that they are behind fences, but can also move with the shifting sand.

- Do avoid drinking brands of hard liquor you are not familiar with.

DON'T

- Don't overestimate your understanding of the Egyptian world

  It seems that as soon as I think I understand what's expected of me, I miscalculate a small item, and there I go again. So, I would have to say foreigners' number one blunder is to think they have actually become multicultural. You haven't and probably won't even approach a good multicultural understanding of the Egyptian world without many years of immersion. But you can avoid some of the most frequent cultural faux pas by remembering that you still have much to learn.

- Don't over- or underestimate your Egyptian colleague's understanding of your language or your culture

  Thinking people understand what I mean when I say or do something ranks number two on my list. Why? On the surface, it seems a simple proposition—say what you mean and you will be understood. Not so! Language is inescapably intertwined with cultural practices and symbolism.

  Let me give you a recent example of how I blundered with this one. Following an email request for information, I mistakenly wrote a response to a very Westernised, educated Egyptian friend stating something to the effect of, 'Oh, by the way, this is what I do for a living. Please tell them we need to negotiate a contract and I will be happy to provide the information'. Because my friend was so aware of Western practices, I assumed we were talking on Western terms, not Egyptian. Big, big mistake! Well, it doesn't take a rocket scientist to figure out my mistake. By assuming we were talking on Western rather than Egyptian terms, I had inadvertently broken all the rules of friendship. He had asked me, as a friend, for information. Yet I responded as a Westerner would in a business proposal. Fortunately, he, too, realised what had happened and started thinking American. In general, however, don't count on most Egyptians thinking things your way. Even if they have a very good command of the language, subtleties will be overlooked! Also, we Westerners, especially Americans, use words in English differently at different times and in different places. Someone whose native language is not English may know only one or possibly two meanings for a word or a 'sound-alike' word. The subtleties of word usage are not always known by someone who is not from where you originate.

- Don't assume you belong
  I recently made the exact opposite blunder. I requested information I needed from an Internet community to which I belong. I assumed that because I was a member, it did not matter that I was American. Wrong again! The list master politely informed me that I needed to take out an advertisement on their webpage if I wanted information from the group to use for 'proprietary' purposes. The cultural blunder? I assumed we were talking in Egyptian terms. I had asked as a friend and member of the community for assistance, and received a response in American business terms. Oh well, live and learn!

- Don't get drunk and rowdy in public, and don't even consider driving drunk in Egypt
  Yes, it is true that Islam forbids alcohol consumption. It is also true that alcohol consumption is legal in Egypt. Do Egyptians drink alcohol? Some do, which explains the need for the new drunk-driving penalties. Am I telling you it is a cultural blunder to drink alcohol in Egypt? Yes and no. What I am saying is that the perception of alcohol consumption is somewhat hypocritical. Egyptians assume that if you are from the West, you must drink alcohol. This is based on overgeneralisation and the practices Egyptians see among tourists. Do bear in mind that alcohol consumption is perceived as a major example of foreign decadence. My suggestion is this: if you are going

to drink alcohol, keep public consumption minimal. No sense asking for contempt or trouble.

- Don't sit on, climb on or touch archaeological monuments. There will likely be someone in a uniform, or a monument guard that will tell you if you make this mistake! And, in no uncertain terms!

- Don't be surprised to see Egyptian men holding hands. Women, too, can hold hands or link arms. It doesn't mean they are gay.

- Couples, don't show too much affection in public. Handholding is OK.

- Don't drive without an international driver's licence. I still don't drive there, but definitely would not want to get into an accident without a proper licence.

- Don't try to come close to diplomatic convoys. Just makes sense—no sense tempting fate!

- Don't swim when and where a black flag is raised; it means the surf is too rough.

- Don't sunbathe topless, though Western-style swimsuits are acceptable on some beaches.

- Don't carry a lot of money, but do carry a lot of small change for tips.

- Don't visit mosques during prayer time.

- Women, don't enter a mosque without covering your head. Make sure your arms and legs are covered as well.

- Don't bring illegal drugs into Egypt and don't attempt to buy drugs there.

- Don't drink on the street—make sure you are at a designated bar, disco or at a private residence—unless you are in a tourist place where this is common.

- Don't smoke, eat or drink in public during the month of Ramadan.

The remains of the storage granaries of Ramesseum. When visiting Egypt's national monuments and treasures, do not sit, climb or touch them. Uniformed personnel will be on hand to make sure that you don't.

GLOSSARY

The following is a list of names and proper nouns which will be helpful to know during your stay in Egypt. Pronuncitation of the words are in parenthesis.

Allah (AHL-lah)	Arabic word for 'God'
Anwar el-Sadat (AHN-wahr al-sah-DATT)	president of Egypt between 1970–1981
Aten (AH-ten)	the Sun God in ancient Egypt
Bahri (BAH-ree)	the dialect of Egypt spoken in Cairo that forms the basis of Egyptian colloquial Arabic
Ballana (BAL-lah-na)	one of the women who prepares a bride for her wedding
Bedouins (BED-wins or BED-oo-ins)	one of a nomadic group of Arabs living in Egypt, North Africa, and the Arabian Peninsula
Diocletian	Roman Emperor who ascended the throne in AD 284 and is known for persecuting Christians in Egypt.
Eid el-Adha (eye-EED el-ODD-ha)	the big feast
Eid el-Fitr (eye-EED el-FIT-er)	the little feast
El Alamein (el-AL-ah-mane)	famous World War II battleground in the northern part of Egypt
En Passant (IN pah-SANH)	a person who is passing through an area

Felafel (feh-LAH-fal)	see *ta'miya*
Fellahin (FELL-ah-heen)	a small-scale farmer. The lifestyle of most *fellahins* has only recently begun to change with mechanised cultivation. The term originates from the Arabic word meaning 'farmer'.
Felucca (feh-LUKE-kah)	a narrow wooden sailing boat with a lateen sail used in Egypt. These boats are of various sizes, often around 7.5 m (25 feet) long, and have been used in Egypt for many centuries. Today, *feluccas* are used to transport goods, tourists, and other people up and down the Nile River.
Fuul hamam (FOOHL heh-MAM)	small, round, dark-brown beans

An Egyptian *felucca*, used as transport along the Nile River.

Fuul or *Fool* or *Foul* (FOOHL)	beans
Galabea (GAHL-ah-BAY-yah)	also spelled *jalabaya*. A loose, traditional garment worn by men and women in Egypt that is ankle length, and usually has long, flowing sleeves.
Gamal Abdel Nasser (guh-MAHL AB-dul NAH-sur)	first president of modern Egypt (1952–1970)
Giza (GHEE-zah)	district of Cairo that begins at the west bank of the Nile River and extends west for 20 km (12.4 miles) to the Great Pyramids
Hadith (ha-DEETH)	the sayings of Muhammed
Hejira (heh-JEER-rah)	the flight of Muhammed from Mecca to Medina in the year AD 622. It marks the first year of the Islamic calendar.
Iftar (IF-tar)	literally, 'break the fast'. Meal taken after sunset during the month of Ramadan to break the fast.
Intefah (EN-te-FAH)	opening
Khamsin (kahm-SEEN)	hot, dry wind and sandstorms during April and May
Khedive (kah-DEEV)	a viceroy or governor of Egypt ruling on behalf of the Ottoman Empire
Khushmaan (kush-MAHN)	one clan among the Ma'aza tribe of Egyptian Bedouins
Ma'aza (MAH-ah-zah)	a tribe of Egyptians living in the Eastern Desert of Egypt

Mahr (MAHR)	a marriage payment from the groom's father to the bride's
Mamluks (MAM-eh-LUKES)	originally slaves of the Ottoman Turks who were converted to Islam, became military officers, and eventually ruled Egypt
Mecca (MECK-kah)	a city in Saudi Arabia that is considered to be the holiest city to Muslims
Medina (meh-DEEN-ah)	holy city to Muslims, located north of Mecca
Messaharatis (MES-sah-ha-RAH-tees)	men who go through the streets before dawn to remind people to eat their *Sohour*
Mosque (MAWSK)	the place Muslims go to worship
Muslim (MUZ-lem)	a person who practises the faith of Islam
Naguib Mahfouz (nah-GEEB MAH-foos)	famous Egyptian author who won the Nobel Prize for Literature in 1988
Nawashef (NAH-wah-shef)	dry foods
Nilometer	a measuring device used by the ancient Egyptians to measure the rising and falling of the Nile River
Nubian (NOO-be-an)	Nubians are a group of dark-skinned Egyptians. Historically, Nubians lived in the area stretching from Aswan to the Sudan border. After the Aswan High Dam was built in the 1970s, most Egyptian Nubians were moved to villages north of Aswan, around the town of Kom Ombo.

Papyrus (pah-PIE-rus)	a tall, aquatic reed (sedge) or paper originally made from the stems of the reed in ancient Egypt
Pharaoh (FAY-rohs)	ancient Egyptian kings
Piaster or piastre (pea-AS-ter)	a segment of the Egyptian pound (E£), Egypt's monetary currency. An Egyptian pound is made up of 100 piastres. One piastre is approximately equivalent to less than one-third of a US cent.
Qur'an (KOOR-rahn)	the holy book of Islam
Ramadan (RAH-mah-dahn)	the holy month of fasting for Muslims
Saidi (sy-EE-dee)	the dialect of Arabic spoken in Upper Egypt
Saqqara (sahk-KAH-rah)	the necropolis (cemetery) of Egypt when Memphis was its capital in the days of the Old Kingdom
Septimus Severus	Roman Emperor who ruled from AD 193–211
Sham el-Nessim (SHEM el-NESS-sem)	'scent of spring'; a festival of spring
Shisha (SHEE-sha)	Shisha is a gummy form of tobacco combined with molasses. Sometimes flavours, such as apple, are added to the tobacco. This Egyptian tobacco is smoked in large water pipes by men at cafés and at home.
Shistosomiasis (SHIS-toe-so-MY-a-sis)	a tropical disease caused by a parasite called shistosome

Shura (SHUR-rah)	the Consultative Council in the framework of Egyptian law. The Shura serves only as an advisory panel to the People's Assembly. The Shura does not pass laws.
Sohour (so-HOO-ur)	meal taken before dawn during Ramadan
Sunna (SOON-nah)	the 'beaten path'. The Sunna refers to the sayings, deeds, and approvals of the Prophet Muhammed.
Tahrir Square (tah-REER)	square at the centre of Cairo
Ta'miya (TA-ah-MEE-ya)	also called *felafel*; a fried bean cake
Wadi (WAHD-ee)	dry stream bed
Waseet (wah-SEET)	a mediator sent to a girl's parents to determine if she is single and/or to ask her parents for her hand in marriage

SOME USEFUL WORDS

English	Arabic-Egyptian
no	*la'*
yes	*aiwa or naam*
absolutely not	*'bitta-kiid la'*
thank you	*shukran*
welcome	*ahlan*
you're welcome, not at all, don't mention it	*afwan* (often shortened to *aff*)
perhaps	*yemken*
possibly	*mumken*

English	Arabic-Egyptian
impossible	*mesh mumken*
necessary	*daruri*
please	*men fadlak* (for males) *men fadlik* (for females)
hello, good to see you	*ahlan wa sahlan*
good morning	*sabah el kheer*
good morning (reply)	*sabah e-noor*
good evening	*mise el kheer*
good evening (reply)	*mise e-noor*
how?	*izzay?*
how are you?	*izzayak?* (to a man) *izzayik?* (to a woman)
I'm fine	*kwiyis* (man) *kwiyissa* (woman) or *el hamdu lilah* ('thanks be to God')
I feel better	*'ahhsan*
what is your name?	*isme ke?* (to a man) *isme ki?* (to a woman)
please	*min'fadhlek*
sorry	*asif*
not at all	*'abadan*
goodbye	*maa e-salemma*
what?	*ay?*
who?	*meen?*
when?	*emta?*
where?	*fin?*
which?	*aya?*
why not?	*'leeh la?*
how much?	*bikam?*
so much	*laa'bas*
that's enough	*'yikfii*

English	Arabic-Egyptian
I love you	*ana ohebak*
I speak English	*ana batkallem englizi*
I don't speak Arabic?	*ma-batkallamsh 'arabi?*
I don't understand	*ana mish fahem*
do you speak English?	*int betetkalem inglizi?*
bridge	*kubri*
today	*en-nahar da*
tomorrow	*bukra*
yesterday	*imbarih*
again	*'marrah 'thaanyeh*
always	*'daayim*
I'm sorry	*ana 'aasif*
Never mind, it doesn't matter	*malesh*
What do you think?	*'wish 'raayak?*
I can do it	*'agder asa'wiih*
I don't think so	*'maaetagid*
Do you mean it?	*ayn 'djid*
I want a...	*ana a-iyiz...* (man) *ana a-iza...* (woman)
I don't want any	*mish a-iyiz*
I want to go to...	*ana a-iyiz arooh...*
a little	*shuaya*
7-Up	*7-Up*
Pepsi	*Pepsi*
Coca-cola	*kakola*
mineral water	*maya ma adanaya*
fresh orange juice	*aseer farowla*
hibiscus drink	*karkaday*
I would like coffee please	*min 'fadhlak aetny 'gahwah*
cappuccino coffee	*ahua 'cappuccino'*
Turkish coffee	*ahua*

English	Arabic-Egyptian
bitter coffee	*ahua sadah*
moderately sweet coffee	*ahua maazbut*
extremely sweet coffee	*ahua ziyadah*
cocoa	*kakow*
tea	*shay*
sugar	*sokkar*
milk	*halib*
hot	*sokhn*
cold	*bared*
God	*Allah*
God willing	*in sha'allah*
There is no other God but God	*la illah illa Allah*
God is great	*Allah akbar; Allah wa akbar*
God, make this a safe country	*haza baladan aminan*
Patience is beautiful	*e-sabr gameel*

DAYS OF THE WEEK

Monday	*El-etnein*
Tuesday	*El-talat*
Wednesday	*El-arbaa*
Thursday	*El-khamees*
Friday	*El-gumaa*
Saturday	*El-sabt*
Sunday	*El-had*

MONTHS OF THE YEAR

January	*Yanayer*
February	*Febrayer*

March	*Mares*
April	*Abryl*
May	*Mayu*
June	*Yunya*
July	*Yulyo*
August	*Aghustus*
September	*September*
October	*Octeber*
November	*November*
December	*December*

NUMBERS

one	*wahed*
two	*etnein*
three	*talata*
four	*arbaa*
five	*khamsa*
six	*sitta*
seven	*sabaa*
eight	*tamania*
nine	*tesaa*
ten	*ashaara*
fifty	*khamsin*
one hundred	*mia*
five hundred	*khams mia*
one thousand	*alf*

RESOURCE GUIDE

I have done my best to get accurate telephone numbers and Internet addresses. However, the reader should note that Egypt is undergoing such rapid growth that numbers and addresses may change by the time you try to access them. If you do find yourself in a situation where a number or address has changed and have access to the Internet, check there first. Alternatively, almost anyone at a major hotel, especially in a business centre, will be able to assist you. You can also check with the folks at the Internet cafés.

GENERAL INTERNET RESOURCE SITES
- Tour Egypt (best site for just about everything in Egypt)
  Website: http://www.touregypt.net
- Arab.Net
  Website: http://www.arab.net
- Egypt Focus
  Website: http://www.egyptfocus.com

GOVERNMENT
- Egypt's Information Portal mainained by the Information and Decision Support Centre (IDSC)
  Website: http://www.idsc.gov.eg/
- Egypt State Information Service
  Website: http://www.sis.gov.eg/En/Default.htm

BUSINESS
- American Chamber of Commerce in Egypt
  Website: http://www.amcham.org.eg/
- Internet Business Mall (Egypt)
  Website: http://www.ibm-e.com/
- German-Arab Chamber of Industry and Commerce: Egypt
  Website: http://www.ahkmena.com/
- British Egyptian Business Association
  Website: http://www.beba.org.eg/index.asp

EGYPTIAN NEWSPAPERS IN ENGLISH (ONLINE)

- Egypt Daily News
  Website: http://www.egyptdailynews.com/
- Al Ahram Weekly Online
  Website: http://weekly.ahram.org.eg/index.htm
- Business Today in Egypt
  Website: http://www.businesstodayegypt.com/
- Cairo Times
  Website: http://www.cairotimes.com/
- Egypt Today
  Website: http://www.egypttoday.com/
- Middle East News Agency
  Website: http://www.mena.org.eg/index.aspx
- The Middle East Times
  Website: http://metimes.com/

EMERGENCIES AND HEALTH

I have compiled a list of emergency telephone numbers for Cairo (unless noted otherwise) that I hope will be of help. Telephone numbers in Egypt change rapidly, so be sure to double-check that prefixes have not changed since publication. Also, Dr Sameh M Arab, MD, wrote a good article entitled 'Medical Emergencies in Egypt', which can be found at:

http://www.touregypt.net/magazine/
mag07012000/mag13.htm.

Ambulance

HQ (Emergency)	123
Giza	(02) 516-5458
Heliopolis	(02) 244-4327
Maadi	(02) 350-2873
Nasr City	(02) 402-7961
Zamalek	(02) 340-1788

Medical Care

The American Embassy can provide you with a listing of hospitals and English-speaking physicians. Check the listing on the American Embassy website at:

http://cairo.usembassy.gov/consular/acslist1.htm

As a general rule, medical facilities are adequate for non-emergency matters; however, emergency and intensive care facilities are limited. People will likely tell you that you should bring your own syringe when you are going to need an injection; however, when I have had to access services of this sort, I found that the modern laboratories/clinics utilise the one-use, disposable syringes so there was no need. When in doubt, just ask.

The *Egypt Daily News* keeps an up-to-date listing of hospitals in Egypt with their phone numbers and addresses at:

http://www.egyptdailynews.com/egypt%20hospitals.htm

A few hospitals are listed below.

Hospitals

- Al-Salam International Hospital
  Tel: (02) 524-0077
- Al-Salam Hospital
  Tel: (02) 346-7061
- Anglo American Hospital
  Tel: (02) 340-6162/ 63/ 64/ 65
- Namero (rabies vaccination)
  Tel: (02) 284-1375/ 76/ 77/ 78/ 79 ext 379
- Nursing Support Services
  Tel: (02) 525-5385

Tourist Police

Emergency	126
HQ	(02) 391-3370
	(02) 393-3000
	(02) 363-3006

Police

Emergency	122
HQ	(02) 590-0122
	(02) 510-0122
Heliopolis	(02) 243-2305
Nasr City	(02) 270-8744
Nazha	(02) 244-5981

Fire Brigade

Emergency	125/ 180
HQ	(020 391-0115
Downtown	(02) 391-0466
Gezirah	(02) 341-9966
Giza	(02) 361-0257
Heliopolis	(02) 243-0954
Maadi	(02) 350-0183
Salah Edin	(02) 415-1590
Zamalek	(02) 341-9966

EMBASSIES AND TOURISM OFFICES
Foreign Embassies in Egypt

Over 100 countries maintain embassies in Egypt. Listed below are some embassies that may be of interest to the reader. All are located in the greater Cairo area. Note that not all embassies have websites, but many do. You may have to do a search to find the place where the embassies are located in Egypt. For a start, try:

> http://www.gksoft.com/govt/en/world.html

- Australia
  World Trade Centre, 11th Floor, Corniche El Nil, Boulak
  Tel: (02) 575-0444; fax: (02) 578-1638
  Email: cairo.austremb@dfat.gov.au
  Website: http://www.embassy.gov.au/eg.html
- Canada
  No 26 Kamel El Shenaway, Garden City
  Tel: (02) 794-3110; fax: (02) 796-3548

Email: cairo@dfait-maeci.gc.ca
Website: http://www.dfait-maeci.gc.ca/cairo/

- France
29 Avenue Charles de Gaulle (Giza Street), Giza
Tel: (02) 570-3916; fax: (02) 571-8498
Email: cgfcaire@link.net
Website: http://www.ambafrance-eg.org

- Germany
2 Sharia Berlin, off Sharia Hassan Sabri, Zamalek
Tel: (02) 739-9600; fax: (02) 736-0530
Email: germemb@gega.net
Webiste: http://www.german-embassy.org.eg

- Ireland
3 Abu El Fida Street, 7th Floor, Zamalek
Tel: (02) 735-8264, 735-8547; fax: (02) 736-2863
Email: irishemb@rite.com
Website: http://www.embassyofireland-cairo.com

- Italy
15 Abdel Rahman Fahmi Street, Garden City
Tel: (02) 794-3194/ 95, 794-0658; fax: (02) 794-0657
Email: ambasciata.cairo@esteri.it
Website: http://www.italembassy.org.eg/

- The Netherlands
18 Hassan-Sabri, Zamalek
Tel: (02) 739-5500; fax: (02) 736-5249
Email: az-cz@hollandemb.org.eg
Website: http://www.hollandemb.org.eg

- United Kingdom
7 Ahmed Ragheb Street, Garden City
Tel: (02) 794-0852–58; fax: (02) 794-0859, 794-3065
Email: info@britishembassy.org.eg
Website: http://www.britishembassy.org.eg

- United States
8 Kamel El Din Salah St, Garden City
Tel: (02) 797-3300; fax: (02) 797-2218
Email: consularcairo@state.gov
Website: http://cairo.usembassy.gov/

Egyptian Embassies and Consulates Abroad

For a complete listing of Egyptian Embassies and Consulates Abroad, see:

> http://www.emigration.gov.eg/EgyptianConsulates/
> DisplayConsulates.aspx

(Country code followed by city code in parentheses)

- Egyptian Embassy: Australia
  1 Darwin Avenue, Yarralumla, Canberra, ACT 2600
  Tel: (61-62) 273-4437/ 38
- Egyptian Consulate: Sydney, Australia
  Level 3, 241 Commonwealth Street, Surry Hills, NSW 2010
  Tel: (61-02) 9281-4844; Fax: (61-02) 9281-4344
  Email: info@egypt.org.au
  Website: http://www.egypt.org.au/
- Egyptian Consulate: Melbourne, Australia
  124 Exhibition Street, 9th Floor, Melbourne, Victoria 3000
  Tel: (61-03) 654-8869, (61-03) 654-8634
- Egyptian Embassy: Canada
  454 Laurier Avenue East, Ottawa, Ontario KIN 6R3
  Tel: (1-613) 234-4931
- Egyptian Consulate: Montreal, Canada
  3754 Cote des Neiges, Montreal, Quebec H3H 7V6
  Tel: (1-514) 937-7781
- Egyptian Embassy: France
  56, Avenue d'Iena, 75116 Paris
  Tel: (33-01) 4720-9770
- Egyptian Consulate: Paris
  58, Avenue Foch, 75116 Paris
  Tel: (33-01) 4500-8464
- Egyptian Embassy: Germany
  Stauffenberg Strasse 6–7, 10785 Berlin
  Tel: (49-030) 477-5470; fax: (49-030) 477-1049
  Email: embassy@egyptian-embassy.de
  Website: http://www.egyptian-embassy.de
- Egyptian Consulate: Frankfurt, Germany
  Eysseneckstrasse 34, 60322 Frankfurt/Main I
  Tel: (49-069) 9551-3410 / 15; fax: (49-069) 597-2131

- Egyptian Consulate: Hamburg, Germany
  Harvestehuder Weg 47, 20149 Hamburg
  Tel: (49-040) 410-1031; fax: (49-040) 410-6115
  Email: gen-kons-et-hh@gmx.de
- Egyptian Embassy: Ireland
  12 Clyde Road, Dublin 4
  Tel: (353-01) 606-566, (353-01) 606-718
- Egyptian Embassy: United Kingdom
  26 South Street, London W1Y 6DD
  Tel: (44-020) 7499-3304; fax: (44-020) 7235-9719
- Egyptian Consulate: London
  2 Lowndes Street, London SW1X 9ET
  Tel: (44-020) 7235-9719
  Email: info@egyptianconsulate.co.uk
  Website: http://www.egyptianconsulate.co.uk/
- Embassy of the Arab Republic of Egypt: United States
  3521 International Ct NW, Washington DC 20008
  Tel: (1-202) 895-5400; fax: (1-202) 224-4319, 244-5131
- Egyptian Consulate: New York, USA
  1110 Second Avenue, New York NY 10022
  Tel: (1-212) 759-7120/ 21/ 22; fax: (1-212) 308-7643
- Egyptian Consulate: Chicago, USA
  30 North Michigan Avenue, Suite 1900, Chicago, IL 60611
  Tel: (1-312) 828-9162 / 63/ 64; fax: (1-312) 828-9167
- Egyptian Consulate: Houston
  1990 Post Oak Blvd, Suite 2180, Houston, TX 77056
  Tel: (1-713) 961-4915/ 16; fax: (1-713) 961-3868
- Egyptian Consulate: San Francisco
  3001 Pacific Avenue, San Francisco, CA 94115
  Tel: (1-415) 346-9700/ 02, 346-7352; fax: (1-415) 346-9480

Egyptian Tourism Offices in Egypt

One source of very helpful information is:
http://www.touregypt.net/tourinfo.htm

- Headquarters
  Misr Travel Tower
  Abbassia Square, Cairo
  Tel: (02) 285-4509, 284-1970; fax: (02) 285-4363

Egyptian Tourism Offices Abroad

Africa

Egyptian Tourist Authority
First Floor, Regent Place Building, Mutal Gardens, Gradock
Avenue, Rosebank, Johannesburg, South Africa
Tel: (27-11) 880-9602/ 03; fax: (27-11) 880-9604

Austria

Agyptisches
Fremdenverkehrsamt Elisabethstresse 4/5/1, Opernringhof,
1010 Vienna, Austria
Tel: (43-1) 587-6633; fax: (43-1) 587-6634

Canada

Egyptian Tourist Authority
1253 McGill College, Avenue Suite 250, Montreal, Quebec
H3B2Y5, Canada
Tel: (1-514) 861-4420; fax (1-514) 861-8071

France

Bureau du Tourisme, L'Egypte
90 Avenue Des Champs Elysees, 75008 Paris, France
Tel: (33-1) 4562-9442/ 43; fax: (33-1) 4289-3481

Germany

Frankfurt Agyptisches Fremdenverkehrsamt
64A Kaiser Strasse, 60329 Frankfurt, Ammain, Germany
Tel: (49-69) 252-319; fax: (49-69) 239-876

Greece

Egyptian Tourist Authority
10 Amerikis Street, 6th Floor, 10671Athens, Greece
Tel: (30-1) 360-6906; fax: (30-1) 363-6681

Italy

Egyptian Tourist Authority
Via Bissolati 19, 00187 Rome, Italy
Tel: (39-06) 482-7985; fax: (39-06) 487-4156

Japan

Cultural Tourist Promotion Office of Egypt
Akasaka 2-Chome, Annex 2F, 19–18, Akasaka 2-Chome,
Minato-Ku-Tokyo Japan
Tel: (81-3) 3589-0653; fax: (81-3) 3589-1372

Russia

Embassy of Egypt Tourist Office
Shatertnyi Pereulok 25, Moscow, Russia
Tel: (7-095) 291-3209; fax: (7-095) 134-4035

Spain

Oficina de Turismo, Egipto
Torre de Madrid Planta, 5 Oficina 3, Plaza de Espana, 28008
Madrid, Spain
Tel: (34-1) 559-2121; fax: (34-1) 547-5165

Sweden

Egyptian Tourist Office
Drottninggatan 65, S-11136 Stockholm, Sweden
Tel: (46-8) 102-548; fax: (46-8) 102-541

United Kingdom

Egyptian State Tourist Office
Egyptian House, 170 Piccadilly, London W1V 9DD, England
Tel: (44-207) 493-5282; fax: (44-207) 408-0295

United States

- Egyptian Tourist Authority in Chicago
  645 North Michigan Avenue, Suite 829, Chicago, IL 60611
  Tel: (1-312) 280-4666; fax: (1-312) 280-4788
- Egyptian Tourist Authority in Los Angeles
  8383 Wilshire Boulevard, Suite 215, Beverly Hills, CA 90211
  Tel: (1-310) 653-8815; fax: (1-310) 653-8961
  Email: egypt@etala.com
- Egyptian Tourist Authority in new York
  630 Fifth Avenue, Suite 1706, New York, NY 10111
  Tel: (1-212) 332-2570; fax: (1-212) 956-6439
  Email: egyptoursp@aol.com

ACCOMMODATION

One of the best ways to secure a flat or villa in Egypt is through word-of-mouth or by asking doormen (*bawwabs*) in a neighborhood you like. For high-end flats, you might want to contact a commissioned broker (*simsar*). As a last resort, you might try checking the newspapers. For a really good article on the subject, check out Cam McGrath's at:

http://www.suite101.com/article.cfm/
cairo_expat_life_retired/56214.

It is not only extremely informative, but very entertaining.

Hotels

Well, like everyone else, I have developed my 'favourite' or most frequented hotel for Cairo. It is the Carlton Hotel near the Cinema Rivoli in Azbakeya. The Carlton is a 3-star hotel located in downtown Cairo. Definitely not a touristy place, but it is convenient to the underground train, taxis, local shopping, pharmacies and Internet cafés. A great market runs along the side of the hotel where you can find just about anything in the way of fresh fruits and vegetables, bakery items and *falafel*. A new restaurant has been recently added and most rooms have now been renovated. It is clean and staffed with friendly people. [Tel: (02) 575-5181, 575-5022, 575-5232; fax: (02) 575-5323.]

I have listed a few of my other favourites below and only wish I could list them all. For an extensive listing of Egyptian hotels and current rates, you can visit one of the following worldwide websites:

- http://www.hotelguide.com
- http://touregypt.net
- http://www.egyptfocus.com/

Alexandria

- Hannoville (3-star)
  El Agami, Hannoville Beach, Alexandria
  Tel: (03) 430-3258
- Plaza (4-star)
  394 El Gueish Street, Zizinia, Alexandria
  Tel: (03) 587-8714; fax: (03) 587-5399

Cairo

- Longchamps Hotel
  21 Ismail Mohamed Street, Zamalek, Cairo
  Tel: (02) 735-2311, 435-2312; fax: (02) 735-9644
  Email: hotel.longchamps@web.de
  Website: http://www.touregypt.net/egypthotels.htm

  A very stylish and elegant 3-star hotel located in central Zamalek, the Longchamps is a short taxi ride to the Egyptian Museum, Al-Azhar Mosque and the famous Khal el-Khalili bazaar. The Roof Garden Terrace faces the greenery of Zamalek, you may enjoy alcoholic and non-alcoholic beverages including local and imported beer. A rich continental breakfast is included in the price of the room.

- Garden City House (no stars)
  23 Kamal ad-Din Salah, Garden City, Cairo, Egypt
  Tel: (02) 794-8400, 794-4969; fax: (02) 794-4126

  With its Old World ambiance, this hotel was once very popular among Egyptologists but now is more favoured by university students, so with its budget pricing it may be a very nice choice for young travellers. There is a restaurant, and some rooms have private baths. Not a place for children or those who don't want something not quite so modern, but it is clean, friendly and a place for pretty good food. It's located behind the Intercontinental Semiramis. Just ask for directions at the Semiramis.

MANAGING YOUR MONEY: BANKS:

For a listing of Egyptian banks, addresses and phone numbers go to:

  http://www.egyptdailynews.com/egypt%20banks.htm

Some Egyptian banks have Internet sites, for example:
- Banque Misr
  Website: http://www.banquemisr.com.eg/index.asp
- Alwatany Bank of Egypt
  Website: http://www.alwatany.net/watany/index.asp
- Banque du Caire
  Website: http://www.bdc.com.eg/

Emergency Numbers (Cairo)

- American Express (24 hour customer service)
  Tel: (02) 569-6111
- Visa Card (Lost Cards)
  Tel: (toll free in Cairo) 510-0200-866-654-0128
         (outside Cairo)   02-510-0200-866-654-0128
- Western Union Money Transfer
  Tel: (02) 755-5165
  Website: http://www.westernunion.com/info/homePage.
  asp?country = EG

TRANSPORT AND COMMUNICATIONS

Train information/reservations
Tel: 147/ (02) 575-3555

Country and City Codes

The country code for Egypt is 20

Selected City Codes

Cairo	2
Alexandria	3
Aswan	97
Luxor	95
Hurghada	65

Telephone Service

- Mobinil
  (Their mobile numbers always start with '012')
  World Trade Centre, Cairo
  Tel: (02) 417-2056, 575 6400
  Website: http://www.mobinil.com/
- Vodafone Egypt
  (formerly Click GSM. Their mobile numbers always start
  with '010')
  Maadi City Centre, Katamiyya Road, Maadi
  Tel: 010-181-9674, (02) 520-4399; fax: (02) 520-4398
  Website: http://www.vodafone.com.eg/

- Telecom Egypt
  (Landline service)
  Email:telecomegypt@telecomegypt.com.eg
  Website: http://www.telecomegypt.com.eg/english/Home_
  Caring_ContactUs.htm

Important Telephone Numbers
- International Operator   120
- Local Operator   110

For Telephone Complaints
- HQ   188
- Maadi   555-5188
- Mohandeseen/Zamalek/Dokki   303-3188
- Heliopolis   254-0188

INTERNET CAFÉS AND SERVICE PROVIDERS
- Internet Egypt
  2 Midan Simon Bolivar, Ground Floor, Garden City, Cairo
  Tel: (02) 796-2882; fax: (02) 794-9611
  Email: info@internetegypt.com
  Website: http://www.internetegypt.com/
  At Internet Egypt, you can get free through DSL service
  (at a reasonable rate) and it has eight cybercafés
  throughout Cairo.
- The Way Out
  45 El-Batal Ahmed Abdel-Aziz Street, Mohandessin, Suite
  1402, Cairo
  Tel: (02) 301-7171
  Website: http://www.wayout.net/
  Check their website for WiFi Hotspots throughout Egypt.
- Netsonic
  10 El Nouwari St. from Ammar Ebn Yasser, (Behind the
  Military Academy) Heliopolis, Heliopolis, Cairo
  Tel: (02) 620-7967; fax: (02) 620-7968
  Email: info@netsonic.com.eg
  Wesite: http://come.to/NETSONIC

- MenaNet
  Heliopolis, Cairo
  Tel: (02) 416-6200; fax: (02) 416-6204
  E-mail: info@menanet.net
  Website: http://www.menanet.net/docs/contactus.shtml

EXPAT SOCIAL CLUBS AND INFORMATION

- American Center in Alexandria
  3 Pharaana Street
  Tel: (03) 486-1009; fax: (03) 487-3811
  Email: AmericanCenterAlexandria@yahoo.com
  The ACA organises a full range of fun activities, including lectures, workshops, exhibits and cultural offerings. It also houses a reading room with a focus on American studies, and provides access to electronic information via the Internet.
- American Research Center in Cairo (ARCE)
  2 Midan Simón Bolívar, Garden City, Cairo 11461
  Tel: (02) 794-8239; fax: (02) 795-3052
  Email: arce@internetegypt.com
  Website: http://www.arce.org/aboutarce/cairo.html
  The American Research Center in Egypt (ARCE) is a private, non-profit organisation founded in 1948 by a consortium of educational and cultural institutions to support research on Egyptian history and culture, foster broader knowledge about Egypt among the general public, and promote and strengthen American-Egyptian cultural ties. The ARCE also has affiliates in the US which can be located by visiting their website.
- American Women of Alexandria
  Membership consists of English speaking women residing in Alexandria who hold non-Egyptian passports. The club meets every Monday morning at 10:00 am at a villa in Roushdi. It has an active charity committee, various social activities and a library. The club also issues a members' telephone book and a monthly newsletter. For more information, call Michel Richard at tel: (03) 420-9690.

- Archaeological Society of Alexandria
  6 Mahmoud Mokhtar Sreet Library
  Open 4:30 pm–7:30 pm. Closed Thursdays, Fridays and
  Saturdays. For more information, call tel: (03) 486-0650
  from 3:00 pm–8:00 pm.
- British Community Association in Cairo
  Tel: (02) 348-1358
  Clubhouse, activities, special parties, barbecues and a free
  monthly magazine. Open 10:00 am–3:00 pm.
- British Sub Aqua Club (BSAC) in Cairo
  Meets every other Tuesday at the British Embassy for
  dive-related entertainment. Divers of all nationalities
  are welcome to join and participate in the monthly
  dive trips and free training courses. BSAC certification
  is internationally recognised, and the club has chapters
  all over the world. For more information contact Gerard
  Challis at tel: (02) 290-2943 or Dave Bayes-Walker at tel:
  (02) 354-0852.
- Cairo Hash House Harriers
  Meets every Friday afternoon, approximately two hours
  before sunset all year round. Run, jog or walk at different
  locations near Cairo such as Wadi Digla or near the
  pyramids, with occasional trips to other sites. Members
  come from many different nationalities, professions,
  ages, sexes and running/walking abilities. For more
  information see:
  http://cairohash.com
  Definitely check their website—this group has fun!
- Cairo Rugby Club
  Tel: (02) 525-3841
  Email: cairorugby@visto.com
  Meets for training at 6:30 pm every Monday and
  Wednesday at the Victory College playing fields, Maadi.
  Training continues afterwards at the clubhouse. All rugby
  players, regardless of experience, are welcome to attend.
  For more information, please contact the clubhouse.
- Cairo Toastmasters Club
  A public speaking forum which meets on the first and
  the third Tuesday of each month at the USIS office

conference room, the US Embassy, North Gate. For further information, contact the Embassy.

- Community Services Association
  Tel: (02) 350-5284, 350-0754
  Open 9:00 am–9:00 pm but Thursdays 9:00 am–5:00 pm. Closed Fridays and Saturdays.
  A non-profit organisation which provides support services to English-speaking expatriates around the Cairo area. CSA offers a variety of classes, tours, lectures as well as arts and hobbies courses throughout the year. Newcomer orientation helps newly-arrived expats adjust to their new home in Egypt. .

- Delta Hash House Harriers in Alexandria
  Tel: (03) 542-7054, 545-4446
  A social running club that goes for non-athletic fun and walks in the countryside surrounding Alexandria. Everyone is welcome to take part. They meet every Friday at 2:00 pm from September to June at the Centro de Portugal, Kafr Abdu Street, Roushdi. Call for more information.

- Rotary Club in Alexandria
  The Cosmopolitan Rotary Club meets at Le Salon Restaurant (tel: (03) 482-0986) at 8:00 pm while the Metropolitan Rotary Club meets in the same place at 9:00 pm

- The Cairo Cyclists
  Meet on Fridays at 7:00 am at the front gate of the Cairo American College (1 Midan Digla). The route and pace is decided by the people on the ride. Two groups with mountain bikes and racing bikes meet at 7:00 am on Saturdays. For more serious cyclists, the club organises long-distance events. Also, the Cycling Merit Badge programme for Boy Scout Troop 701 is conducted each year by club members. Call Richard Beck at tel: (02) 350-6647 or Edwin Crosswhite at tel: (02) 352-6310.

- The Egypt Exploration Society (EES) in Cairo
  Holds various lectures and organises field trips to visit British archaeologists at the EES Cairo office

[tel: (02) 301-8319]. Open 10:00 am–2:00 pm. Closed Fridays and Saturdays.

- The Middle East Wives Club
  This is a social club of foreign women (non-Egyptian, non-Middle Eastern) married to Egyptian or other Arab nationals. The club aims to help its members live happily in Egypt. Meetings on the second Tuesday of each month at 10:00 am at the Saint Germain Coffee Shop, Le Meridien Heliopolis.
- The Maadi Women's Guild in Maadi, Cairo
  Welcomes all women to their meetings, coffee mornings, activities and tours. Meetings are held on the third Tuesday of every month, unless otherwise noted, at 9:30 am. Call tel: (02) 351-2755 for more information.
- The Women's Association of Cairo
  21 Boulos Hanna Sreet, Ground floor, Dokki
  Tel: (02) 360-3457
  The club meets on the second Wednesday of every month (September to April) at the Cairo Marriott Hotel at 10:00 am. All English-speaking women are welcome. Activities include monthly programmes focusing on Egyptian culture, day trips, lectures, classes and demonstrations. Open 8:00 am to 2:00 pm in the winter and 9:00 am to 1:00 pm in the summer. Closed Fridays, Saturdays and Sundays.

Christian Churches

- All Saints Cathedral
  5 Michel Lutfallah Sreet, Zamalek
  Tel: (02) 341-8391
  Anglican/Episcopal church which conducts services in English on Sundays at 8:30 am, 10:30 am and 7:30 pm; from Mondays to Thursdays at 9:00 am; on Fridays at 9:30 am with a programme for children; and on Saturdays at 6:00 pm, together with a praise fellowship. Holy communion on Sundays at 8:30 am.
- Cairo Christian Fellowship
  At Saint Andrews United Church hall, corner of 26th of July and Galaa streets

Tel: (02) 350-5708
Reverend Russell Skaggs is the resident pastor. Services are held in English. Worship on Sundays are at 6:00 pm. Christian education (September to May) on Saturdays at 6:00 pm. All are welcome.

- Christian Science Society
  3 Midan Mustafa Kamel, Downtown
  Tel: (02) 392-9032, 525-3781, 525-0670
  Sunday service and Sunday school at 7:00 pm. Testimony meetings are held on Wednesday evenings at 7:00 pm. The reading room is open one hour before services. All are welcome.

- Holy Family Church
  55 Road 15, Maadi
  Tel: (02) 350-2004
  Roman Catholic church which has Masses (French or English according to attendance) from Mondays to Thursdays at 7:00 pm and on Fridays at 9:00 am. English-language weekend Masses are at 5:30 pm on Saturdays and 6:00 pm on Sundays. There is also a service in French on Saturdays at 6:30 pm as well as one conducted in Spanish on Sundays at 5:00 pm. Father Oscar is the parish priest.

- Maadi Community Church
  Corner of Port Said Street and Road 17, Maadi
  Tel: (02) 351-2755 (office)
  This interdenominational church, headed by Senior Pastor Dave Petrescue, conducts services in English on Sundays at 7:00 pm and on Fridays at 8:30 am and 11:00 am. Communion is given every first weekend of the month. A nursery is available on Fridays while a church school runs every Friday at 9:45 am.

- Saint Andrews United Church
  38, 26th of July Street (located between Ramses and Galaa streets)
  Tel: (02) 350-6295 (pastor's home), 575-9451 (office)
  Pastor David Grafton heads this Protestant/International church. Services are held on Sundays and Fridays at 9:30 am, in English.

For a list of other churches in Cairo and other cities in Egypt, see:

> http://ww3.interoz.com/hotels/toursearch8.ihtml?
> cityl = Cairo&search = Search&step = 2

Bookshops

- Anglo-American Bookshop
  165 Mohammed Farid Street, Downtown
  Tel: (02) 391-4337
  Open 9:00 am–1:30 pm and 4:30–8:00 pm. Closed Sundays
- Aly Masoud
  159, 26th of July Street, Zamalek (the entrance is from Behler Street)
  Open 9:00 am–9:00 pm. Closed Sundays
- International Publications (IPL)
  95 Road 9, Maadi
  Tel: (02) 351-6244
  Open 9:00 am–5:00 pm
- Isis
  88 Road 9, Maadi
  Tel: (02) 350-6034
  Open 11:00 am–3:00 pm and 6:00 pm–9:00 pm. Closed Sundays
- Lehnert and Landrock
  44 Sherif Street, Downtown
  Tel: (02) 393-5324, 392-7606
  Open 9:30 am–2:00 pm and 4:00 pm–7:00 pm. Closed Sundays
- Madbouli
  6 Midan Talaat Harb, Downtown
  Tel: (02) 575-6421
  Open 9:00 am–11:00 pm
  45 El-Battal Ahmed Abd El-Aziz Street, Mohandseen
  Tel: (02) 347-7410
  Tiba Mall, Nasr City
  Tel: (02) 401-5602
  Open 10:00 am–10:00 pm

- Shady
  26th of July Street, Zamalek
  Open 10:30 am to 9:30 pm
  29 Abd El-Khalek Tharwat Street, Downtown
- Shorouk Bookshop
  1 Talaat Harb Square
  Tel: (02) 391-2480
  Open 9:00 am to 10:00 pm
- Zamalek Bookstore
  19 Shagaret El-Dorr Street, Zamalek
  Open 8:30 am to 8:00 pm. Closed Sundays

Western Schools

- British International School of Cairo, Gezira
  Tel: (02) 736-5959, 735-6674; fax: (02) 736-4168
  Email: info@bsic.edu.eg
  Website: http://www.bisc.edu.eg
- British School of Alexandria
  Tel: (03) 544-5426, 544-8199; fax: (03) 544-5426
  Email: bsaalex@yahoo.co.uk
  Website: http://www.britishschoolalex.org
- Cairo American College, Maadi
  Tel: (02) 755-5555; fax: (02) 519-6584
  E-mail: support@cacegypt.org
  Website: http://www.cacegypt.org/
- El Alsson British International School, Cairo
  Tel: (02) 388-8510; fax: (02) 386-8414
  Email: info@alssom.com
  Website: http://www.alsson.com
- Maadi British International School
  Tel: (02) 516-4144, 516-3965, 516-3967
  Fax: (02) 516-4239
  Email: mbis@mbisegypt.com
  Website: http://www.mbisegypt.com
- Modern English School, Cairo
  Tel: (02) 617-0005 to 617-0011; fax: (02) 617-0020
  Email: mescairo@mescairo.com
  Website: http://www.mescairo.com

- New Cairo British International School
  Tel: (02) 758-2881; fax: (02) 758-1390
  Email: recncbis@intouch.com
  Websie: http://www.ncbis.org
- Schutz American School (in Alexandria)
  Tel: (03) 574-1435; fax: (03) 576-0229
  Email: scgytz/2schutzschool.org
  Website: http://www.schutzschool.org.eg

Language Schools

- Arab Academy (Cairo)
  Located in Garden City, Cairo
  Tel: (02) 218 0305; fax: (02) 589-1499
  E-mail: arabic@arabacademy.com
  Website: http://www.arabacademy.com
  You can start your Arabic language training before you get to Egypt. Call or email Sanaa Ghanem who started and runs the Arab Academy, which has both online and on-the-ground courses.
- Arabic Language Institute
  The American University in Cairo
  Tel: (02) 797-5055; fax: (02) 795-7565
  Email: alu@aucegypt.edu
  Website: http://www.aucegypt.edu/academic/ali/
- Arabic Language Centre
  Tel & fax: (02) 257-1926
  Email: info@arabic-in-cairo.com
  Website: http://www.arabic-in-cairo.com/
- International Language Institute (ILI)
  Website: http://www.ili.com.eg

FURTHER READING

Cairo: 1001 Years of the City Victorious. Janet Abu-Lughod. Princeton, NJ: Princeton University Press, 1971.

- Out of print, but you may be able to find this in a second-hand bookshop. I found some copies listed on Amazon.com. It remains probably the best history of the development of Cairo.

Veiled Sentiments: Honor and Poetry in a Bedouin Society. Lila Abu-Lughod. Berkeley, CA: University of California Press, 2000.

- This is a compelling ethnography based on the author's living with Bedouins in the Egyptian Western desert that is hard to put down.

The Koran Interpreted: A Translation. Arthur J Arberry. New York, NY: Touchstone, 1996.

- Many scholars regard this as the most literary English translation of the Qur'an.

Egyptian Religion Egyptian Ideas of the Future Life. E A Wallis Budge. New York, NY: Cosimo Books, 2005.

- Originally published in 1899, you may find this book tedious, but it is worth it if you are interested in ancient Egyptian religion. In particular, this book discusses how ancient Egyptians regarded resurrection and future life. The major source is the collection of religious papyri named the 'Book of the Dead'. If you are interested in the topic, see also Budge's works entitled *The Book of the Dead* (New York, NY: Gramercy Books, 1995) and *Egyptian Magic* (Whitefish, MT: Kessinger Publishing, 2003).

Islam: The Straight Path. John Esposito. New York, NY: Oxford University Press, Inc, 2004.

- Put together with Esposito's *Islam and Politics* (Syracuse, NY: Syracuse University Press, 1998), you can get a good introduction to Islam and the issues related to modern Islamic activism.

Kafr El-Elow: Continuity and Change in an Egyptian Community. Hani Fakhouri. Longrove, IL: Waveland Press Inc, 1987.

- Dry reading in a standard anthropology ethnographic style, but informative. What is important about the information in the book is its analysis of change occurring in an industrial, urban village that has a traditional folk-peasant cultural base.

Middle Eastern Muslim Women Speak. Ed. Elizabeth Warnock Fernea and Basima Qattan Bezirgan. Austin, TX: University of Texas Press, 1978.

- Fernea (B J to friends) is known for her warmth and humanistic style of writing which gives the reader an in-depth understanding of women throughout the Middle East. This anthology, edited by Fernea and Bezirgan, addresses areas other than Egypt, but has several poignant articles directly related to women in Egypt. Highly recommended for anyone interested in women in the Middle East. Also, try looking at other books written by Fernea (such as *Guests of the Sheikh* or *Women and the Family in the Middle East*). Once you start reading, you will find her powerful work difficult to put down!

Nubian Ethnographies. Elizabeth Warnock Fernea and Robert A Fernea. Longrove, IL: Waveland Press Inc, 1990.

- For anyone interested in this important subculture within Upper Egypt, the Ferneas' description of life and hardships associated with being Nubian during this century captures your imagination and provides intricate details on this important group. You will gain exhaustive information about the Nubian relocation that resulted from the building of the Aswan High Dam.

Managing Cultural Differences: Leadership Strategies for a New World of Business. Philip R Harris. and Robert T Moran. Burlington, MA: Gulf Professional Publishing, 2000.

- For those who anticipate conducting any international business, this book provides a basis for understanding the nature of cultural differences as they affect business. It has specific sections for the major areas of the world, and one short section specifically addressing Egypt. It is also the book probably used most frequently in MBA programmes to introduce professionals to the art of cross-cultural communications in business.

Valley of the Golden Mummies: The Greatest Egyptian Discovery Since Tutankhamon. Zahi Hawass. New York, NY: Harry N Abrams, 2000; London, UK: Virgin Books, 2000.

- An exciting find in 1999 located in the Bahariya Oasis west of Cairo has yielded numerous golden shrouded mummies. 'In the winter of 1996, a guard at the temple of Alexander the Great near Bahariya, Egypt, reported an astounding discovery: during a routine patrol, he had been startled when the donkey he had been riding fell into a hole. Helping the donkey out of its predicament, the guard saw that the hole was in fact an opening into a tomb–and one from which a mummy's golden face peered.' I can hardly wait for more publications on this important new site.

Bedouin Life in the Egyptian Wilderness. Joseph J Hobbs. Austin, TX: University of Texas Press, 1992.

- This book is an interesting study of nomadic life among the Bedouins of Egypt. Not nearly as readable as Mahfouz or Fernea, it still provides important information on the beliefs, values, folklore and ethnobotany of this small group of Egyptians.

A History of the Arab Peoples. Albert Hourani. London, UK: Faber and Faber, 2005.

- Actually, reading any of the myriad of articles or books written by Professor Hourani will give you an outstanding synthesis of 1,400 years of political, cultural and social events in the Middle East as well as useful information regarding more specific issues in the region.

Ancient Egypt: Anatomy of a Civilization. Barry J Kemp. London, UK & New York, NY: Routledge, 1992.
- This book provides an excellent summary of what we currently know and understand about ancient Egyptian culture and society.

Lonely Planet: Egypt. Andrew Humphreys. Siona Jenkins, Gadi Farfour, Anthony Sattin and Joann Fletcher. Melbourne, Australia: Lonely Planet Publications, 2004 (7th edition).
- Of the basic travel guide books, I like this one best. This book is quite helpful and easy to carry around. It has no in-depth information on the antiquities, but has a wealth of information on places to go and see other than Egypt's ancient past. The maps are all right, but difficult to read.

The Cairo Trilogy: Palace Walk, Palace of Desire, and Sugar Street. Naghib Mahfouz. London, UK & New York, NY: Everyman's Library, 2001.
- Naguib Mahfouz was the first Egyptian author to win the Nobel Prize for Literature. Start *The Cairo Trilogy* with *Palace Walk* and work your way through all three. In addition to these, *Respected Sir* (1986) is an excellent example of his later writing. These books address one of the most characteristic features of dealing with contemporary Egyptian life: the labyrinthine bureaucracy. Actually, you will enjoy anything he wrote. His style is clear and you always think you are part of the scene.

The Arabs. Peter Mansfield. *Penguin History Series*. London, UK & New York, NY: Penguin Books, 1992.
- This is a good, readable introduction to the political and social history of the modern Arab world. Important because Arab society affects Egypt and the modern Middle East.

A Short History of Modern Egypt. Afaf Al-Sayyed Marsot. Cambridge, UK: Cambridge University Press, 1985.
- For a good general history of Egypt since 1800, read this book. It is a good place to get an initial familiarity with the political and historical forces that shaped contemporary Egypt.

Understanding Arabs: A Guide for Westerners. Margaret K Nydell. Boston, MA: Intercultural Press Inc, 2002.
- This book is especially helpful for total newcomers to the cultures of the Middle East. Although most of the examples are general and not specific to Egypt, much of the content applies throughout the Arab speaking world. It is particularly useful as a quick guide for understanding many of the linguistic nuances in the region.

Egypt: The Blue Guide. Veronica Seton-Williams and Peter Stocks. New York, NY: W W Norton Co, 1993 (3rd edition).
- This is probably the best, in-depth coverage of any of the guidebooks related to Egyptian Antiquities, though it will not have coverage on the more recent archaeological finds. It focuses a lot on architecture and includes copious details and maps, but is rather heavy to drag around with you.

The Oxford Illustrated History of Ancient Egypt. Ian Shaw. New York, NY: Oxford University Press, USA, 2002.
- Written for someone who truly wants accurate history. Very accurate based on the contemporary archaeological record, but some may find it dull reading.

Global Studies: The Middle East. William Spencer. New York, NY: McGraw-Hill/Dushkin Publishing, 2004.
- This reader is short, sweet, and to the point. It provides a series of articles for understanding events in the Middle East and a country report with pertinent data for each country in the region. Not a hardcore academic's choice, but excellent information. The 11th edition is expected out sometime in 2006.

The Egypt of Nasser and Sadat: The Political Economy of Two Regimes. John Waterbury. Princeton, NJ: Princeton University Press, 1983.

- This book addresses the socialist transformation of Egypt during the regimes of Nasser and Sadat and discusses many reasons for its failure. If you are interested in political economy, also see Waterbury's other works on the area.

ABOUT THE AUTHOR

Susan L Wilson is currently assistant professor of public health at East Tennessee State University in Johnson City, Tennessee, USA. Wilson has worked as an educator, advisor, negotiator, business consultant, planner, and intermediary since 1979. She began working in Egypt in 1987 while serving as a health and human resources delegate to Egypt from the Texas Senate where she was on staff. Since that time, Wilson has continued to actively assist development between Egyptian and American interests. She has written numerous publications, led university-based training programmes to Egypt, and conducted research in Egypt and the Gulf States. In 1994, she created, organised and directed a new international field school programme conducted in Egypt for the University of North Texas, Institute of Anthropology. Currently, she is exploring new ways to collaborate with Egypt through student and professional exchanges in medicine, nursing and public health.

Wilson was previously on the faculties at the University of Texas Southwestern Medical School (Dallas, Texas), the University of Texas Medical Branch (Galveston, Texas), the University of North Texas (Denton, Texas), and the Ecole Supérieure Libre Des Sciences Commerciales et Appliqués (Mohandiseen, Cairo, Egypt).

Wilson's areas of speciality are:

- Public Health Policy
- International Health and Epidemiology
- Peoples and Cultures of the Middle East
- International Business Communications, Styles and Negotiations
- Cultural Diversity
- Development Strategies in the Middle East

Wilson holds a BA from the University of Cincinnati, Ohio and MA and PhD degrees from the Southern Methodist University in Dallas, Texas.

By the way, Susan Wilson would love to receive email from you! Contact her at: cs.egypt@gmail.com.

INDEX

Titles in the CULTURE**SHOCK**! series:

Argentina	Hawaii	Pakistan
Australia	Hong Kong	Paris
Austria	Hungary	Philippines
Bahrain	India	Portugal
Barcelona	Indonesia	San Francisco
Beijing	Iran	Saudi Arabia
Belgium	Ireland	Scotland
Bolivia	Israel	Sri Lanka
Borneo	Italy	Shanghai
Brazil	Jakarta	Singapore
Britain	Japan	South Africa
Cambodia	Korea	Spain
Canada	Laos	Sweden
Chicago	London	Switzerland
Chile	Malaysia	Syria
China	Mauritius	Taiwan
Costa Rica	Mexico	Thailand
Cuba	Morocco	Tokyo
Czech Republic	Moscow	Turkey
Denmark	Munich	Ukraine
Ecuador	Myanmar	United Arab
Egypt	Nepal	Emirates
Finland	Netherlands	USA
France	New York	Vancouver
Germany	New Zealand	Venezuela
Greece	Norway	Vietnam

For more information about any of these titles, please contact any of our Marshall Cavendish offices around the world (listed on page ii) or visit our website at:

www.marshallcavendish.com/genref